STAY

STAY

A Story of Family, Love, and Other Traumas

JULIE FINGERSH

ROWMAN & LITTLEFIELD
Lanham • Boulder • New York • London

Published by Rowman & Littlefield
An imprint of The Rowman & Littlefield Publishing Group, Inc.
4501 Forbes Boulevard, Suite 200, Lanham, Maryland 20706
www.rowman.com

86-90 Paul Street, London EC2A 4NE

Distributed by NATIONAL BOOK NETWORK

British Library Cataloguing in Publication Information Available

Library of Congress Cataloging-in-Publication Data

Names: Fingersh, Julie, 1966– author.
Title: Stay : a story of family, love, and other traumas / Julie Fingersh.
Description: Lanham : Rowman & Littlefield Publishing Group, [2024] |
    Summary: "This book delves into family complexity, mental illness, and
    the struggle to aid loved ones without losing oneself. Julie Fingersh's
    journey, haunted by her brother's tragic depression, resurfaces when her
    daughter battles chronic illness, unlocking a poignant past and offering
    a second chance at love and life"— Provided by publisher.
Identifiers: LCCN 2024015495 (print) | LCCN 2024015496 (ebook) | ISBN
    9781538195284 (cloth) | ISBN 9781538195291 (epub)
Subjects: LCSH: Families of the mentally ill—United States—Biography. |
    Chronically ill—Family.
Classification: LCC RC455.4.F3 F56 2024 (print) | LCC RC455.4.F3
    (ebook) | DDC 616.890092 [B]—dc23/eng/20240516
LC record available at https://lccn.loc.gov/2024015495
LC ebook record available at https://lccn.loc.gov/2024015496

♾™ The paper used in this publication meets the minimum requirements of
American National Standard for Information Sciences—Permanence of Paper
for Printed Library Materials, ANSI/NISO Z39.48-1992.

To Danny, may his memory be a blessing.

To Jesse, with love and gratitude for the gift of sharing her story.

And to my parents, Pella and Jack, whose love and trust gave this book life.

PREFACE

I know this sounds fishy coming from the author of a memoir, but I don't like talking about myself. I figure, I'm with myself all day long. What I want to know is, what about you? That's *always* interesting to me.

I'm also a little phobic about all eyes on me because I was raised to believe that personal privacy is sacred. *What happened to Danny*—which is how my family often refers to my little brother's life story—has always been private. It was a fourteen-year odyssey that began forty years ago, but few people will have known about it until they read this book.

Any reader whose family member has coped (or is now coping) with any kind of serious personal struggle—mental illness, medical illness, addiction—will understand all too well how this could happen, how a story like this one could unfold, year after year, under the noses of everyone around, including closest friends, extended family, neighbors, roommates, and co-workers, without their knowledge and without anyone in the family turning to them for support.

People walking a path of living with or supporting loved ones who struggle will also nod their heads and understand *why* this would happen. At the time, we fervently believed that keeping our family's privacy airtight was best for everyone. Mostly we thought we were protecting Danny—we were certain that one day he would find his way to the other side of his struggle, and we wanted him to be able to return to life free of baggage, without the weight of judgment from everyone from friends and community members to potential employers.

No doubt it was also simply easier for us if people didn't know what was happening. *We* didn't know what was happening. And since, to the outside world, we were the kind of family pictured on a Raisin Bran box, our odyssey was easily concealed. Things like this did not happen to people like us. No psychiatric hospitals for us, thank you.

And by the time things became serious, our thinking was that most people were just making conversation when they asked how Danny was doing or where he was living. Who wants to have a bomb dropped at a tea party?

Then, decades later, a *different* something happened, but this time I wasn't a sister; I was a mother, and it was my own child whose life suddenly careened off track. Like Danny, it was a confusing, scary reality to navigate, let alone talk about. The path forward seemed obvious in the exact same way: *this is no one's business.*

It took life throwing brick after brick at my head to finally realize the profound and generational cost of family secrets.

That's why I wrote this book. But I need you to know: This is my story. It's extraordinary enough that my parents and older brother gave me their full and loving permission to write what they knew my soul yearned to understand the only way I knew how. In return, I've done my very best to share my heart without exposing theirs.

My brother Danny's part in *Stay* is for everyone struggling to help loved ones plagued by mental illness—and to light the way for those of us left behind if the battles are lost.

My daughter Jesse's part in *Stay* is intended to give voice to the legions of people who cope with the isolating, often invisible veil of chronic medical illness.

And my part in *Stay*? My wrestling match with the empty nest, midlife ghosts of buried dreams, the twin pillagers of self-judgment and fear? Well, you're holding it in your hands.

May my family's story entertain and inspire you to perhaps look at your own life's trajectory and path forward with new eyes.

Danny and Julie, 1977

One

My soul sister, Lucy, was unfazed on hearing the news. "I'm a horrible mother!" I called out as we started our run up the dirt trail behind our Northern California homes.

"Go on," Lucy said.

"It's too horrifying."

"Julie, c'mon," she yelled as she huffed up the hill. "Tell me!"

"Once you hear, you're going to want to break up with me."

For almost twenty years, I thought I'd been a pretty great parent. But in the past several months, I'd ventured into new and ugly territory—so ugly that it was polluting my psyche, so shameful I hadn't told a soul.

"I swear, I won't break up with you," Lucy said as she made her way down the hill and jumped over a little river of dry rocks. "Just tell me!"

I followed her leap. "I don't have to tell you how insanely proud I am of Jesse, right?"

"Yeah, she's amazing," Lucy said. "But? And?"

"But oh my God, lately, and especially since she's been working at the Hillary campaign, I can't help it."

"Can't help—"

I pushed the words out in a rush. "It's like . . . it's like, I'm *jealous* of her. Literally jealous of my own child. It's sick. I'm sick!"

Lucy chuckled.

"Come on!" I shouted, grasping for common ground. "Isn't there some secret part of you that feels like the older our kids get and the more they expand, the more we *contract*?"

"I mean . . ." Lucy was pushing up her bright-orange, cat-eye glasses, her sign that she was struggling with diplomacy.

I forged on breathlessly. "Like we're animals on some depressing National Geographic special where the mother who is finished raising her young goes off into the forest alone and crumples up under a log to die?"

"Wellllll," Lucy said, turning her head enough so that I saw her wincing, "not really, because I love what I do. I wake up excited to go to work and teach kids and make art."

Clearly, Lucy was not a good enough friend to torture herself with me.

Torture, along with heart-bursting joy, is par for the course with parenting. But an unholy clashing of the two had nearly blown me off my feet when, a few days before that run, Jesse had walked into the kitchen, tossed her wallet right onto my pile of sliced red onions, and announced that she'd just gotten off the phone with the Secret Service.

I cocked my head. "Okay, wait? Like, *the Secret Service* secret service?"

She squatted down and patted her leg, trying to get Scotch, our emotionally distant Brittany spaniel, to come over and give her some love.

"Here, Scotchie! Come here, you good bad boy!"

Our family constantly pined for our dog's affection, usually to little avail. He was like a bad boyfriend we couldn't quit.

"Yup, the Secret Service secret service," Jesse said, standing up, as Scotch trotted off in the opposite direction. "Hillary's coming to the Bay Area next week, and guess which intern was asked to drive the White House press van in her motorcade?"

"Jess!" I yelled exultantly, my heart filling with joy.

Classic Jesse. Whatever she fell into, she rose to the top. *Of course* she was the one asked to drive in Hillary Clinton's motorcade.

Nineteen years old and a four-week-old high school graduate, Jesse was now a five-foot-two version of just what she'd looked like as a little girl: freckled, creamy skinned, big slate-green eyes, thick spun-copper hair.

I shook my head and smiled. She was a treasure of a human being, and her spirit radiated in every part of her life. She'd sailed through school and was beloved among her peers. She was guided by a fierce and old-soul inner compass. Her life stretched before her—everything possible, everything yes, everything why not.

I looked at my beautiful girl, shining and proud. And that's when it happened—when the verdict came down about what a terrible mother I was. As I looked into Jesse's face, that time in my life—so filled with clarity and ambition, exactly like hers was now—rose to my mind like a ghostly mirage.

The mirage then, horribly, turned into a wave of envy that swept through me like a dirty tide. And right under its crest, like a black ocean at the bottom of my consciousness, churned a quiet, aching grief. It was a grief steeped in shame—shame about how my own young promise, year by year, had slowly and inexplicably drained away.

I had done this to myself, that much I knew. And now it was coming back to roost.

Two

When you turn fifty, your friends, basically by law, must do anything you want, no matter how miserable it makes them.

I'd been thinking about my fiftieth birthday for a long time. In my mind, each new decade brings with it huge grist for the psychic mill, a chance to reflect, celebrate, and dream up what's next.

My fiftieth year, I had decided, should be used both to help me out of my precipitous mental free fall and to get to the bottom of something larger—namely, what is the Meaning of Life?

It seemed like a reasonable question, but no one else seemed to be talking about it. Was it love? Success? Achievement? As the years unfolded, my search had evolved into a search for peace—in part, perhaps, because the Meaning of Life remained too elusive.

After twenty-five years of marriage, miraculously Dave was still happy to accommodate my relentless interviews on the subject. He loved me, yes, but clearly the man was exhausted.

The Meaning of Life was not a new question to me. When I was a kid growing up in Kansas City, I started carrying around a yellow legal pad roughly the size of my torso, pretending I was writing a story for my school paper.

"I'm writing a story about life," I'd say to my involuntary subjects, who became instantly alarmed. "First question: How do you actually *know* how to live your life? Like, how are you supposed to know *what to do?*"

After assaulting people of all ages with unanswerable questions, I'd say casually, but with big hopes, just when they thought they were done, "One last thing . . . *what do you think the point of the whole thing is?*"

No one had much to report on this question. My father began and ended our interview with the words "Honey, just take two and hit to the right." But who the hell knew what that meant? I kept asking my mom what the Meaning of Life was, but she always said, "Just a minute!" When I asked my older brother, Red, he told me I was weird and he was doing homework.

Then I asked Filmore, whom I'd known since I was five years old. Technically, Filmore was our housekeeper, but there really wasn't a name for what Filmore was to our family. He was everything.

He came to our house three days a week to help my mom. He'd fix things and return things at the store, drive me to tap dancing, and help with big family holidays. Filmore and my mom often worked side by side, planting the spring garden or cutting onions and carrots for chicken soup. He'd answer the phone if my mom was busy and, if she gave the signal, tell the person we weren't home when we were.

In between everything else, Filmore moved from room to room cleaning floors and bathrooms and counters and making order. He sang while he worked. His big brown eyes were always laughing. The best days were when he and I could sit at the kitchen table together while my mom made us lunch. That's when we had a chance to talk things over. Being around Filmore was like wrapping myself in a cozy blanket. He was a cross between my uncle, Dear Abby, and a really nice rabbi. He always had an answer that made me feel better. He was the happiest person I knew.

One day, I burst through the front door after school. Filmore stood up tall in his powder-blue, short-sleeve shirt and bellowed his usual greeting.

"Well, helllllllo, sweetheart!" he sang in his warm, raspy voice. "How're you *doing*?"

My soul rose as it always did at the sight of him, and I gave my usual response: "Good, but hey, Filmore? What do you think the Meaning of Life is?"

Without taking even a second to think about it, he smiled broadly and bent over to look me in the eye. He put his soft chocolate-brown hand on my shoulder and gave it a squeeze.

"To live, baby. *Just to really live.*"

I didn't happen to have my legal pad with me, but even if I did, I wouldn't have bothered to write this one down. I loved Filmore, but . . . *just to live? That's it?*

Having been raised at the altar of productivity, the mere concept ran counter to everything I knew. My dad worked like a crazy man. My constantly-in-motion mother would rather skin herself than take a nap. It seemed terribly obvious that *just to live* couldn't possibly be the answer. How indulgent and possibly even illegal in its lack of ambition.

I filed Filmore's answer away in my mind just in case, but I kept on asking people.

For around fifty years, I'd been asking. Yet, somehow, I was no closer to the truth—or maybe just an answer that satisfied whatever it was I was looking for. Which is how I decided to turn my fiftieth birthday party into a secret mission to get to the bottom of the Goddamned Point of It All.

A week after Jesse's call from the Secret Service and on the morning of my birthday party, I shoved a mini peach-colored, frosted rose cupcake in my mouth and looked at my watch.

My guests were on their way, speeding obliviously toward a gathering of involuntary soul-searching around the firepit in our backyard that, if all went well, would help subdue my secret existential breakdown and bring me closer to the Meaning of Life.

Yes, Jesse was just weeks away from leaving home for college, and our son, Sam, was just a few years behind her. And yes, I was just shy of being a half-century old, right on schedule for the clichéd midlife crisis. But the truth was, I'd been wrestling with a deep angst for years—even before this new, hideous emergence of envy toward my own offspring had recently surfaced, even before I had a family. So it felt less like a midlife crisis than it did an animal force of grief, folded in shame.

Guilt wrapped around my good fortune with slimy, muscled tentacles: Who was *I* to be unhappy? But I was. Behind the rosy skin of my happy family, I'd been sinking into a river of dread and anxiety, and the source of it was a mystery.

To make matters worse, most of my friends and I were slogging through what I'd come to call the Year of Lasts, which any parent of a college-bound kid could tell you is a guilt-edged grief-fest in which you're supposed to be all joy and pride for your kids—*You did it! You're graduating!*—but secretly you're bleeding from the heart. The last Halloween, the last Valentine's Day, the last birthdays celebrated as a family. As each event came, I couldn't help it: I was stupefied with nostalgia, reliving all the years that had come before.

I checked my watch again. Fifteen minutes until everyone arrived. I walked outside into our backyard to rest my eyes on the hills nestled above our valley. Golden and undulating, they stretched for miles in the sharp light of the waning autumn sun. Giant stands of dark-green oaks dotted the beckoning landscape.

I put my hand on the cool, gray trunk of our ancient bay tree, so massive it seemed to hold up our whole backyard. I looked up into its deep-green, leafy canopy. *Goddamn it, this is the year I have to figure things out*, I thought.

The doorbell rang. The party was on.

Thirty minutes later, my friends had all arrived.

"Okay," I announced, "time for our Wisdom Circle!"

Everyone took their seats around the firepit, mojitos and wineglasses in hand.

I started.

"This is not about you having some giant pearl of wisdom to impart!" (Except it was.) I looked around the fire and read the collective change of expression on my friends' faces as they realized that I was about to ask them to publicly emote.

"Okay, can you please not be miserable?" I pleaded.

All ten of them looked back at me, miserable.

"Here's my question for you," I continued. "When we were kids, we all wondered what our lives were going to be: What would we do when we grew up? Who were we going to be? And then the years unfolded. And now here we are, smack in midlife, and a lot of those questions have been answered."

The light had started to fade, and the air was getting still. Flames danced in shades of orange and white. I had their attention now.

"So, tell me, are there parts of yourself that got buried along the way? Are there parts that you long for? And how are you doing here, in the middle of your life? Have you gotten any closer to what the point of it all is?"

One by one, voices rose in the gathering darkness.

"I've always felt like a hippie inside," Gina said. "Like, I wanted to be a social activist. So what did I do? First I became a corporate lawyer, and now I'm the communications director for the temple. What the fuck?"

Everyone chuckled.

"I feel lost," said Grace, a social worker originally from New York City. "After Dylan, my youngest, left for college this year, it felt like the bottom fell out of my insides. Aside from my job, my focus has been on raising my three kids for so many years. I've always been so sure of who I am. Now I wake up in the morning and I just feel like I'm floating. Floating away."

Ilana raised her hand. "Me too. I figured I'd go back to work after the kids left home. But I've been looking for a job for the last two years, and it's a joke. I've got two degrees, but after this many years out of the game, I'm looking at nanny listings."

It was my turn. "Well," I started, "when I was a kid, every Thursday, I waited for Anna Quindlen's column in the *New York Times*. She was the only regular female columnist they had, and she wrote about life. All I wanted was to grow up and do what she did. And now, here I am, fifty years old, and I never became the writer I always thought I'd be—like, not even close. It's as if at some point along the way, I just blocked myself out from my own calling. And now it feels like it's all too late—it's over, I'm done."

I looked over at Lucy, whose silvery, shoulder-length hair had been released from its usual ponytail for the occasion. She sat cross-legged, knitting furiously.

"Look," I went on, "I know we're all *supposed* to be having a midlife crisis right about now, but this feels different, deeper. On the other hand, compared to the rest of the universe, I know how insanely lucky I am to have all that I have. Unfortunately, that just adds more self-loathing to the shit pile."

Lucy pushed up her glasses. I waved to my right.

"Next!"

Judy raised her glass. "Well, I've got a little bit of a different perspective. I'm seventy-five years old and buried Jack last year. Married fifty years. I miss him so much, but what I feel—well, what I'm working on feeling—is a deep sense of gratitude. Gratitude for all we had together, gratitude to be alive. My next chapter is focused on gratitude. I think that's what matters most."

I looked at Judy and my heart ached for her loss but also yearned for her clarity. What a relief it must be for her, in some way, to be in the homestretch of her life. No more pressure. No more expectation of who she was going "to be." Simply permission to be in her life, to just be, and to hold it all with love and grace.

The conversation went deep into the night and left everyone filled with the magic of what happens when women and generous amounts of time coalesce. We learned about one another, driven by the electricity of connection and how deep and complex humans are, how mysterious.

After the last, long hug goodbye, I closed the door. The silence in the house surrounded me. Soon, Dave, Jesse, and Sam would return from their party exile.

I looked out at the darkening sky beyond. The joy and energy of the evening were still palpable, but as wonderful as our time together had been, no revelatory answers had emerged. I felt no closer to clarity, no wiser regarding the Meaning of Life.

Still, I was determined in this fiftieth year to once and for all figure it out for myself. But how? And why did I think this year would be any different from any that came before it? I looked through the window for our bay tree, but by now it was indistinguishable from the black sky. I could already feel the quiet return of the familiar ache.

As I turned back toward the kitchen, my eye caught the photograph that sat on my desk. I bent over.

"Danny," I whispered to my little brother, meeting his gaze. "I'm fifty. *Fifty years old.* Can you believe it?"

In the image, Danny was eight years old. His halo of hair was thick and brown; his brown eyes were huge and soulful. He was tan and smiling shyly in his red-and-white basketball jersey, frozen in time.

Danny had died eighteen years after that photo was taken. Adulthood had been just a dream back then. Now here I was, married with two grown children, entering the last third of my life.

"I miss you, Danny."

My eyes filled as I touched his smile, encased in glass and memory. A lifetime had passed without him.

Three

If childhood is meant to be wrapped in love and play, I'm lucky because ours is.

My father's devotion is a river running beneath our family, constant and deep. He leaves for work early and comes home late, and each night the lurch of the garage door announces his return. The moment never fails to fill me with a sense of relief and comfort, like something has been restored. Before anything else, he trudges up the stairs, wood creaking beneath the red shag under his feet, to visit each of us in our bedrooms as we do our homework and to ask about our day.

As a kid, my father wasn't so lucky. He was raised by a mother known for stepping on a mouse with her bare foot to get rid of it. When my father left his pet snake's cage open one too many times, she flushed the snake down the toilet. She kept a hawk eye on my aunt's every bite of food, admonishing her that if she got fat, she would never marry.

My grandfather was a kind man, but his gentle nature was overridden by my grandmother's dominance. When they bought a grocery store in Springfield, Missouri, several hours away from their home in Kansas City, they sent my aunt to live with a cousin and left my father to live alone, at sixteen years old, in the family's apartment. There, my father skipped school and passed the time with his friends on the open porch, smoking cigars and drinking whiskey.

How my father somehow managed to eventually pull it together enough to go to college, graduate from law school, and go on to become an accomplished attorney, no one can say, least of all him. "I didn't have the faintest idea what I was doing," he'd always say.

But to me, far more extraordinary than his professional accomplishments is the person my father became in spite of his upbringing. His exterior can be rough and his wit often biting, but on the inside he is like soft gold: incredibly loving, devoted, and pure of heart. Our family is his center.

Our mother is Sophia Loren–kind–of–beautiful, and her velvet heart is her beauty's perfect match. She is my father's counterpart. While my father speaks his love in hard work and parental oversight, my mother speaks hers in affection and caregiving, which she does with the light of a thousand suns. She is a blur of cooking and carpooling and doing craft projects with us. We make tiny ceramic figurines together. We make candy houses. She helps us with our homework. She runs from one thing to the next, driven by an energy that never lets up, doing mysterious and endless mom things that we can never really identify. We are steeped in love.

My brother Red is funny and smart and my idol for the way he makes life look easy. He is always off with cool friends doing cool things. And Danny and I—we're a team. We're allowed to watch TV for only thirty minutes each week. Together, we agonize between *Mork & Mindy* and *The Love Boat*. In a time before smartphones and tablets and a developed social life outside the house, we're partners and conspirators, happily thrown together to make our own fun.

Saturday mornings are always the same—no school, no plans, the whole day before us.

"What should we do, Stiggy?" This is my favorite nickname for Danny, given to him by our great-uncle. No one knows what it means.

"Let's get the hat!" he says on cue.

Danny is a beautiful boy, almost more pretty than handsome. He has planet-wide eyes and thick, dark lashes, a perfect little nose with triangle nostrils. His shy half smile shows his Chiclets-white teeth. He is thin and lithe and always tan, muscular in that young-boy way—without trying to be. He is always the fastest runner in his class but doesn't brag about it.

I run to fish the old Kansas City Royals baseball hat out of the coat closet.

"What are you two doing?" Mom calls from the kitchen sink.

"I don't know!" I call out. "Something!"

When I get back to Danny, he's sitting on the floor in our wood-paneled family room, his long brown legs extended in a *V*, already ripping up the little pieces of paper. He hands me a stack.

"Okay, let's think of really cool stuff this time. No poppycock!" *Poppycock* is one of Danny's favorite words. He says it as often as possible, whether it makes sense or not.

"Yeah, yeah," I say. "No poppycock."

Then we do what we always do. We write down every activity we can think of on little slips of paper, throw them in the hat, and then pick them out one at a time and do them. But first, as an opening ceremony to the festivities, we sit at the very top of the red shag-rug-covered staircase and make giant carpet puffballs by stripping the wool from the strands (an illegal activity that is kept off the official list).

Official activities include:

1. Bike racing around the block, offering house commentary along the way: "That's ugly" or "I bet it smells in there" or "I could live there."

2. Hide-and-seek with our Brittany spaniel, Alfie, who sits patiently as we blindfold her with a handkerchief, and then we scatter to hide from her. The moment we call her name, she paws off the cloth and tears through the yard at lightning speed, finding us one by one.

3. Lemonade stand. A frustrating activity, since we are only allowed to set up shop in front of our house, which is in the middle of a quiet suburban street. "Mom, what do you think is going to happen? We live in *Prairie Village, Kansas!*" "That's all right, just go in front of our house. I'll call the neighbors and tell them you're selling." "But Mom, that's fake!" "Go on, just go." No sooner than we've lined up our little Dixie cups, our next-door neighbor Carole dutifully walks over, acting all surprised and thirsty.

4. Picnic, which consists of raiding the refrigerator for random items (white bread, pickles, apples) and walking to the end of our block to lay down our spread on a blue-flowered blanket in the middle of a tall stand of trees that feels like it's a world away from home.

5. Mary Poppins. For this, we take turns climbing our backyard swing set and standing on top of the monkey bars, which of course aren't meant for standing on. We open our umbrella and jump off the

swingset, yelling, "Mary Poppins!" as we pray like crazy that this time the wind will carry us up, up, and away into the sky.

Today, Mary Poppins is the first activity out of the hat, much to Danny's delight.

"Yessss! Mary Poppins!" he cries.

"Let's go!" I say.

After completing our carpet-stripping, puffball-building opening ceremony, we run to the coat closet, wrap our arms around every umbrella we own (for variety), and head for the backyard.

Our swing set has all kinds of fun things on it, including swings of differing heights, monkey bars, and a little red car thingy suspended from two iron bars that two people can fit into, cable-car style. The car thingy is our favorite. Danny and I sit across from each other and push down on the foot pedals to propel us back and forth so fast that we are certain the thingy will eventually shoot us off into space.

We are a joyful duo. We are a two-person pack, playmates on an endless playdate.

Outside, umbrella in hand, I climb to the top of our swing set and say my silent little prayer. *This time, please, God, let me fly.* "Here I go, Stiggy!"

"Lulu!" Mom calls from the kitchen window. Our family is full of nicknames, and Lulu is one of my mother's many for me. The one she chooses at any given moment is dependent on her mood. Lulabelle is for when she's happiest, and it's my favorite.

I see her craning her head out the window.

"Lulu, you know I don't like when you do that!"

There's no stopping me.

"But Mom—this time, I might fly!"

All I want is to fly.

Four

As I sat at my kitchen desk post–fiftieth birthday party and looked at the picture of Danny in his red tank top, my mind drifted back.

Danny's downward spiral started with barely a whisper. I was a senior in high school, working on the school newspaper and busy with college applications. Red was a junior at Swarthmore College in Pennsylvania, and Danny was a high school freshman.

After school, Danny and I had always hung out in the kitchen together, kicking the day around, playing with the dogs. But by his freshman year, he was becoming increasingly withdrawn. Instead of meeting me in the kitchen after school, he'd walk through the front door and plod slowly up the red shag stairs, straight to his room. He'd stay alone there for hours, listening to Pink Floyd, Metallica, and Deep Purple.

Finally, I brought it up with my mom, lamenting that my playmate had started to disappear lately.

"I don't know, Lulu," she told me. "He's fifteen. It's the age, I guess." I wondered whether her words were a decoy, a disguise to the concern I could swear I felt gathering in the space between us.

After weeks of the same behavior, I knocked on Danny's door. "Hi," I said, opening the door and looking around his room.

"Hi," he said flatly. He was lying on his bed with a Pink Floyd album cover on his chest, looking up at the ceiling.

"Is something going on, Stiggy?" I asked. His childhood nickname was awkward on my tongue.

"What do you mean?" His eyes darted above my head.

"I mean, you seem down lately. Is something going on? Is everything okay?"

"I'm fine," he said, eyes fixed on the ceiling. But I knew my brother. Something was working inside him. Something new, something dark, had begun to brim behind his gaze.

"Well, I'm here, okay?" I said, sitting down on his bed. "I know starting high school is hard, and I'm here if you want to talk."

"Yeah, thanks, Sister Julie," he said sharply, his nickname for me sounding equally forced. I could feel him waiting for me to leave.

A few weeks later, Danny told my mother, "I don't feel good." *I don't feel good.*

Those four simple words would begin a story that would change our family forever.

As the months passed, Danny's withdrawal turned into a shadowy energy that settled around him. He stopped joking around with me. A grimness set in around his mouth. His presence in the house took on a new life—murky and inscrutable, heavy and dark. I grew into a new habit of checking to see whether he was home the moment I walked through our front door. Over time, the sight of his closed bedroom door triggered a Pavlovian response of concern laced with a secret resentment for the anxiety he was spreading in our family.

When I graduated high school that summer and left home to join Red at Swarthmore College, it was with a heavy heart.

"Mom," I said, "do you think Danny's going to be all right? Do you think this is just a phase?"

"I hope so, Lulu." But by now, my mother could not hide her worry. It was sinking into us both without a sound.

Standing next to my desk on the night of my fiftieth birthday party, I brought the childhood picture of Danny closer to my face and stared into his eyes, searching for signs.

If only we could have known what was to come.

Five

As the buzz of the party settled into memory, I replayed in my mind what my friends had shared around the fire that night.

Clearly, most of us were trying to make peace with this middle space of our lives. We'd all spent the last two decades shaping our days, psyches, and souls around raising our children. As that part of our lives wound to a close, we were trying to make contact with who we were now, what remained of us.

My great-aunt Etty floated to mind. She was one of the few people in my young life who seemed to understand my tireless search for the Meaning of Life.

Etty had a heaping hive of copper hair, a deeply lined face, and giant green eyes set behind huge, square-framed, fire-engine-red glasses. She always wore flamingo-pink lipstick that matched her extra-long nails.

Although she was my great-aunt, she always insisted that I call her by her first name—I think to make the point that she was too young to be a great-aunt, although she was in her seventies when I was a kid.

Every few months, Etty would call me up and take me to lunch at the Dragon Inn, a family-run Chinese restaurant that had been around forever and had an ominously dark-green carpet that hid who-knew-what secrets.

Coming from a family that was always too busy exercising its relentless work ethic to go out for lunch, Etty's invitations felt joyfully decadent, sanctioned by a family member who was so different in nature from my parents.

Etty always took a great and constant interest in my activities and opinions, even though I didn't have many of either. She was especially fond of imparting pearls of wisdom about how to live.

"Honey!" she would say routinely and with great seriousness, putting her wrinkly, powdery face right up to mine. "Just remember one thing: we only go around this life once. *But if you do it right, once is enough!*"

Each time she told me this, I had new hope, like I might finally be inching closer to understanding the Meaning of Life.

"But Etty, how *do* you do it right?"

She would nod at me with a glint in her eye and say, "Remember what I keep telling you? It takes time, honey! *Time!*"

Over egg rolls at one of our lunches, Etty gave me a pearl of parenting advice that I would take to my grave.

"Think you want kids, baby?" she asked in her deep, papery voice. Etty had one son who aggravated her to no end.

"Well," I said, "I don't really like little kids, but I guess I'll have them."

She took a bite of her egg roll and chewed slowly. "Well, sweetheart," she began in a whisper.

I leaned in, knowing I needed to listen hard.

"You just take your sweet time."

"I mean, I'm pretty young, so—"

"I know *that!*" she said with fanfare, reaching her hand out between us until her long, flamingo-pink index fingernail was right between my eyes. "What I'm saying is, you just take your sweeeeeet time, because once those little *fuckers* are out of you"—and now she was yelling, and the ladies at the next table jerked their heads around to look at us—"they're on your back for the rest of your life! *For the rest of your life!*"

Etty's finger was now jabbing the air up and down wildly, pointing to the dark-green carpet. "They're on your back 'til they put you in the hole, honey! *Till they put you in the hole!*"

I was twelve years old. I tried not to shriek.

Eighteen years after Etty died, I was put to the test. Pregnant, with my due date speeding toward me, I was obsessed with one terrifying question: What happens when your identity has been built around one set of things—academic and professional achievement, let's say, grades and career and productivity—and then, all at once, you consider trading that for what society has deemed the polar opposite thing?

I called my brother Red. We were both theoretically full-fledged adults by then, but he was still my cool big brother whose opinion I revered. That day I called in hopes that he would help me grapple with whether to stay at my job as the founding executive director of my Boston community service organization or leave the workforce and stay at home with my new baby.

I had no idea at the time that I had unwittingly wandered into the heart of what became known as the Mommy Wars debate. This, I would eventually learn firsthand, was a war in which both sides lose: The working moms lose at the hands of a corporate system built for full-time workers. The stay-at-home moms lose at the hands of a society that worships working, productivity, and financial earnings and in which motherhood is an invisible given.

And so on the day that I made that SOS phone call to Red—a call that would ultimately lead me to decide to leave my job and the working world—I had no idea that I was about to pull the plug on my professional future, in some ways irrevocably.

I laid out my dilemma: "I can't imagine not working. I can't imagine who I would be without a job. But I'm so scared I won't be able to balance it. And also, working like maniacs is what our family does, isn't it? How can anything else not feel like shit?"

"Julie," Red said, "it's true, but this is different. Your kids are only going to be young once, and you've got your whole life to work. You're lucky enough to be able to have a choice."

Ah, a choice. Another thing I didn't realize: Over time that privileged choice would pave the way for writing myself out of my own life. The choice I ultimately made would also mean losing contact with an incalculably deep part of myself, my professional identity, and my dreams and aspirations beyond the province of my family and friends.

In the moment, it seemed so logical.

"I know how lucky I am that Dave earns enough for me to be able to stop working, Reddy," I told my brother. "And in some ways, it makes staying at work almost seem selfish, since the expense of childcare would probably be more than I'm making now."

"Is that really true?" he asked.

It *was* true, and many of my childbearing Gen X friends were in the same boat. Some of us may have had the privilege of choice, but, especially when our own earnings were modest, that choice seemed to render our own careers little more than indulgent.

If my salary didn't make a material difference to the family bank, was my career really more important than being able to be the primary caregiver of our children in those early years? Was my professional fulfillment really that important in the grand scheme of things?

I did not yet have the insight or self-value to realize that the answer to that question was *yes*. But my soul must have known enough to put up a little fight.

"Reddy," I yelled into the phone, "haven't I worked my ass off all these years to become something in the bigger world? Am I really going to give that all up to be a stay-at-home mom? Which basically means you're invisible and shat upon by society? Also, I'm afraid being home with a baby full time might bore me into a coma."

"Listen," he said, "no one's making you. Do you think you can do both well?"

I was quiet. I knew I *could* be a working mother. But I was only half-joking about the coma issue, because at the heart of my struggle was a dirty little secret that went beyond societal expectations or politics. I was afraid of myself.

I had already proven that despite my best intentions, I usually chose work over everything else—self-care, time with friends, even at times my marriage. So why did I think a drooling, pooping baby was going to compel me to make better choices? If left to my own devices, what evidence was there that I wouldn't choose the excitement and stimulation of work over my child, again and again? *Whoops, sorry, hon, I have to work late. Damn, I missed her bedtime . . . again!*

Did I really think I'd have the discipline to draw healthy boundaries around work when the simple, guilty truth was that I would most likely find work far more compelling than taking care of a baby? The answer was a thundering no, and our children would be ruined because I was a selfish person and a terrible mother.

Maybe I needed to give in to my black-and-white nature—make a choice that would take my future choices away.

"It would be hard," I said.

"Look, you could definitely do both if you wanted to," Red said. "But just remember, you've got the rest of your life to work."

I wanted to believe the logic in Red's words. It seemed so rational. But my chest constricted with the next question that surfaced in my head: *Once I'm out of the working world, will I ever be able to get back in?*

We sat on the phone in silence. Red's words reverberated in my mind. *It'll only be a few years. I can go back once they're in school. My kids will only be young once.*

I used my brother's words to silence the voice inside.

"Okay, you're right. That's what I should do, even if I do completely lose my identity," I said, only half-joking.

And so that was it. I gave notice to my organization's board of directors.

When I did, I felt two things:
I am doing the right thing for my family.
I am making a huge mistake.

Two epidurals and twenty-three hours of labor later, a nurse placed in my arms a pink, breathing being with a tiny face, tightly wrapped in a flannel hospital blanket . . . like a holy, living burrito, packaging a million dreams. Jesse Danielle.

Dave lay in the hospital bed next to me and leaned his head against mine. I turned to seek out his luminous hazel eyes, and I saw the tears falling gently down his face.

There are times in life when love feels so palpable, so fully manifest in a space, that you can almost hold it in your arms. Like this. Like the love I felt for this man to whom I had pledged my life, whose tears, I knew, maybe even more than joy, were tears of relief. Relief that both Jesse and I had come through the hard labor unharmed, relief that all the things he'd imagined could go wrong hadn't. This was one of the albatrosses that Dave carried in his profession as a doctor, I had learned—the knowledge of the body's fragility and the endless ways in which life can change on a dime.

Something strange happened next. Newborn infants cannot see more than a few inches in front of them in their first few weeks of life; their eyes during that time period appear blurry and unfocused. But the moment I took Baby Jesse in my arms, she looked straight at me with a gaze that I could only describe as otherworldly.

There was nothing about her eyes that was infant-like; there was no sign of the fog of childbirth. It was as if she was already an old person, so old, and urgently trying to communicate something. I just didn't know what.

She held my gaze in hers for what was probably five seconds, but it felt like five minutes. Then her old-person eyes moved slowly over my shoulder and upward to Dave, and she rested her gaze on him for a long while.

There was no sound. Just a complete and knowing being boring its soul into ours, seemingly trying to share something—a message, a prayer, a blessing, perhaps.

And then it was over and our baby was just a baby again, erupting into little, urgent newborn cries, eyes suddenly blurry and filling with tears.

"I have something really weird to tell you, and you're not going to believe it," I said to Dave that night. I was hesitant to tell him because, as is the case for many doctors, the spiritual world inspired in him little more than an eye roll and the label of psychobabble.

"What?" he asked.

"When the nurse first gave Jesse to me—"

"I know. . . . I saw," he said quietly, his eyes flickering. "She looked right at you and then at me."

"Her eyes were like an old soul speaking," I said. "Do you think . . . ?"

But I felt too silly to finish my sentence, to admit that I longed for this brief flash to be Danny's soul. Danny, for whom she was named. Danny, who had been gone for two years. Danny, who I so badly wished could be with me now. Had that been him looking out of the eyes of Jesse Danielle, his new niece, his flesh and blood, whom he would never see and who would never know him?

"I saw it," Dave said. "I don't know what to say. I saw it too."

What were we to do with that moment? We had no idea. We just put the memory aside and became fumbling new parents, crazy in love.

But right off the bat, there were little arrows pointing to how eventually it was headed secretly south. I had landed in a surreal alternate reality that had seemingly sprung up in Technicolor overnight. One day,

I worked a very respectable job with an office and a business card and a title and people who were waiting to talk to me. I'd been spearheading community projects, meeting with CEOs, sharing an event stage with Secretary of State Colin Powell, fielding questions from the press. And now? Now I sat cross-legged in a circle of new mothers singing "Ring Around the Rosie" with a drooling baby on my lap. Now I was "Jesse's mom," walking around with little cascades of dried vomit down my shirt.

It was clear . . . before, I was many things: executive director, writer, strategic planner, program developer, fundraiser, community leader. Now I was one thing. I lived in a seven-day-a-week world of singsongy, high-pitched tones. Conversations were limited to baby talk. Days of all the same thing: caregiving. No matter how I sliced it—or how much I loved being with Jesse—a stay-at-home mom was a fraught designation.

A few months into the gig, in a desperate effort to have a conversation that didn't include sleep schedules and mortifyingly named products like My Brest Friend, I called up one of my former board members to say hello.

Jim answered with a warm, familiar voice. We'd worked together for years.

"Hey, Jim!" I said, heart lifting at the sound of my old life.

"Ah, it's Julie Fingersh!" he laughed with a breezy edge. "Back from the dead?"

My heart stopped. Did he really just say that?

Back from the dead?

My mind replayed it. *Yes. Yes, he did.*

"I didn't *die,* Jim," I said, a little too loudly. "I'm just home taking care of my daughter for a while. . . ."

"Oh, of course!" he said quickly. "Most important job in the world!"

There it was: the fake marketing campaign for motherhood subverted by society's real opinion on the matter.

There seemed only one way to feel good about this new, blessed, complex reality. I channeled my joy—right along with my low-level grief—into a hyperfocus on my baby and the walls around me. I learned that it was easier to let go of my lost world entirely and immerse myself in my new twilight-zone universe.

It took time, but eventually I did lose myself in that world. And I was surprised to find how much pleasure there was in how the days unfolded, one by one, in a pleasing and unfamiliar clarity of microscopic focus. *Is Jesse up? Is she hungry? Do I nurse lying down? And if I do, will I roll over and kill her? Okay, she's up! Now for a walk! Now for a few swings in the park. Now she's crying. Get the bottle! What'll I make for dinner? Better clean up the mess before Dave gets home from work so he doesn't see what a wreck I am!*

Although I couldn't escape the feeling that I'd become a 1950s housewife, I also couldn't help but appreciate, after having lived my entire conscious life thus far in a sprint to achieve and produce, the secret freedom that came from walking off the working field.

I discovered a sunny, surprising relief in the simplicity of my new world. No more Excel spreadsheets. No more presentations, grant deadlines, or board meetings. No more strategic plans and the constant stress of keeping our company coffers full.

I felt at once liberated and isolated—irrelevant to the rest of the world but filled with a novel clarity regarding what to do in every next moment. All the daily angst that attended working in my old world evaporated. My endless striving to follow my family's credo of *Do, Do, Do* had been dismissed; my endless searching for the right next step had been suspended.

Big thing of the week now? Miss Katherine's music class! And yay, Baby Jesse was a star! Look how Jesse clapped up a storm while her fellow students were slumped over, snoring.

Wow, I marveled, *she's so bright!*

And so it went, year after year. Days disappearing into a blur of mealtimes and naps and developmental milestones. Holidays, birthdays. One week folded into the next. Life fell into a rhythm that felt as solid and predictable and existentially peaceful as any days I'd ever had.

And then, in what seemed like a flash, Jesse was two years old. After being cloistered at home for months, it was time to pay a visit to the real world. As fraught and surreal an occasion as it threatened to be, my fifteenth high school reunion in Kansas City was upon me, and I forced myself to go.

High school reunions can be great fun. They can serve up an opportunity for the ultimate revenge on the people who made you miserable back then—that is, if you're going back in triumph, with great success to report. But beware of going back when you're feeling small.

My former classmates and I—the thirty of us brave enough to show up—sat in a circle. Our host introduced an icebreaker exercise in which we were to give a one-minute summary of our lives since we'd left one another all those years ago.

I felt the familiar pit in my stomach. At the time of our graduation fifteen years earlier, the other girls in this circle had voted me, among our sixty classmates, "Most Likely to Succeed."

I looked at the faces around the circle, each of which had aged in a way that felt strange, like we were in the second act of the theater production of our lives.

Oh God, now what? How could I possibly spin an impressive version of myself to my former classmates when my days were currently centered on keeping the house from imploding from the circus of toddler mayhem?

What do you do? For me, the words never failed to land like a hand grenade—an impossibly casual but loaded challenge to account for the very worth of my life. How could I make my life sound like it had a shred of value in a society that paid little more than lip service to the importance of motherhood? When far too many people judged a woman's choice to leave the workforce as an opting out from the real world?

No matter how many times I had been asked the question, I could not find words that felt anything but uncomfortable and pathetic. A ticket to being dismissed.

My turn in our circle came, and this time would be no different.

Well, a little different. Worse.

"Hi guys," I said, laughing nervously. "It's so great to see everyone. Wow. So I'll try to sum up my life story in under a minute. I know the last time we saw each other, I was editor of the school paper and on my way to a giant career as a writer. And, well, here's what happened. I was right on the path after college. I moved to New York City and wrote for *BusinessWeek* and *Billboard Magazine*. Then my husband and I met at a bar in the West Village, fell in love, and moved to Boston. I took a break from journalism to become the founding director of a community organization. And don't ask me how this happened, but now I'm a stay-at-home mom with our two-year-old daughter, driving a minivan, and chairing her preschool's annual campaign . . ."

My mouth was going and going and I could not stop it. I could feel my self-deprecation backfiring miserably, my cheeks reddening, but there was no turning back.

"Yeah, so no letters after my name, no breadwinning, no column in the *New York Times*. But I do have a really, really cute little girl!"

The group laughed politely. I wanted to shoot myself.

The evening only got worse from there, as I was forced to have the same awful catch-up conversation with one former classmate after another, each of whom kept saying things like "Wow, I'm really surprised you don't work."

The entire event felt like one gargantuan indictment, a pounding verdict that I had failed my potential and abandoned my ambition. The Mommy Wars were kicking the shit out of me.

The next morning, I boarded a plane back to Boston. I could not wait to get home, where there was no trial and no judgment and where Dave was waiting for me. There, in my cozy little world, I could lose my-self in Jesse's radiant being—her endless chant of "Mama Mama Mama," her little hands grasping for my face, never wanting to let me go.

Eventually, I started to figure it out. Here's the deal with parenting, as far as I could tell: You give birth to a baby, and this baby takes you places you never thought possible. This baby makes your heart burst and heave in ways you never imagined.

If you have a spouse, sure, you love him or her or them. But let's face it, love them all you want, the sound of their chewing still bugs you. Or they always get you terrible birthday gifts. Or they don't get you any gifts. Or they don't notice when you've dressed up for them, or they reach for the bigger piece of meat.

But your babies, your children?

I mean, yes, there are moments when you want to kill them, but that's because you're sleep deprived and have no idea what you're doing. Those moments aside, you love them like you've never loved anything in your whole life. You're a new mother, and you don't even think it's weird to stick your nose in their little mouths to smell their milky breath, because that smell is some kind of magical elixir to all else that's wrong in the world.

You don't just love them. You are *in* love with them. It's a romance you've never known, and, unlike with everyone else in your life, you *stay* in love with them. You follow them around the house as they crawl and then walk and then talk. You cry through their recitals, marveling at how they are growing and growing into amazing, independent beings with thoughts and lives—first little, and then big—of their own.

And then the years zoom past in a blur, and you look back and wonder why you wanted their naps to last longer and why you were always in such a hurry.

"Mama," Jesse said to me once when she was about seven years old, "why are we always in a rush, even when we aren't really in a hurry?"

But you were, see? You were.

Jesse's Latvian babysitter, Frida, who escaped the Nazis and never stopped rushing around, explained it to me.

"Julie? Vee are running to de grave," she always said, laughing, even though we both knew it wasn't funny. "Vee can't help it. Vee run."

And then, before I knew it, Jesse's high school senior year was upon us and we were neck-deep in learning which school was the right "fit" and trying to help her reduce her whole life into a story that would capture the vote of some twenty-three-year-old college admissions officer with the life perspective of a kiwi.

And then there she was, walking down that grassy-green walkway in a cap and gown and Ray-Bans and Vans, sharing smiles and laughs with childhood friends she would never share life with the same way again.

In just a blink or two, she would be off to college.

Six

B ut not quite yet. Because now that my birthday party was behind me, it was time to take Jesse to Silicon Valley, where she would drive the White House press around in a massive van during Hillary Clinton's campaign events.

As we got our things together, our Brittany Scotch briefly took note of our burst of activity by ambling up to me and poking my knee.

The thing about Scotch was, even if he was the one who approached us, if we responded too enthusiastically, he instantly lost interest. We'd coo and smother his mahogany-brown face with kisses while he looked blankly off into the middle distance. Eventually, if you played your cards right, with a perfect balance of attention and detachment, he'd hand you a paw or give a cursory lick to your face with his dry, papery pink tongue, just to keep your addiction to him going. Scotch's aloofness only increased his lovability. We were in a constant state of longing.

Like everyone lucky enough to have pets in their lives, each member of our family shared a deep, joyful, private language with him. During all of Jesse and Sam's childhood, he was my copilot, riding shotgun for hours in my black minivan while the kids talked to him from their car seats in back. Nearly every day, he would run with me in the Marin County hills, sticking his nose into various holes—his tiny, cropped stub tail wagging madly—hunting insects and rodents since he was denied the dignity of the real hunting he was bred for.

Unfortunately, he also routinely surfed through the garbage, rolled in rotting carcasses, wolfed down horse poop, and Houdinied his way out of our house so often that after a while our neighbors just let him back into the yard without telling us. "God, you're such a pain in the ass," was muttered in our house plenty.

But then there was his constancy and the way his presence was instantly grounding, calming, and comforting. There was the smell of his fur and the pleasure of his beauty. There was the sight of him bounding in the hills with a strength and jubilance that never failed to make people stop and watch. And there was the way he taught us all to strive less and savor more and that lying in the sun was a worthy, and maybe even the worthiest, endeavor.

I bent down to him. "We'll be back soon, Scotchie." I applied a battery of kisses to the top of his soft head before, with a brief, slightly gratifying wag of his stubby tail, he trotted off.

We pulled out of our driveway and headed for the Four Seasons in Palo Alto, where Jesse was to meet the Clinton campaign entourage. I looked over at her in the passenger seat, putting blush on in the sun-visor mirror. She looked like a miniature senior executive in her black Ann Taylor suit, copper hair gleaming and almost straight from my blow-dry job.

Her eyes shone beneath her mascaraed lashes, but her face was pale. "You all right, Jess?"

"Yeah, just my stomach."

"Nervous?"

"No, I'm really not. It just hurts."

We stopped twice for a bathroom on the way.

"I can't believe I have a stomach thing today of all days," she moaned.

I tucked my anxiety into advice. "Yeah, it sucks, but just remember, Jess, if you have to pull over, you have to pull over. The press will just have to wait."

"Yeah, but what a nightmare," she said, shaking her head.

I winced at the prospect of Jesse needing to stop a van full of reporters and interrupting the Clinton motorcade because she had the runs. "It really is."

We made it just a few minutes before her briefing began. As I started to turn into the parking lot of the hotel, a large man in a black suit and mirrored sunglasses walked directly in front of my car, holding his hand up like a big stop sign.

I put down my window.

"You here for the motorcade?" he asked, looking past me to Jesse.

"Yep," Jesse said without a beat.

"Joe, Secret Service." He reached across me to shake her hand.

I tried not to be a pathetic, passive-aggressive mother, but I couldn't help it. "Yeah, and hi, Joe, I'm Julie Fingersh, Jesse's mother."

Joe looked at me, bored. "Hello, ma'am. You're going to need to stop right here. Can't go past the gate. Jesse? Why don't you come with me?"

Then Joe somehow looked both back at me and through me at the same time.

"Ma'am, you don't need to be back here to pick her up until 4:00 p.m. Please make sure you stop at the gate when you come."

Jesse was already out the door. "Bye, Mom!"

"Okay, bye, Jess. Be really, really careful! Love you!"

But she didn't hear me. She'd already slammed the door and was running carefully in her high heels, catching up to Joe.

I looked at the dashboard clock. It was 7:40 a.m.

While Jesse was getting debriefed by the Hillary Clinton campaign chair and about to be flanked by a presidential candidate and White House reporters, I had nowhere to go and nothing to do.

I looked across the highway and saw the familiar bull's-eye logo. Target. I knew their hours by heart. They would be open in twenty minutes. *Always shit to get for the house!*

I pulled into the giant, empty parking lot and turned off the ignition. I looked down at myself in my navy sweatpants covered in dog fur, my black tank top, and sweatsuit top that I'd worn in case I got inspired to take a run in some random Palo Alto neighborhood. I looked at my watch. Still fifteen minutes until Target opened.

"I guess this is my fucking life!" I told the steering wheel.

I looked in my rearview mirror and saw Jesse's face, but thirty years older. I had two deep grooves between my eyes—the ones that Sam said made me look angry. My formerly (theoretically) adorable freckles now just looked like sun damage. My hair was gray at the roots, overdue for a dye job.

I looked at myself. How was it that I, who by now was supposed to be Anna Quindlen, or at least one of the White House reporters, was sitting in an empty parking lot at 7:45 a.m., waiting for Target to open so I could browse the housewares aisle?

I thought back to that conversation I'd had with Red when I was pregnant with Jesse about whether to stay at my job or quit and become a stay-at-home mother. When I decided on the latter, I planned to be out of the workforce for a few years at most. But in the interim, Dave finished his medical residency and we moved to San Francisco for his new job. By then, Jesse was three and I was pregnant with Sam. I kept thinking about my writing but never seemed to find the time.

By the time Sam arrived, we'd moved to the Bay Area suburbs and I'd sunk into a community of stay-at-home moms who became a shield of permission that I used to silence my ambivalence about giving up my professional and creative life outside my family.

Soon, the voice of the ambitious young woman I'd once been became like one of those old AM radio stations: crackling, remote. *I'll get back to it when Sam's a few years older*, I told myself. Then eighteen years passed.

I thought about Etty and how right about now she would raise her long, flamingo-pink nail and stab the air in front of my face. *Honey? We only get one life. But if you do it right, once is enough!*

Oh, Etty, with her copper beehive and giant green eyes. I wished I could talk to her now. *What does it even mean to do life right? And how do I do it? How?*

I looked up at the mirror again. I saw Jesse's face in mine, the haggard version, looking back at me, waiting for the answer.

I picked up the phone and called Dave.

"Hi, hon," Dave said in his warm-but-pressed doctor voice.

"Hi. I know you're working."

"No, it's okay, I have a little time. How's Jess?"

"She and Hillary are probably having coffee as we speak."

"What're you doing?"

"Sitting in a parking lot, waiting for Target to open and wanting to toss myself off a cliff."

Dave knew my self-deprecating SOS code, and his translation was eager and instant.

"Is it because she's leaving in a few weeks?"

"Yes, but also more and worse than that."

"What?"

"It's because I'm a horrible, selfish mother who is basically jealous of my own daughter for some sick reason. I already told Lucy."

I could hear Dave running my fake joke through his mind, trying to trace it to its origins. "Because she's having coffee with Hillary and you're at Target?"

"Pretty much." And now I couldn't talk because I was trying not to cry.

"Hon?" Dave said.

"Yeah?" I whispered.

"What is it?"

The gentle care in his voice made the tears come. "I just see myself in her so much—all that energy and focus and ambition. I was just like her, with everything before me. I was on my way to becoming a writer, headed for the stars."

"I know."

"And then, I don't know. I just don't know what happened. I don't know why . . . why did I just let it all slip away, that whole, huge part of myself?"

Dave was quiet, but I could feel him there.

"I'm sorry, hon," he finally said, and I could feel him searching for something more to say.

"It's okay," I said quickly, "I'm fine. I know you have to go."

"Yeah," Dave said. "I should—but we'll talk later, okay?"

"Yeah, okay. Love you."

"You too."

Even twenty-five years after our serendipitous meeting in a dusty New York City bar, my heart sang when Dave walked through the door at the end of each day, clad in blue hospital scrubs, holding the mail. The lines of his face were my daily bread. But sometimes even the people we love most can't soothe our pain.

I threw my phone in my purse and looked out my front window.

A man in a red-and-white Target bull's-eye T-shirt opened the double doors in the distance.

Seven

The moment Target's doors swept open with their mechanical *whoosh*, I was awash in a sea of calm, ready to let my gaze glide through the colorful, orderly aisles.

To me, Target is a giant dopamine bath, a chance to escape the outside world. I love taking in the rows on rows of products bursting with design, color, and creativity. I find comfort in sailing around a big, clean, well-lit, all-American space where all life's needs and choices are distilled into neat little rows.

I pulled out my phone and looked over Jesse's dorm room list. Only one major thing left: a duvet cover. We had already been to Bed Bath & Beyond several times that month, and let's just say they had not been fun outings.

During the month before kids left for school, Bed Bath & Beyond felt less like a store and more like a scene of psychological warfare. Tense, sad parents trailed their kids down the aisles, doing their best to keep their mouths shut as their children trudged on, pretending they weren't overwhelmed and sad too. As I passed fellow parents, our eyes would sometimes meet and exchange a knowing look that said, *This is the fucking worst.*

It occurred to me that I might avoid another trip to Bed Bath & Beyond if I picked up this last item on the list, but I also knew that without Jesse there to choose for herself, she was bound to veto my pick on principle.

For one thing, it had to match a specific and alarming color scheme, based on what Jesse had told me the previous day after speaking with her new roommate, Leila, for the first time.

The report had been characteristically brief.

"I don't know, she seemed nice," she said. "Except that she sent me a picture of her room and it was all hot pink."

Dear Lord, hot pink? Jesse was the opposite of a hot-pink girl. I hoped it wasn't a bad omen.

As I rolled my cart toward the bedding section, I thought back to my freshman roommate. Caroline was from Stamford, Connecticut, preppy and chipper, seemingly unmoved by the act of leaving home and starting college. She handwrote her class schedule in neat block letters and taped it up on our lemon-yellow, cinder-block walls. She spoke to her family every Sunday night at 5:00 for twenty minutes before heading to the dining hall with the freshman gang. Within a few weeks, she had a boyfriend who frequently slept over in her skinny twin bed, about thirty-eight inches away from my head.

More than anything, living with Caroline woke me up to just how different I was from the people around me. Age teaches us that we don't really know the secret lives of the people around us. But back then, Caroline seemed to fall into that enviable category of people who had been unscathed by life. Everything about her said *normal*, a life lived at low volume in a palette of beige and pink.

I, by contrast, felt like I was living inside one big secret. As the news from home got worse—Danny withdrawing further into a state of depression and isolation—my daily life felt increasingly distant. Classes were interesting and the people were nice. Having my big brother at the same school was a comfort. But the knowledge that Danny was at home, descending into a psychological state we didn't understand, took on a life of its own inside my mind.

Every morning, I woke to a feeling of suspension, followed by the dawning of a dread that washed over my consciousness: *Danny*. Most mornings I'd jolt out of my bed and gallop down the three flights of gray-speckled linoleum stairs to the basement, which was home to Dana Hall's only two phone booths. I would step inside the tiny dark booth in the far corner and slide the ancient door across its rusted steel tracks until it screeched shut . . . and for a moment, standing in that tiny wood-paneled booth, I'd feel safe, contained. No more news to face until I picked up the phone.

If I was lucky, it would be a Filmore day.

Filmore knew every inch of our house, as well as how to make the people around him feel better about the world. He was my comfort and touchstone, unfettered by the riffraff and worries that governed my little universe.

Filmore was a deacon at his church, and he was filled with the peace and wisdom of the Great Book. He was a member of our family, without the family baggage. He sat with us, at the end of the row, for every graduation and dance recital. When I did poorly on a test, he told me all that mattered was that I chose to be a good person. When I complained to him that I was fat, he told me I was beautiful, inside and out. I tried to believe him.

At the beginning of that second month of college, with everything feeling so new and so raw, the sound of Filmore's voice on the phone was a balm.

"Nyelllow?" he answered one morning when I called.

"Feeeeellmooooorrrrre!"

"How you *doin'*, sweetheart?"

"I'm all right, Filmore, but what about you?"

"Just peachy. Just peeeach-y!"

We went into our routine.

"I'm so glad," I said. "So you know I like to hear you tell me: What's the Meaning of Life again?"

He laughed. He knew. "Well, you know what I say. Just to live, baby . . . *just to live.*"

He said it the same way every time. I laughed at how lovely it sounded, how impossibly simple.

"I love that, Filmore. I wish it were true. Hey, is my mom home?"

"Sure thing, baby."

The conversation with my mother always started out the same. But during these past few months away from home, I'd learned to run both my mom's and Danny's voice through my own private soundcheck, looking for trouble.

"Hi, Lulu," she said today.

"Hi, Mama," I said. "How's everything?"

Her strain came in through her pause. "Okay. How is school going?" I could feel her thoughts were elsewhere.

"I'm fine, Mama." But I was far from fine. Leaving home increasingly felt like a family betrayal. In the few weeks before my departure, Danny had all but stopped leaving the house. His friends had seemed to call less and less. I'd left filled with a sense of foreboding about what would be next. And now the foreboding was taking shape into a new chapter, in both Danny's life and mine.

Once I got to college, I became seized with a regular and overwhelming urge to stuff myself with food. Having grown up in a family in which food was love, my weight had always been a struggle. But at school, eating veered into foreign territory where food became both a refuge and a tool of self-destruction. With increasing frequency, I would walk to the corner store after class and fill my arms with junk food.

"How's it going?" I'd ask the one clerk who always seemed to be working when I came in, forcing me to engage him in small talk in hopes that he didn't notice that I was alone and once again buying a small boatload of junk food. Doritos, Twinkies, Hot Tamales, Pop-Tarts, Diet Coke—the mere sight of that combination of fat, sugar, salt, and caffeine would light up my brain with a pre-binge giddiness.

"Oh, you know, all right," the clerk would always reply as he packed the brown bag with my booty. "Just another day, warmed over."

I'd take my stash back to my dorm room and eat everything from that bag, one package after another, barely tasting any of it, until I fell into bed to sleep off the post-binge coma. I would wake up numb and distantly sad, my mind a hazy chamber.

It would be decades before I would be able to let that pattern go.

"So tell me how you are, Lulu," my mother said, not taking "fine" for an answer.

I stared out of the little phone booth at the lemon-yellow walls of the basement. I knew she cared and wanted to know how I was. She was my mother, my rock. She loved me more than anyone in the world.

I thought about telling her about my alien roommate, my blooming habit of binge eating, the new arrival of a daily, morning dread. But her voice was so thick with anxiety that giving her another kid to worry about felt wrong—selfish.

"Mom, really, everything's fine here," I said, holding my head, which felt heavy from yesterday's hangover. "There's nothing to talk about. Just tell me what's going on with Danny."

And with that, it came pouring out. My mother's voice went from strained to almost relieved at being able to let go and shape her torrent of anxiety into words.

"I just don't know, Lulu," she said. "He's only got this year left to pull up his grades and apply to college, and he just doesn't seem to care about anything."

It hit me then. "Mom, maybe he's worried about going to college. Maybe he's acting out so that he doesn't have to go."

"I don't know," she said. "It feels like more than that. It's like he's becoming a different person. He's not himself."

By now, we'd had dozens of these conversations: *He's getting worse. He's not himself.* No matter how long we talked, there was no relief. We didn't know how to help Danny. *I* didn't know how to help Danny. We talked and talked until one of us had to go.

"I'm so sorry, Mom, I have class. But do you feel any better after talking?"

"Yes, Lulu, thank you, my love. I do."

Sometimes I knew she did, and sometimes I knew she didn't.

Early the next morning, there was a knock at my dorm room door.

"Hey, Julie! You in there? Your mom's on the phone."

I jumped out of bed and ran to the end of our floor to pick up the phone receiver, which was hanging upside down by its cord.

"What, Mom, what??"

"I found drugs in Danny's car," my mother said. Her voice sounded like stone.

"Are you *sure*? I don't believe it," I said—and I really didn't. It was the 1980s. Weed was for problem kids, burnout kids. "Are you sure that's what it was?" I repeated. "How did you find it?"

"I don't know; something in me just carried me to his car. You know I never snoop, but I just needed to see if I could find something to explain what's going on."

My mind sprinted to think of the right angle, the right line of reasoning. *Mom, it's going to be okay.* I bobbed and weaved. *I just talked to him yesterday and he definitely wasn't stoned. We'll get him help.*

"Maybe this is actually good news, Mom," I said, landing on what I hoped was the right tack. "At least we know now what's been going on."

We talked and talked and talked, our anxiety and fear rising and merging.

That's how it is when a family member descends into illness. Everyone falls into a pattern of coping. You learn who will be the talkers, who will be the listeners, who will be the ones who prefer to cope alone.

As Danny's illness unfolded, my father and Red turned inward. I rarely raised the subject with Red at school or with my father when we'd speak on the phone. Our shared avoidance became a refuge in which it felt okay to discuss normal life, even though we all knew what was happening in our other life.

When it came to Danny, my mother and I turned almost only toward each other. Soon, her pain merged into mine. Her moods became mine. Only the external obligations of my life—classes, coffee dates, exams—brought me back to my own world. Dread's swirl became like air.

"Mom, I'm so sorry," I finally said, realizing the time. "I'll call you right after class, but I'm already late. I should go."

"Go. Go, Lulu."

"Okay, but I'll call you after class, Mama."

"Okay, love."

It would be many years before I would begin to appreciate the cost of our interdependence—the cost of my urgent, endless need to try to ease my mother's pain.

Dear Sister Julie,

Happy Birthday. I can't believe it's been one month since you've left for college. Thanks for calling me all the time. Have a nice day and thanx for being there.

Love,

Dan

Eight

At Target, I hovered over the duvets and picked out one with a Harry Potter theme. It seemed like a safe bet, given Jesse's lifelong devotion to the series, and we could always bring it back if she didn't like it. It just made me feel better to check it off the list, even temporarily.

One hour later, after having filled my cart with groceries, cleaning supplies, and a new stash of tank tops, I rolled my cart to the car, unloaded, and climbed inside.

I checked the time.

By now, Jesse was probably driving the White House press to their first campaign event at the home of Tim Cook, Apple's CEO. I thought about her upset stomach. I imagined her behind the wheel of a giant van and hoped she was okay. Then I fished my phone out of my purse. Days after my fiftieth birthday gathering, Danny was still heavy on my mind.

Mom, I texted, *when can we talk? I want to ask you some things about Danny.*

The three dots responded with their little wave.

We can talk about Danny, she texted back, and my heart swelled at the love that I knew was required to say those words.

It had been twenty years now since Danny had died. Even all these years later, we were still like birds that had flown into a window: blinking and stunned, not knowing what had hit us.

Funny, I thought. After all those years of daily conversations about Danny, trying to navigate his illness together, we seldom spoke of him after his death, beyond the tearful toasts to him at holidays.

I dialed my mother, imagining her picking up the phone as she sat at her kitchen desk in Prairie Village, in front of glass shelves packed with rows of family photographs. A disproportionate number of photos were of Danny—the paper remains of a life.

"Mom," I said, not bothering with small talk, "I just don't remember much. It's like there's a whole series of years I don't remember."

"It's okay, Lulu. We can talk about it."

I was stung by the softness in her voice, the opening up of the tenderness and strength that had held her up all these years in the wake of the death of her youngest child.

Slowly, we went there.

"Danny was my boy, my sweet, sweet boy," she said. "The world was too much for him. It was like he had no skin."

I listened and she went on.

"But, you know, he's with me, Lulu. He's always with me. He's always sending me signs, you know that. Just the other day he sent me a dragonfly right as I was thinking about him."

The day Danny died, dragonflies covered the windows of my parents' house and stayed for days. No one had any explanation for it. Since then, dragonflies had continued to appear in my life—over and over, and often when Danny was in my thoughts.

"A few years ago," she continued, "I was looking through some old albums from when you were all little. . . . Danny was maybe five or six. For the first time, I noticed that in every photo Danny and I were holding hands, even behind people's backs or under tables. He was always holding on to me, like I was his lifeline. It was like he knew what was in store for him." Her voice broke.

"Yeah," I whispered, thinking about Danny's wide-open face and exquisitely sensitive eyes, the way he was always so eager for all of us to do things together as a family.

"And we just didn't understand what was happening," my mom said. "We thought if we kept imposing our answers on him, he would come out of it. But it was like a tunnel he couldn't get out of, and we just didn't understand. And it made it so much worse that *he knew* we didn't understand. That's what breaks my heart. How alone he was. How hard he tried."

My mother's voice was getting further away now, and I wished I could reach across the miles and hug her.

"All these years later, there's still a sense of disbelief and wonder," she said. "All these years later, Daddy and I still talk about it all and ask ourselves, 'How did it happen?' It's like stringing beads on a chain, trying to understand how it all came together like that. There are kids who are abused and live through horrible circumstances who survive. Why couldn't he survive when there was so much love?"

Her question hung in the silence between us.

"I don't know, Mama," I said, wiping my tears, grateful she couldn't see me. "I don't know."

Nine

I've just come home for the summer after my freshman year of college. While I take a summer job and Red gets ready to go on a road trip with friends, the plan is for Danny to join a youth group program to Israel for high school juniors, a four-week rite of passage for kids from around the country. For Red and me, the trip was a highlight of our high school years.

Despite Danny's struggle over the previous few months, my parents have pushed him to go.

"I don't know if I can do it," he's told them more than once.

"Of course you can do it," they keep saying. "Once you get there, you'll be happy. You'll see."

We all know that the trip is a gamble, and the stakes seem frighteningly high. Danny has been to Israel many times before to visit family, so it shouldn't be so scary. But he's isolated himself for so long at this point that his whole energy has retracted into a tight opaqueness, and it's hard to imagine him in a structured program filled with strangers.

If he can't rise to the occasion, it means that he will spiral alone, 6,500 miles from home. Still, my parents summon all their powers of reassurance to ease his doubts. I marvel at their courage. I know they are reassuring themselves too.

After a few pep talks, hope takes hold of him. He wants to believe he can do it. He wants to believe it's just what he needs.

We want to believe it's just what he needs.

And so he goes.

Just six days into the trip, my mother gets the phone call from Alan, the program's trip leader.

"Danny's coming home," my mother tells me as she stands at my bedroom door, holding on to the knob, a sharp fear shining in her eyes.

"What?" I say, my mind freezing. "He's leaving already?"

The group had just arrived at their hotel in Jerusalem when Danny grabbed Alan's arm and said his heart was racing; he couldn't breathe.

We would later learn the name for this experience: panic attack. It would be his first of many.

"He told him that it felt like he was going to die," my mom tells me. "All the kids saw it happening and it scared them. Alan said that Danny has been keeping to himself right from the beginning of the trip. He said it was clear that Danny is depressed, and he just can't take on the responsibility."

"So that's it?" I ask. "He's coming home right now?"

"Yes," she answers, her face gone white. Alan will leave the group to take Danny to Ben Gurion airport, where Danny will catch the night flight out.

The next afternoon, my father leaves for Kansas City International Airport to pick up Danny. For two hours I sit in my room and wait for him, listening for the sound of the garage door opening. I wait and wait and finally hear it, my stomach turning at the sound of the door cranking up into its metal housing.

Raw fear reels through me as I take the staircase two steps at a time.

My father walks in, silent, his face white. Danny follows behind him. His color is ash; his planet-wide eyes are cast downward.

I hold out my arms and he walks into them avoiding my gaze, hugging me stiffly. He's been taller than me for years now. He hasn't been that little boy I played Mary Poppins with for what feels like a lifetime. But standing on my toes to hold him, his height makes me even sadder, and I don't want to let him go.

"Hi, Sister Julie," he says quietly into my hair.

He is still Danny, and his hollow voice directs a laser into my heart.

"Hi, Stiggy," I say, trying to sound natural, trying to talk past the knot in my throat.

I follow him up the stairs, not wanting him to go alone to his bedroom, where just one week ago he packed his bags for the summer. I don't want him to sit alone with the enormity of having been expelled from the trip, his summer plans evaporated because of . . . what? We have not even begun to understand that yet.

I sit with him on his bed, my hand on his back. I feel the heat under his hooded sweatshirt. With the other hand, I smooth his chocolate-brown comforter, searching for the right words.

"What do you think happened, Stiggy?" I ask softly.

"I don't know." He stares ahead. Water begins to pool in his eyes, but the tears don't come.

I touch his cheek, hot and rough with stubble, and I'm struck, as I always am, by the dark beauty of his angular face.

"I heard you had, like, some kind of episode?"

"I guess. I couldn't breathe. I couldn't stay. I just couldn't do it. I was too scared."

I was too scared. They are the words of a little boy, the words he would have used, say, on one of those Saturday nights when my parents went out and it was just the two of us. When a news flash on the TV would report that there was a tornado watch in the next county and I'd say, "Don't worry, it won't come to our neighborhood," and he'd say, "But Julie, I'm scared."

I look at him now, lying on his bed, his eyes glassy, fixed on the ceiling. I lie down next to him in silence, and we breathe.

After his return from Israel, my parents kick into high gear. *There is something wrong with Danny.*

It's been eight months since my mother found drugs in his car. She confronted him then, and he had promised that it was no big deal . . . that he'd just been messing around with a friend. He promised to stop smoking—but who knows?

Maybe the panic attack was really a drug overdose? Maybe he's become addicted?

Whatever the cause, a metamorphosis is taking place in my sweet, loving little brother, with whom I used to build forts and escape into the forest for secret picnics. With whom, as we grew older, I took walks around the block and drives to 7-Eleven, where we'd browse the candy aisles and eat in the car, talking through life. Where did he go?

The summer wears on and Danny continues to fold into himself— away from us, away from his friends.

My parents insist he see a therapist. He goes, reluctantly, but nothing seems to change. There is no discussion about his getting a job or doing anything else for the rest of the summer. The focus is on him getting better.

A few weeks later, after I return to college, I dial home from my little wooden booth.

"What's happening over there?" I ask my mother.

"Well . . ."

I can tell she is trying to steady her voice.

"Just tell me." The dread rises in my throat.

"We came home from a party last night." Pause. "He'd taken a baseball bat and smashed the kitchen windows," she says quietly.

"Oh, God, Mom." I feel lightheaded. "Oh, God."

Danny's therapist is judged to be unfit, and my parents take Danny, against his will, for an extensive psychological evaluation.

Words float up one by one. *Depression. Addiction. Borderline personality.* His symptoms fit some of everything, but there is no definitive diagnosis, just speculation and guesses.

A new milestone is reached: he will start medication trials.

It is the beginning of a march into psychotropic drugs that will last the rest of his life.

After the party incident, Danny rarely returns my calls. When we do talk, our conversations are short and his voice is hollow.

One day, as my spring semester is winding down and I'm contemplating returning home for the summer to live once again with Danny, I gingerly try a direct approach. "Stiggy, do you have any sense of what's really wrong?"

"Stop asking me, Julie," he says to me, a sharp edge in his voice. "I don't know. *I don't know.*"

Somehow he manages to finish his senior year and apply to the University of Kansas. But anger seems to have seeped into the energy around him; a quiet rage is growing within.

Red and I fly in for Danny's graduation—Red from his new post-college life in New York. We sit in our folding chairs on the green grass in front of the graduation stage. After the parade of speeches, the students cross the stage to accept their diplomas. I don't take my eyes off Danny. For the entire ceremony, his expression is flat, his face white and taut. His mouth is stretched into a straight line, and he stares ahead, unseeing.

Over the months of medication trials, it has become hard to separate the drugs' side effects from his feelings. The head of school calls Danny's name and my heart beats fast. *God, please get up.* He rises from his chair and walks woodenly across the stage in his oversized cap—his graduation gown fully unzipped, his face motionless against the backdrop of his smiling, jubilant peers.

After the ceremony concludes, the new graduates flood into the reception hall in packs. They fly into the arms of their waiting families and friends. They throw their caps in the air.

As we wait and wait, a feeling takes hold of me that will become familiar over the years. It's a feeling of dread that slowly trickles into my body at the realization, the possibility, and, finally, the certainty that something terrible is about to happen.

We continue to stand there, waiting, as the other families wander off to the parking lot.

I look at my parents and Red. They are frozen and silent, searching the crowd.

We stand there together. I look back at my mother and see the bouquet of red roses hanging downward in her hands. Danny never shows up.

We drive home, and as we walk through the garage door into the house, we can hear the blasting of Pink Floyd.

He is up there in his room. His door is shut.

Ten

With Jesse's motorcade success behind her and summer winding down, reality settled in. Only three weeks remained until she would leave home. Three weeks until this era of her childhood would officially end.

I lay in bed in the dark as Dave slept next to me, turned toward the wall.

So what? I thought. *Every parent faces his or her kid leaving home. Of course we're sad. Of course we'll miss her. But what the fuck is wrong with me? What am I so afraid of?*

I envisioned the road ahead. We would leave Jesse in her new college home, ensconced, happy, and excited for her new chapter. We would take great pleasure in knowing all that awaited her. She would come into her own, explore parts of herself and the world she had yet to touch. We knew and we were proud of how ready she was for it all. How confidently she would go forth, so strong in her firstborn skin. *I knew this.*

And so? I asked myself in the dark.

The answer came: *I am afraid of the void she will leave behind. I am afraid of reeling in the months that lay before us.*

For eighteen years Dave and I had built a tiny civilization: David, Julie, Jesse, and Sam. We had been a family, a unit, a measurement of four. We were spokes on a wheel, shooting off by day but always coming back to one another—homework and dinner, safe and cozy, *goodnights and love yous* under one roof each night.

I knew it was the natural course, but still, my mind asked: *What happens when one of the legs is sawed off a table? How does one keep it from tipping over and crashing to the ground?*

My mind wandered back to the scene of me sitting in that circle of women at my high school reunion, confessing, embarrassed, that I had abandoned my career, along with my earliest dreams of becoming a writer. Had it really been almost two decades? Had I really let it go so long?

I stared into the dark and conjured the image of myself as a teenager, angsting up a storm, lugging around a legal pad, asking people about the Meaning of Life.

Although punctuated by constant tiny and large joys, motherhood's packed days and endless responsibilities had all but extinguished my writing ambitions, along with my search for meaning. And now here I stood on the precipice of that role ending in just a few years, after Sam left home too. Now what mattered?

The next day, Jesse and I sat at our backyard firepit, feet up on the concrete ledge.

"I've got a weird question," she said as she chewed on a straw.

"Go ahead," I said.

"Like, how's it going to work?"

"What do you mean?"

"I mean, how are we going to communicate when I'm at school?"

"You mean, like, how often are we going to talk?"

"Or anything."

"I don't know. It's really up to you, baby," I said, kicking a pinecone off the firepit's edge.

"No. I don't want it to be up to me. I want you to tell me."

I was startled to hear this from a girl who always knew what she wanted. I rooted around in my head for my mom bag of wisdom.

"But Jess, there's no right answer. It depends on how you feel."

"I mean, now we're all together all the time. I know what you're doing. You know what I'm doing. We're never going to know that anymore."

We're never going to know that anymore.

"Well, not in the same way, right?" Quickly I stuck my index fingers in the corners of my eyes to stop the tears.

"So, like, am I supposed to call and, like, give you a daily report?"

"You'll decide what you want; you'll figure it out, Jess. You'll probably want to talk more in the beginning, but it'll change over time, I'm sure, and that will be natural, too."

Man, I was good. Then I quickly turned my head up to the sky so gravity could help push the tears back in before she could see.

That afternoon, I met Lucy up in the hills for a run.

"Lucy, I have *got* to get a grip!" I huffed and puffed. "I can't be sitting in my house pining away for Jesse, hoping she's going to call! But I know that's what's going to happen. Is that so stupid? First, I'm jealous of my own offspring, and now I'm dying of separation anxiety. What in God's name is wrong with me?"

"Nothing's wrong!" She waved at the sky from the trail ahead. "You're just sad!"

"No, but that's the thing—I'm *not* just sad. It's like I've got this awful feeling of dread and foreboding. Like a feeling of doom. It feels like it's precipitated by Jesse leaving, but Jesse's leaving is not where it's coming from."

"Have you ever felt like that before?" Lucy asked, slowing down to a walk.

I walked beside her. "I mean, for like fourteen years." Humor was my shield.

"You mean when Danny was sick?"

"Yeah."

"Well . . ." Expert advisor though Lucy was, I could tell this crisis was out of her league. "I don't know. Maybe you should write about it?"

"That would mean I still remember how to write."

"Oh, c'mon. You're an amazing writer. Just follow your thoughts. See where they take you."

Maybe she was right. Maybe I should try to write this dread out of me. Couldn't hurt to try.

Once I got home, I sat down at the kitchen table and opened my laptop. I reflexively scanned my messages for anything good and landed on one from a sender I didn't recognize.

"This can't be real," I said to my laptop.

I read the tiny black script: *Writing Retreat in the Woods: Claim your voice. Join us for seven days that just might change your life. Haven Retreats. Whitefish, Montana.*

Obviously, my first thought was: *I am a walking cliché, going on a writing retreat to try to "find myself."* Then I clicked through. There was one retreat date available, starting twelve days after we were scheduled to drop Jesse off for college. Lucy's words were still in my head. *Whaaattt?*

Maybe it was one massive cliché, but aren't clichés clichéd because they're true? Because they work? Maybe this was the answer I had been looking for. Maybe I just needed to get out of Dodge and force myself to somehow write my way back to some sense of peace.

Every ounce of dread I'd carried around for so long, every tentacle of that animal force inside that had increasingly taken hold of me over the Year of the Lasts, called out.

I clicked on the "Register" button.

Magical thinking or not, the next chapter of my life suddenly seemed to depend on it.

Meanwhile, with three weeks and counting until college drop-off day, I was desperate to cram in as much family time as possible.

We'd lived in the Bay Area for sixteen years, surrounded by sights and natural wonders that people from all over the world flock to see. Naturally, we'd rarely made the time to enjoy—or even visit—many of those sights.

I wondered how common it was to coast blindly through time, only to look up and see that you'd almost run out. Why was it so hard to truly savor, to pay attention to, the finite amount of time we had with those we loved?

Now that it was almost over, I saw how I'd pissed away the summer. We'd all burrowed into the tunnel vision of our work and lists. Screens and routines held us in their autopilot trance, enslaving us with dings and pings and Snapchat streaks and posts.

I'd woken up that morning with a sense of the clock ticking. I walked into the family room to find Jesse and Sam sprawled on the couch watching an episode of *The Office*. Just as my father used to do to us (which as kids we hated, and yet I nonetheless felt compelled to repeat), I stood in front of the TV to make an announcement.

"Pause this for a second, will you?" I asked, throwing my hands in the air for emphasis. "Did you know there are seventy acres' worth of wild animals from Africa only forty-five minutes away from here? All these years, we've basically had a small African safari less than an hour from our house—isn't that insane?"

"Really?" Jesse said with tepid enthusiasm, looking past me to the screen.

"Yeah, and we've never been," I continued, undeterred. "Which is why I made reservations for this weekend. Isn't that *so* fun?!"

"Oh no, Mom," Sam said, throwing his head back on the couch. "It's supposed to be 104 degrees this weekend. Plus, we've already gone on two family outings in the last week, and they were great. You know that no matter how many family outings we do, *Jesse's still leaving*, right?"

Sam. My blue-eyed, redheaded boy. My sage, forever the deliverer of the miserable truth.

"I do know that, Sam," I snapped. "And put a sock in it, because we're going!"

Sam was right, of course, because the day did come. But before it did, we went to Safari West, and although it was too hot for the giraffes to come out of their fake caves and the safari Jeep's pleather seats burned the backs of our sweating thighs, we still had fun—sort of.

We also sort of enjoyed the unreasonable number of other tourist attractions I forced us to cram in. But a collective, undiscussed sadness permeated every outing, every hike, and every festive meal, as they marched us closer to the end of an era in our little family's life.

Eleven

The taxicab swung through to a stop in the U-shaped driveway of the Hotel Orrington. Here we were, finally, in Evanston, Illinois, home of Northwestern University.

Early that morning, Jesse, Sam, Dave, and I had walked through the San Francisco airport, two by two, our carry-on bags noisily rolling behind us, just as we had done dozens of times before when going on a family trip. But this trip, of course, was different.

This trip I had anticipated—and dreaded—for about eighteen years.

I remembered that first moment when I held Jesse in my arms—that tiny face with those old-soul eyes. I remembered having the thought, horrible even so far off, that Dave and I would have her to ourselves for only her first chapter of life. And now, just this morning, we'd watched Jesse hand over a one-way ticket.

As soon as we checked into our hotel, Jesse wasn't feeling well.

"I don't know what's wrong with me," she said as she put her bags down on the hotel bed and headed for the bathroom. "My stomach really hurts again."

"Really?" Dave asked. He tried to sound casual, but I heard the alarm in his voice. "The same kind of feeling you've been having?"

"Yeah."

This problem hadn't let up since she'd first mentioned it on the way to Clinton's motorcade the previous month. Her stomach had been hurting her a lot, and she often felt nauseous. We'd both noticed her getting up to go to the bathroom way more than was normal in recent weeks. But we'd all decided, since Jesse almost never got sick, that this issue had to be a normal manifestation of pre-college jitters.

The toilet flushed and Jesse emerged from the bathroom and climbed into bed in her clothes. She was pale and her eyes were dull.

When it came time to get ready for family orientation two hours later, Jesse balked.

"I'm sorry, guys, I just can't. I just can't." She shook her head.

"Okay," Dave said. "You two just stay here and rest, and Mom and I will go. These orientation things are bogus anyway. Jess, see if you can sleep it off."

Holding hands in silence, Dave and I walked down the broad sidewalk, following big, purple signs directing us to the massive school auditorium.

"Hon, are you worried?" I asked.

Throughout his many years in practice, Dave had developed the ability to tell just enough truth to be honest but not so much as to cause undue worry before a full medical workup had delivered its verdict. I'd honed the ability to read between his lines.

"A little bit," he answered in a voice slightly higher than usual, which was his worried voice. "I just can't imagine what it would be. She's had no history of gastro issues, but this has been going on for longer than I would expect from a stomach bug. I wish our move-in time wasn't so early tomorrow morning."

As we approached the swelling crowd at the doors of the auditorium, I glanced over at Dave for a read of his face. On it, I found a look that I had come to know well. He was casting his mind like a fishing line into the future. Brow furrowed, he filtered through the range of medical conditions that might lay hidden in the depths.

In that moment, I could feel a familiar distance forming between us. When I was anxious or worried, my instinct was to draw close, to talk through, and to huddle. When Dave worried, he wanted the opposite. He disappeared into what I had named his "silo." He slammed the windows and sealed the doors, and there his emotions and spirit took cover until the source of stress had passed.

Dave could be in the silo for days or weeks. All the while, I'd yearn, I'd spin, I'd turn to my holy tribe of friends. I would withdraw so I didn't feel his withdrawal. This difference in our natures, this pattern we fell into in times of stress, was the Achilles' heel of our relationship. So far, we'd been lucky; we'd not had to weather anything too long or intense. But in the back of my mind, I'd always worried what would happen if we did. I closed my eyes and willed this new storm to pass quickly.

When the next morning came, Jesse struggled out of bed, holding her stomach.

"I can't," she said to us, noting our long looks. "I'm sorry; I just can't leave." She'd been to the bathroom three times in the last hour.

I looked at Dave. "This is nuts. Shouldn't we take her to health services?"

Dave nodded. "Yes, but our move-in slot is in an hour. Jess, you stay here, and we'll take you after we're done."

Jesse climbed back into bed, huddling in the corner, her arms wrapped around her knees. She rested her back against the plaster wall. "Okay, Dad. Sorry."

And so, move-in day, the iconic beginning of college, turned out to be a tense and grim experience, executed without Jesse present. Luckily, Leila, Jesse's pink-loving roommate, hadn't yet arrived, allowing Dave, Sam, and me time to set everything up uninterrupted.

As soon as we were done, we picked up Jesse and caught an Uber to university health services.

One hour later, the doctor came back with a diagnosis of gastroenteritis. "It's been going around like crazy," he assured us. "She just needs to wait it out."

This verdict meant Jesse would need to wait it out alone, because we were scheduled to fly back home the following morning after the drop-off ceremony.

Dave floated the idea of us staying an extra day or two until she felt better.

"That's ridiculous," Jesse said. "I'll be fine."

Dave and I looked at each other. This was the classic, clichéd moment when parents are supposed to let go. But this was no normal letting go, and we were stuck, not knowing whether to trust our instincts to stay and make sure she was okay or trust what Jesse was telling us.

Looking at her pinched face, the best course of action was not in any way clear. I could feel the effort it took both of us to bow to her word. That was our job, at least for now. We had to go.

Early the next morning, Jesse left the hotel room to meet her new classmates and to prepare for the March Through the Arch, where the school's entire, two-thousand-person freshman class would walk through a stone arch on campus to mark the moment when they officially become Northwestern's class of 2020.

An hour later, Dave, Sam, and I walked out the hotel doors and into the blazing sun. We navigated our way down the unfamiliar streets, taking in Jesse's new world. We crossed Sheridan Road and joined the mass of parents gathered before the stone and cast-iron arch, waiting for the band to start up.

"Ready for our cue?" Dave smiled. He was trying to lighten the mood, and I loved him for it.

"What do you mean?" Sam asked.

"Basically, this whole production is the school's way of saying, 'Buck up and cut the cord, people! Leave behind your wallet and get out so your kids can move on!'"

He was right, which only made me more depressed. This would be the site of the next big letting go. I thought back to the many goodbyes we'd lived through—the first day of preschool, kindergarten, summer camp, and high school. I saw Jesse's bronze, bouncing curls and tiny, upturned smile; I saw all those little dresses she used to wear with her shiny, black patent-leather Mary Janes.

My heart rose into my throat, and I felt Sam's sky-blue eyes on me.

Like me, Sam had a bionic radar that alerted him to the feelings of those he loved, especially the sad feelings. I hated that I'd somehow passed this codependent trait onto him—I knew too well the cost of that trait and the damage it could do—but there was no undoing it.

I put my sunglasses on hastily, and Sam put his hand on my arm.

"Hold it together, Mom," he said jauntily, trying to defuse the sadness. "Remember, you still have me!"

I pulled him to me in a hug. "I sure do—and don't you worry about me, okay, Sam? I'm fine, I really am, and so is Dad, and so are you. We all are going to be fine. We're going to be *good*."

He nodded without looking at me, a sure sign that he'd heard what he needed to hear.

Suddenly a band of purple-clad upperclassmen walked down the parent-lined path, shouting in a chorus, "Kleenex? Anyone need a Kleenex?"

Parents raised their hands and little white Kleenex packs soared through the air like bags of peanuts. A cheerful, blonde-haired girl handed me a pack and I squinted to read what it said on the neat little package: *This is a big day for you and your Wildcat!*

I had two thoughts. First: *Oh really, you junior in college? How would you know how big a day it is?* And second: *Really? My child is a Wildcat? I barely know the Giants from the Cubs. Now my child is your school's new walking brand strategy?*

I imagined that this March Through the Arch tradition had been invented in the 1940s, when pomp and circumstance subjugated what was really going on: parents leaving their children behind. As a result, now *we* had to stand here in the blistering heat, watching two thousand students walk past and trying to spot the speck among them who was our kid.

Finally, the marching band started up their jolly horn racket, and we pumped our fists in the air as the class of 2020 paraded past us, a river of Northwestern purple, a sea of parents trying to sing a new fight song, donning sunglasses, straining to see our babies, trying to pretend we were one solid channel of happy.

Forty-five miserable, sweltering minutes later, Sam pointed into the crowd. "Look, there she is!" Yes, there she was. Wearing her purple Northwestern shirt and her Ray-Bans, Jesse walked toward us, not seeing us, a grin plastered across her face—except that it was not a grin but a grimace. A grimace of pain.

"Hon," I whispered loudly to Dave, "I'm really worried. Look at her. Are we seriously just going to leave her like this?"

My stomach churned as a feeling of dread climbed through my body. I watched Jesse disappear down the wooded path and thought suddenly of Danny. I saw his tan face, those giant brown eyes. I thought about how his illness began—just a gradual emergence, and then a settling in of a reality that took us months to recognize. By the time he'd started college—right around the age Jesse was now—he'd begun to free fall. *Please God, let her be okay.*

The ceremony ended and we waded through the crowd, dodging the little flags and Kleenex packs folks were waving, making our way to one of the main quads where the students gathered to say goodbye to their families before heading off for their orientation activities.

We found Jesse waiting alone on the hot, green field at our predesignated meeting spot. As we walked toward her, I could see her standing stiffly, fists balled. She was still in her sunglasses, which I knew wasn't an accident. She was in game-on mode. She didn't want eye contact. It was time to separate, and even if she was sick, she was ready.

Like so many other milestones I'd anticipated leading up to the actual occasions—my college graduation, our wedding day, the birth of our children—the moment of saying goodbye to Jesse felt like a movie in which we were acting out scenes I'd rehearsed a million times. It was a moment that seemed to hold all the preceding years of dread, the ultimate symbol of the end of her childhood in all formal respects.

As I looked at Jesse standing before us, pale and poker-faced, it was hard to breathe. This part—leaving her to fend for herself while feeling sick—I had not rehearsed. And yet our next step was clear. My parent instinct kicked in and yelled into my brain: *Do it. Just do it and go.*

And we did.

Twelve

Back at Chicago's O'Hare Airport, we boarded the plane home to San Francisco—a blinking, numb family of three.

I followed Dave and Sam down the aisle and took the window seat. I wished I could be alone so I could cry if I needed to, but turning toward the window was as close as I could get.

Sam sat down and put his headphones on. I could feel him retreating into his music, as he often did, away from whatever feelings he was having of leaving his sister and starting a new version of his life at home without her.

I leaned forward and stole a quick glance at Dave. His face was tight, on his way to his silo.

As the plane gained elevation, I watched the city shrink below. I followed the serpentine curves of the cars on the highways and byways, the patchwork of parks and buildings that gave way to Lake Michigan, glittering in the afternoon sun.

I searched for a sign of the part of Lake Michigan that the school was on but couldn't locate it. My heart caught at the thought of Jesse, somewhere down below in one of those buildings, about to start her new life, sick.

As much as I wanted to, I couldn't stop my mind from drifting into a river of memory.

It's one week after Danny's graduation, one week since he left the ceremony before it ended.

My mother and I are in the kitchen, and I'm fighting to stay calm.

"An antipsychotic, Mom?" I ask, trying not to raise my voice.

As she cuts carrots and adds them to a big, steaming pot, I'm struck by how bizarre it is to hear my voice say those words in the company of her chicken soup, the consummate symbol of comfort and care in our loving, healthy family. "That's what they're telling you to give him? What, now they think Danny is psychotic?"

She raises her index finger to her mouth, signaling me to lower my voice.

"Oh, Lulu, they don't know," she whispers. "They don't know. They're just trying everything they can to try to get him back to where he was."

That night, when my father gets home from work and we gather for dinner, my mother hands him an envelope. It's Danny's final high school transcript.

My father takes out the folded paper, scans it quickly, and then looks at Danny, squinting and incredulous. "You finished high school with *two Fs?*"

Danny is standing at the kitchen counter, looking away.

"What is going on with you?" my dad asks sharply, and my heart starts beating fast.

Danny does not answer, but I can see the bones in his jaw clenching as he stares straight ahead of him.

"Danny, you *failed* two classes," my father says, his face screwed tight, shaking his head in disbelief.

"Jack," my mom says quietly, and I can see her alarm. She is stepping into her role of peacemaker, assuager. Her eyes are fixed on Danny as she puts her hand over my father's hand, which grips the edge of the counter, his knuckles white.

When my father gets mad, it's scary. That's when his mouse-squashing mother's meanness spews out of him like blistering lava, usually flattening whoever is in his path. In these rare moments, his fury is blind and ruthless.

And the worst anger of all is when he feels one of us is exhibiting any of what he considers the greatest of moral defects: sloth, disrespect, or weakness of character. He cannot see beyond the immediate crime before him—cannot see, in this case, that the perpetrator is acting not from defiance but from helplessness.

"How are you going to make it in college, Danny?" he says in a low voice. I look into my father's eyes and see my grandmother's—dark and mean.

I can't breathe. *How can he say that? Why would he say that?*

Danny's eyes widen and his jawbones jut in and out. He does not say a word.

"Danny!" My father raises his voice. "What is wrong with you?"

Danny physically recoils at the words. *What. Is. Wrong. With. You.* He glares downward, and his face flushes a deep red. He is silent.

"Jack!" my mother says in a guttural tone. "*Stop it.*"

But my father's own pain and impotence has boiled into anger. He is worn down by months of worry and has become hardened by not being able to figure out how to shake his son out of a state he cannot understand, one that he can only imagine is a lack of will and motivation. At my mother's relentless insistence to keep his thoughts to himself, he's held his tongue too long.

"DANNY!" my father shouts. "Are you listening? Answer me! What is going on? *What is wrong with you?*"

Suddenly, Danny convulses into a rage I've never seen in him before. In one swift motion, his hand shoots down to the counter, grabs a long chef's knife, and then swings in the direction of my father. Danny's eyes are dark and wild.

The air goes flat. I am floating, frozen, seeing but not seeing.

"Danny!" my mother screams as she grabs the knife out of his hands and throws it in the sink as if it's on fire.

"Stop it!" I hear someone scream, out of control, before realizing it's me. "*Stop it!*"

Danny's eyes go dead. He turns and walks out of the kitchen, out of the house. The front door slams behind him with a sickening thud.

My heart is beating in my head, and I am shaking. I look at my father. His face is ghost white. No one moves. Not my father. Not my mom. Not me. No one says anything.

My father goes to the table. He is broken, slumped, his face slack with shock. My mother has shrunk into her chair. I imagine her anger, her confusion, her fear. I am lost. I can't see anything but the clenching of Danny's jaw and the knife in his hand. I can't think about anything except the powerlessness and fear and anguish of my parents.

An hour later, the front door opens and shuts loudly. We are cleaning the dishes. After pounding up the stairs, Danny's bedroom door slams shut. I look at my mother, who is looking at my father. *What is happening? What is going to happen?*

After we finish cleaning, I stay in the kitchen. I am afraid to go upstairs to my bedroom. I am afraid to be on the same floor that Danny and I have shared all our lives.

Later, I walk into the study and see that our gun case has been emptied of my father's collection of bird-hunting rifles, a fixture in our house for as long as I can remember.

I find my mother in her bedroom.

"Mom, did Dad really take the guns out of his case?"

"Yes," she says quietly.

I walk into the foyer and look up to Danny's closed bedroom door. Dread thickens in my throat. For the first time in my life, I am afraid to walk up the stairs and knock on his door and check in, as I have most days since coming home from school for summer break.

I am afraid of what Danny will look like now. I don't know how to act with this person who pulled a knife on our father. I don't know how to begin to bridge the widening chasm forming between us. I feel a fear I've never felt before. I do not go up.

My father walks out and sees me standing at the bottom of the stairs. He puts his warm, strong hand on my shoulder and says in a low voice, "Come on, Jules, you're going to sleep with us tonight."

My strong, fearless father is afraid of his son . . . afraid for our safety.

It's a turning point in my family's life I will never forget.

That night I sleep in my parents' bedroom, the three of us in their king-size bed, me now a junior in college. A new darkness has come to our family.

When I wake up in the middle of the night, something leads me to check the bedroom door. My father has locked it.

The next day, Danny apologizes woodenly to my father, who hugs him stiffly. But it is too late. There is a new energy in our house. The very air around us feels wild and threatening.

My heart-splitting sadness for Danny's struggle has begun to fuse with a new, awful emotion: rage. I don't know when my worry for Danny started mixing with anger and resentment. I just know that it is an exquisitely painful element of the punishment of having a sibling who is ill.

When Danny first started becoming depressed, I didn't know yet that this was the easy part. The part when especially we siblings get to feel only what we're supposed to feel—nothing but empathy, worry, and sadness. It's only now, as the illness has proven to be endless and seemingly intractable, that my resentment has set in—resentment at Danny for hurting our family; for sucking all the oxygen out of our home life; for making our parents miserable; for robbing Red and me of their attention and, in some ways, of our own young adulthood. It's a toxic brew of bitterness and shame that will never leave me.

I am enraged that Danny has brought fear into our loving family. I am enraged that suddenly it feels dangerous for my parents to be in their own home. I am terrified of what he is capable of.

"I'm glad he's leaving for school," I tell my mother as we take a walk just to get out of the house, away from his closed door. It is easier to be angry than to be sad and afraid, and I lean in. "I'm *so* glad. It can't come soon enough. I don't want him in our house with you. I want him out, Mom. I want him *out*."

But he stays, because we don't know what else to do.

Somehow, we get through the summer. Red calls periodically to see how things are going, but we don't tell him much. There is an unspoken and tacit understanding between my parents and me. Without discussion or perhaps even consciousness, and without consulting Red, we act in lockstep: We will protect Red from the bunkers of this new war. We will not share the details. He needs to focus on his new job and adult life in New York City, and he can't do anything to help anyway.

But I am already in deep. After witnessing Danny so close to violence, I am more desperate than ever to help. The helping comes easily to me, and I find that the more I turn away from the emotional needs of my own life and into the storm of Danny's, the more relief I feel. This matters more than anything else could. I can go back to my life later.

My parents spend the summer researching new avenues of treatment for Danny. Eventually, they find a doctor who promises a new approach.

As the summer heat wanes and the time nears for Danny to leave for college, he is put on a new medication trial with lithium—a drug used to treat major depressive disorders. The transformation is almost instant. Within days, Danny's entire energy lightens. His face opens and he begins to smile for the first time in months. He starts seeing friends again. He holds his summer job at the pretzel store.

"Hey, sister," he says to me one day a few weeks before we are both due to leave for school. "Let's go for a drive."

We hop into my mother's car and steal away for one of our favorite secret pleasures: the drive-thru lane at McDonald's, where our large fries and giant Diet Cokes await.

We pull into a parking spot and unpack our little white paper bag.

"Danny," I say, reaching out to ruffle his hair. "It really feels like a miracle, doesn't it? I mean, you just seem like yourself again."

Danny dips a fry into the pool of ketchup on the napkin between us. "Let's just not jinx anything, okay? I do feel a lot better. I'm even kind of looking forward to getting the hell out of Dodge and going to college in a few weeks, can you believe that?"

I take a big gulp of my drink for cover, trying not to dissolve into the tears of relief that I feel rising.

"It's awesome, Stiggy. It's just awesome. I'm so grateful."

Dear Julie,

I feel nervous now about the new medications. But you have lifted a wave of anxiety from my mind since being able to talk to you. I thank you, for I found a temporary miracle drug relief, and it was you. I would love it if you would accompany me for a walk just me and you tonight after din-din. Things are happening fast and your level-headed coolness with dealing with me has given me a chance to tolerate my anxiety. Please sit by me during dinner.

D.F.

Two weeks later, I return to Swarthmore, and Danny leaves for the University of Kansas, reassured by the fact that school is only forty-five minutes from home.

Three weeks after I return to school, I call my mom from the wooden phone booth to see how things are.

Instantly, I can tell something is wrong. "What is it, Mom?"

My mother's voice is flat. "Danny just called. I don't know exactly what happened, but he told me that he can't stay at school. I'm picking him up this weekend. He doesn't want to go back."

My heart stops. "Oh God, Mom. Can't you make him at least try to stay?"

Her voice is distant. "He told me that I didn't understand—that none of us understand. He just kept saying, '*I can't do this, I can't do this, you don't understand.*'"

And so begins the next chapter in Danny's story.

From the very beginning, institutionalizing Danny has been the last resort on the list. But after his breakdown in Israel, the knife incident, and so many drug treatment failures, the doctors and my parents agree: it is time for him to go someplace where he can have a full-time team of doctors working on his case, which still has no confirmed diagnosis beyond a seemingly untreatable depression.

And so my parents pick him up at his college dorm in Lawrence, Kansas, and drive him directly to Topeka, where he is admitted to Menninger Psychiatric Hospital.

Oddly, our grief and anxiety over this spine-chilling new step is met with palpable relief by Danny. Even a few days after my parents leave him there, he sounds buoyant.

"I feel good, Jules," he says to me through the phone receiver in my little wooden booth.

"Do you, Stiggy? You're not afraid to be there?" It's the second time I've used his nickname since our McDonald's outing, the second time in what feels like a century.

"No, I think maybe this is going to be a good place for me. I feel comfortable here."

My little brother, my childhood playmate, is in a mental institution. *He feels comfortable.*

I roll that reality around in my mind. *What does it mean? How can he feel comfortable in a locked psychiatric ward? What will make him ever want to leave? How did this happen to our family?*

"Okay, well, that's great, that's really great," I say, trying to sound upbeat. As I stare out the paned phone-booth window at the tenement wall, the ceiling seems to move above me. It feels as though a block is pressing on my chest.

Menninger specializes in progressive treatments for difficult cases, and so each week the treatment deepens with new medications and strategies.

Most days, I gallop down the stairs and call Danny, running his voice through my mental sound check.

"So Stiggy, tell me, really, how are you?"

"I'm okay," he says. "I'm getting these weird facial tics, but it's okay. I think the medications are working."

"Well, I guess it's worth it if it helps you feel better."

"Yeah, it is. It is worth it. I just wonder when I'll be normal again."

"Well, as we know," I say with a forced laugh, "no one's actually normal, right?"

"A lot more normal than me," he says. "I mean, look at me, here in the loony bin, Jesus."

"Don't say that about yourself, Stiggy. I love you and we all love you."

"You too," he says, and I hear him stifling his tears. I swallow mine.

Dear Loving Sis,

I just got your wonderful picture and it is the first and only objet d'art on my wall in my room over my bed. Needless to say, your letter sent chills of good feelings and of total acceptance down my spine.

I'm waiting for the weather to get hot. It hasn't happened yet. I'm becoming friendly with two guys at Derham House—Peter Addison—age 29—comes from New Canaan, Connecticut—graduated from Kenyon College in 1988—played baseball—all the girls even my social worker are in love with him. Fernando—age 22—last name too hard to spell. Very smart, short, stocky guy—from Colombia —another heartthrob with the girls—His current girlfriend had a book written about her ballet career when she was 11. They are both accepting, non-judgmental guys and are fun to be around.

There has been much excitement at Derham House lately. Santiago was court ordered—forced by the law to stay at Menninger's Case Hospital because he threatened to kill his mom and he had a loaded 44 magnum gun in his car. It was a scary night for everyone at Derham House. I have seen every movie (not artsy but trashy-pop films like Leprechaun*) by myself lately. Sincere good luck in your job quest—may God bless your resume.*

   P.S. I'm at One Derham House 2221 SW 6th Topeka, KS 66066

I want you to come to visit me and give me support.

When you explain things to me, I feel better.

Love, D.F.

As the plane from Chicago back to San Francisco sliced through a bank of white cirrus clouds, I wiped the tears off my cheeks with my sleeve and glanced over at Sam and Dave sitting next to me, both wearing their giant Bose headphones and watching movies.

Looking at my boys, it seemed like Danny was from another lifetime. I studied Sam's profile. Danny and Sam would have been so close. Both old souls, both so sensitive to the world. And Jesse, too—Danny would have adored her. That their lives never overlapped was a source of deep sadness for me. Jesse came along two years after Danny died. Her middle name of Danielle, a Jewish tradition of naming a new life after a lost loved one, felt in this moment like a cross to bear.

Jesse. I pictured her in her dorm room, lying on her new Target Harry Potter duvet cover, which she'd happily approved. I wondered what she was doing . . . how she was feeling. My mind zoomed onto the image of her grimacing in that sea of purple. I hoped she was okay. I prayed she was okay.

"Hi, Sam," I said, putting my hand on his solid, warm arm.

He nudged his left headphone off his ear with his shoulder.

"What, Mama?"

"Just hi."

"Hi, Mama," he said, examining my face. "Is something wrong?"

"No, no," I said quickly. "I'm good. It's just that I adore you."

"You, too, Mama."

I laid my head on his shoulder as the plane tipped down toward its descent.

Thirteen

It'd been three days since we'd dropped Jesse off at Northwestern. Every day I texted, *How are you feeling?* And every day she texted back, *Eh*.

We told her to go back to health services; finally, she went. The doctor reassured her it was gastroenteritis, which was still raging through campus.

That night, though not in much of a party mood, we went to our friend's fiftieth birthday bash. We'd been going to a lot of these milestone parties lately, and, just like my party the month before, they often landed somewhere between a celebration and a thinly veiled midlife crisis.

Happily, this one leaned more toward celebration. It felt a lot like a bar mitzvah, complete with a candy buffet, novel activities for the grownups, and a video montage of the birthday girl's life.

"Hon," I said to Dave the moment we arrived, "I'm getting a huge margarita and getting in line for the psychic."

Dave gave me a look. "Seriously? A psychic?"

I shrugged. "Why not? Might as well see what our future holds."

To me, psychics occupied the province of the great divide between reason and hope. I assumed it was all just a big racket, but *maybe* it wasn't, in which case, why not give it a whirl?

In the years since Danny's death, my mother had increasingly become a believer in other realms. "Who says we know everything?" she often said. As the years passed, it was getting harder to argue with that.

To my mother, the dragonflies that covered the window the day he died were just the first signs from another world—little flares sent up by Danny to assure us that all was well, that he was good, that she and we should go and live our lives.

I couldn't bring myself to be an all-out believer, but I had come to a point where I was not *not* a believer. Let's say I was an ambivalent believer. Just ambivalent enough to stand in line for twenty minutes to talk to a psychic.

"So?" Nadine the psychic said as I took my seat across from her in a low-slung chair and set my margarita on the little wooden table between us. "What would you like to talk about?"

Now that I was there, I was embarrassed. *Am I really going to strip my psyche naked in front of a complete stranger? Especially when she has a clearly fake red jewel glued to her forehead?*

It somehow helped me feel better that Nadine was young and beautiful, with one of those pleasant faces you'd see on the side of a bus advertising a help hotline.

"Well, um . . ."

"What's on your mind?" She smiled at me with bright-blue eyes lined in thick black. "Work? Family?" She pulled her large, peacock-sequined scarf around her bare shoulders so that only her perfect, swan-like neck was exposed.

"Okay, well, yeah, sure." I hesitated. Might as well come out with the big guns. "So this is sort of heavy and absurd to talk about here . . . in this setting . . . at our friend's birthday party and all . . . but I kind of feel paralyzed. Like, paralyzed in my life."

Nadine leaned forward and knitted her brows together earnestly. "Yes?"

Is the leaning forward and being earnest thing part of the act? Also, where did the jewel come from? Michaels?

"Well, I feel blocked—like, barred in some way from my own life. It's like this weird dark animal force that's wrapped around me."

Nadine appeared intrigued. "Can you say more about that?"

"It's like . . . I wake up in the morning with a feeling of rootless dread."

Nadine nodded. "Tell me, what do you do for work?"

Instantly, I felt flooded with the familiar shame attached to this dreaded question. Despite all my resources, all the investment in my education, all my ambition—despite my certainty in my youth that I could do or be anything—I continued to feel that I'd failed to reach my professional potential.

I looked at Nadine. "Well . . . that's the thing. From when I was a little girl, I knew I wanted to be a writer—to write about things that mattered, about life. I wanted it more than anything."

"And?"

"And I worked in journalism in New York after college for a few years, but I just . . . kind of lost my drive for it before I made any real progress. And then we moved to Boston for my husband's job and I got offered a job to be the director of a new nonprofit, so I took it. I gave up writing, just like that."

I shook my head. I really didn't get it. Why *had* I given up on writing so easily?

At the time, it seemed so practical. The process of writing had become increasingly painful. My once-boundless mojo was dissipating into a Herculean struggle to meet deadlines. The job as an executive director sounded easy in comparison. No more wrestling for hours with the blank page, engaged in a constant battle with distraction. No more pressure to get national bylines on stories that were becoming harder and harder to focus on. No more pressure to follow my dreams.

I remembered hanging up the phone after accepting the offer and being overcome by a strange combination of relief and loss. I remembered putting my head on my desk and crying.

After leaving the working world entirely for fifteen years, I'd finally mustered the energy to try my hand at freelance journalism. But even after scoring initial success as a new writer for the *Huffington Post*, I'd slipped back into silence—letting the opportunity pass.

"The point is," I said, trying to make light of it, "I never answered my calling as a writer, even though I knew then, and I still know, that's what I'm meant to be. And that haunts me, and I don't understand it."

I looked down into my giant margarita. *Am I simply a midlife crisis in Spanx and a black dress? Is that what this is?*

But at this point, I was on a roll. "And in the last few years, when I've tried to get back to it, I just haven't been able to stay the course. Every time I sit down to write, I just . . . can't . . ."

"What exactly happens?" Nadine asked.

The question pressed on my chest. "The moment I open my laptop, I'm crushed. It's not about performance anxiety. It feels like something terrible is going to happen and I have to flee. Even when I get a little bit of traction, inertia and procrastination take over like turbo-engined twin enemies that never let up." I paused, considering for a second. "Oh, and then there's the Committee."

"The Committee?" she asked.

"What?" I joked. "You mean *you* don't have a committee living in your head, judging your every move?"

Nadine laughed. "Tell me."

Was she a psychic or a therapist?

"Oh, you know, it's this chorus of old white men telling me that everything I'm doing is pointless and frivolous and indulgent. They're probably all variations of my dad," I chuckled. "They have gavels, they wear robes. Basically, I'm on trial. Like, you know, at all times." I was trying to be funny, but it was true.

"Oh, wow," Nadine said. "That doesn't sound very fun. What do they say?"

"Mostly things like 'What's the point?' and 'Why do you even try?' One of the big favorites is 'Why do you think that's going to work when nothing else has?'"

Again Nadine knitted together her lustrous brown eyebrows. "What do they mean by 'Nothing's worked'?"

"Like, nothing's worked to break through this block in my head. Like, I'm stuck in a feeling of powerlessness and uselessness, no matter how much I do or how great the feedback on any level. And I'm so good at covering it up, no one would ever know."

As if on cue, the Committee piped up. *You shmuck! Why are you telling this to a psychic? Why are you telling* anything *to a psychic?*

My old, mean friends had a point. They always did.

They raised their collective gavels. *Shame on you! Look at your charmed life! What about people with real problems? Lucky you, to have the good fortune of your little existential crisis!*

I took a swig of my margarita and decided to spare Nadine the Committee's latest report.

"Look," I said, "I know how blessed I am, but I guess the truth is just the truth."

Nadine nodded empathetically as she fanned the tarot cards out in front of me, face up. She studied the exotic faces etched on the cards, scanning them, back and forth, in silence.

The Committee weighed in. *Freaking cards?! Like some voodoo cards are going to solve the mysteries of life?*

I felt stupid. And hopeful.

Nadine closed her eyes for a full minute and then opened them. "Julie, what I see here is that you have built an identity around a block."

I craned forward. "What do you mean?" The mere idea of an actual explanation for my state of mind sent a surge of energy through me.

"The cards show a blockage to the soul that's enveloping your life. I can see that you're a writer. I can see the words floating all around you, but they're out of reach. The block inside you serves a function."

Nadine may have been wearing a fake jewel from Michaels, but what she said hit a nerve that felt dead on, even if I didn't quite understand it.

She leaned forward and put her hand on my knee. "I believe that you will find the answers in silence." She looked at me intently. "I believe that you must go to nature, away from here. See if you can take a week away. There you will begin to learn what this is. I think you may begin to see how to find your freedom."

I stared at her. In nine days, I was scheduled to go on my weeklong writing retreat in Montana.

Dear Sister Julie,

This Menninger thing is hard. I feel scared. After I talk to you on the phone I feel better—

Have you ever heard of the word altruistic? That's what you are. Beautiful inside and out. It means so much to me when you take time out of your life to talk to me, make me feel good, give great advice and love me unconditionally. When I have felt so low you have been there, been nice. You understand me—understand what I'm going through.

I will always remember when you talk to me. I'm ready for a nice friendship with you but as you say, take it slow.

I love you and care for you deeply. You are like an oasis in the desert or like a beacon in the fog (my head-thoughts). I'm getting closer to the light of the beacon—getting closer to home where I belong. It makes me feel warm and secure, like a Sunday afternoon nap while it's snowing outside.

Fourteen

The morning after my interlude with Nadine, my phone buzzed.

It was another text from Jesse: *Mom, my stomach really hurts*.

It had been only a few days since we'd left her at school, but already it felt like an eternity had passed since I'd sat on that flight and looked down at the busy patchwork of Chicago, tears blurring my vision as I imagined my daughter somewhere in that shrinking puzzle thirty thousand feet beneath us, alone and not feeling well.

How could *only four days* have passed?

I read the next text as it buzzed in; Jesse was going to the bathroom so often that she was afraid to leave her dorm room.

For days she'd been texting me that she felt worse. Each text deepened the well of worry forming inside of me, but I did my best to text back variations of encouragement, assuring her that she'd get through it.

As hard as I knew it was for Jesse to be sick so far from home, it felt like the first test of independence for all of us.

I'm so sorry, baby, I texted back, impressing myself with the show I could put on when just a few layers down in my heart, the pool of anxiety was growing. *I'm afraid there's nothing to do for gastroenteritis but rest and drink a lot of fluids and let it run its course.*

When I came home from running errands later that afternoon, Dave was waiting for me in the kitchen. I took one look at him standing there stiffly in his blue scrubs, and I knew something was wrong.

"What, hon?" I went to give him a hug, but he put his hand out to stop me. "What is it?"

"I think you should go back there," he said in an urgent monotone.

"What are you talking about?" I asked, shaking my head. "I thought it was a stomach bug. Don't you think she would be humiliated to have me fly back four days after drop-off because she has a stomachache?"

Dave's lips were in a tight line. He took his phone out of his back pocket and held the screen up to me. I looked at the little black text.

Daddy, it read, *there's so much blood in the toilet. Help me please.*

Dave spoke evenly. "I'm on call. I can't go. I'm telling you, she needs to get to the hospital, and we need to find out what's going on. You need to fly there tomorrow morning. You need to fix this."

You need to fix this. Dave's doctor poker face was gone. His words were a command; this was a tone I'd never heard from him before.

I looked at him. Fear glowed in his eyes.

And so, a mere five days after watching Jesse grimace through the March Through the Arch, I boarded a 6:10 a.m. flight to Chicago.

On the way from the airport to Jesse's dorm, I called my parents and shared what was going on. They were both on the line.

"Jesse's never been sick," I said. "She's never broken a bone. The last time she was at a hospital was when she was born. That's a good sign, right?"

"Absolutely, it is," my mother said.

"She'll be fine," my father said.

I heard right past his words to his worry. He'd been here before with a child, I realized with a sick feeling. They both knew too well what it was to live in uncertainty.

"Remember to call us when you know something," my mother reminded me before we hung up.

Within two hours of my arrival, Jesse and I were in the emergency room of NorthShore Evanston Hospital.

"Thanks for coming, Mama," Jesse said to me. She was pale, so pale. She reached for my hand.

"Don't thank me, Beauty," I said. "I adore you, and I'm so happy to see you."

"I don't want you to miss your writing retreat because of me."

I looked at my girl. "Jess, please take that out of your mind. I just want you to feel better."

Obviously what mattered above all was to help Jesse. But on the flight, I did wonder—and not without guilt—whether I was going to end up missing the retreat. It seemed impossible that Jesse was sick at all, let alone so sick that she would miss college orientation while I missed my chance to expel my demons and lay the groundwork for my next stage of life.

But looking out the window and thinking back to the Danny years, I thought about how life always made sure to point out that anything was possible.

Jesse's blood work came back, and a colonoscopy was ordered for that afternoon.

"What does that mean, hon?" I whispered to Dave on the phone. "That they'd want this done so quickly?"

"Well, it's not good," he said grimly. "She must have lost a lot of blood."

The verdict came swiftly. Not gastroenteritis, not the flu. Jesse had the presenting symptoms of ulcerative colitis, a debilitating inflammatory bowel disease that was chronic, unpredictable, and incurable. A lifelong sentence of disease. Her next step was to be transferred from the emergency room to the main hospital.

"Okay, Jess," I said after the doctor left the room. I put my hand on her cheek. She was numb. I was numb. I put on my strong-mom voice. "You will manage this. Everyone's got something. Everyone. It sucks, but it could be so much worse."

"Yeah," she said like a soldier, looking straight ahead. "Yeah."

I called Dave.

"Okay," he said when he heard the diagnosis. I could feel him working it through in his mind.

"I mean, it's a miserable thing, but it could be worse, right?" I asked.

"Yes." His voice was measured but clear. "But it's a serious disease. And there's no way to know how it's going to play out over time."

A serious disease. A familiar dread crept over me.

The start of an illness. Future unknown.

I shook my head back and forth violently, emptying Danny's name from my head. I needed to think only about the now: getting Jesse admitted to her hospital room, letting her resident advisor know that she would not be back for orientation week, calling my parents and Dave's.

"Goddamn it," my father said bitterly when I told him the diagnosis, as if God Himself were to blame.

I had not been in a hospital since I'd given birth to Sam, and as I unpacked my things onto the narrow windowsill, I tried to absorb the moment.

This was not an overnight stay. This marked a new chapter in our lives. Jesse, who'd soared through the last eighteen years, faced living the rest of her life with a serious disease.

Jesse got into the hospital bed, and I went in search of some extra blankets.

As I walked down the hallway, I took in the ecosystem of the hospital. The packs of doctors in white coats doing rounds. The clusters of nurses sitting in their stations, staring at screens. Maintenance staff and aides rolling mops and carts through the corridors. Phlebotomists rattling down the hallway with their carts, knocking on doors before they entered.

Visiting family was easy to spot. There was a huddled energy to them. *All hands on deck.* We nodded and smiled at each other, a wordless exchange of support. I realized now . . . this was us. We were all in this together. Our lives zoomed down right now to just this—our loved ones, our hospital rooms, our fates.

As the evening wore on, it seemed like every hour a new resident came in checking his or her clipboard, looking for all the world like a middle schooler, and repeating the exact same questions.

"So, Jesse, can you tell me what happened?"

"Uh, yeah. Sure." And Jesse would tell her story all over again.

That night she and I slept inches away from each other. Me in my reclining chair, her in the hospital bed turned toward me, facing the metal guardrails. I kept waking up and looking over at her, trying to absorb into my brain what had just happened.

By the next day, both of Jesse's arms were already so sore from being stuck for blood that she couldn't lift them.

When it came time for dinner, I sat next to her hospital bed, feeding her applesauce and soup.

"Mom, slow down," she said.

I had to laugh. I used to feed her too fast as a little girl, too. I'd start out all joy and delight at the fun of it, but halfway through the mound of baby food I'd get antsy about how long it was taking and start heaping the spoons too high, putting them right up near her mouth in an effort to get her to hurry up and finish chewing. *What was my hurry?*

All these years later, here I was spoon-feeding my eighteen-year-old, still too fast. Can we ever really change our nature? I thought about this question and hoped the answer—in Jesse's case, at least—would be *no*. In the span of just a few weeks, Jesse had gone from a carefree, self-assured high school graduate ready to take on the world to a weakened and vulnerable patient unable to feed herself.

And yet somehow, miraculously, just four days after she'd been admitted, the doctor came into our hospital room with great news. The prednisone was working; her symptoms were being reined in. She was weak but stable. She would be discharged that afternoon.

Jesse and I decided that she would come back with me to the hotel for a few days. She would rest there until she was ready to return to the dorm.

I went into the hallway to call Dave and give him the update.

"That's so great," he said, his relief washing over me and leaving me instantly lighter. "Thank God she's responding to the medicine."

"It's almost scary how powerful those drugs are and how fast she turned around," I told him. "She's like a different person even compared to yesterday. It's like she woke up. She's hungry and eating and nearly back to herself."

Then it occurred to me . . . "Hon, if Jesse really is strong enough and wanting to go back to the dorm in a couple days, do you really think it's okay for me to leave for the writing retreat on Monday?"

Dave was resolute. "Yes, you should go. Definitely go. You've been looking forward to this for weeks—and the truth is, there's really nothing you can do for her now. It's better for her to get back into her routine."

A strange combination of relief and guilt washed over me.

Relief and guilt. A combination of feelings both ancient and fraught. Danny and the changing tides of his needs. The struggle to remember my own. The occasional reprieve into my own life.

For three days, we rested in our room at the Hyatt House. Jesse spent most of the time on her phone—filling in her resident advisor on what had gone down and sending notes to her teachers (first introducing herself, then apologizing for missing her first week of classes).

I listened in amazement as she started to build her new world with words. A grenade had been dropped in her path and she was taming the explosion, steering the narrative. I could feel her fighting against the new label as a person with a serious chronic illness. Instead of awkwardness, she saturated her conversations with dark humor.

"Yeah, I know it's kinda radical," she said during one call, "but I decided I'd spend my first week of college at Evanston Hospital. No biggie. I'm fine. I'll see you in a few days."

As I listened to her navigate each conversation with skill and humor, imparting the necessary information without any overlay of struggle, my heart swelled with sadness and pride.

We were all just at the beginning of this new story, but, already, Jesse was making her way.

One week after my arrival in Chicago, I swung the rental car around the driveway in front of Jesse's dorm, where Leila waited for her to help get her bags.

I looked at Jesse's roommate, with her tiny figure and waist-length brown hair. Her parents were Brazilian and, though raised in America, she emanated that culture's exuberance and warmth. With her swing skirt and high-heeled boots, she looked like a high-fashion Tinkerbell. I thought back to Jesse's first conversation with her, when Jesse was upset to learn that Leila wanted to decorate their room in hot pink. Already I was nostalgic for a time when the big dilemma was decor.

Now all I wanted, and desperately so, was for Leila to like Jesse enough, to be generous enough, and to be kind enough to her newly diagnosed chronically ill roommate. I prayed for that college thing when first-year students skip the usual social steps of friendship and become insta-families.

"Leila," I said, trying not to sound too heavy, "thank you so much for everything. I'm so glad Jesse has you here. Please call if you need anything!"

"Oh, don't worry!" Leila cooed. "We're going to have a great time!"

"Bye, Mama." Jesse gave me a peck on the cheek and a quick look. "Love you. Thanks for everything!"

I was filled with gratitude at the returning swagger in her voice, even if it was a little forced.

"Bye, beautiful girl," I said, holding back my tears and turning forward to drive back to the airport, back to my own life, without her.

Fifteen

As my rental car barreled down the highway toward O'Hare, I leaned my head back on the seat.

Maybe this was it. Maybe we were getting a free pass: the medication would keep working and that would be that. Jesse would be healed and go back to her life as it was. Maybe this last week had been no more than a temporary, if hellish, detour.

It was true that she'd been diagnosed with a chronic disease known to be debilitating, but thankfully there was a spectrum. There must be people, lucky people, who found the right medication and just went on with their lives normally, forever. Right?

I looked at my phone to check for texts from Jesse. Nothing. How many times, in those years of Danny's illness, had I waited for a call, a sign, something that would tell us that it was all over, that it would all be okay? A thousand times? A hundred thousand times? Magical thinking. It never came.

I boarded the plane. I pressed my face against the oval window as we took off. In the span of just a few short hours, I would go from an antiseptic, white hospital room in suburban Chicago to the dark woods of northern Montana.

I would spend four days at a writing retreat, followed by three days on my own at a nearby hotel in the town of Whitefish, trying to get back on track with my writing life. Maybe, just maybe, this one week would help me connect with a new version of myself—or maybe an older version of myself—that could help me into this new chapter of my life.

I'd tried so many things to rid myself of the feeling of paralysis, the ancient force of dread. Therapy, medication, meditation. None of it had worked. Weirdly, even trying to beat myself out of it with the privilege baton—*how could I be unhappy when I looked at my beautiful life?!*—only compounded my shame and self-loathing.

Maybe Nadine was right. Maybe these days away in Montana would give me a rehab of the soul. In my past—albeit my distant past—writing was always the thing that had felt most like me, the purest expression of potential that I had. I had already lost so much time flailing around, never finding my grounding. Maybe finding my way back to writing would be my ticket to the self I once knew, the person who lived in a sense of excitement and possibility rather than paralysis and dread about the future.

I shook my head. I had to laugh at myself. I was like a literal cliché in flight—a middle-aged woman on my way to a writer's retreat "In Search of Answers." Pinning my hopes on transforming my inner life in seven days. *Good Lord*, the Committee and I said in chorus.

And yet! As we descended over the necklaces of silvery lakes ringed by thick, emerald forests, I guarded a little tendril of hope that, as unlikely as it seemed, maybe, just maybe, I could pull it off.

That evening, I sat in a circle set up for the requisite icebreakers. I looked around.

There we were, nine middle-aged women, all looking slightly worn out. The Committee hissed in my ear, *Look at this scene! Look what it's come to for you! Pathetic.*

And where were the men? I wondered. Were men just too proud to come on retreats like these? No doubt many couldn't get the time off from work, but seriously? None? Were they just all too busy hurtling obliviously through the cosmos of middle age to notice they were also lost? Apparently.

A woman in a black-felt cowboy hat sitting across from me raised her hand to go first. Maybe she was that bold simply because her name was Candace Camden Jones.

Unlike me, Candace did not feel pathetic. Her taupe eyes slowly made their way across the room ceremoniously. Her lashes, which she batted slowly, were encased in mascara as black and thick as porcupine needles. She crossed her legs, bouncing her sharply pointed cowboy boots stitched in bright-blue embroidery. No, Candace was not pathetic. Candace was here to *shine*.

She tipped up her hat so that we could enjoy more of her long blonde hair. "Well, hello, everyone. *I* am Candace Camden Jones, and *I* am a novelist and short story writer."

I looked at the feather earrings dangling down her neck, waving in the wake of her declaration. Candace Camden Jones. Woman balls, Candace Camden Jones. With a name like that, she didn't even need to be a novelist and short story writer. She could just walk around, enjoying her name. In fact, maybe her name *allowed* her to claim herself as novelist and short story writer, never mind that she had yet to publish a book either.

Perhaps if I had her name, I, too, would have woman balls. But as it was, along with everyone else who schleps around with a terrible name, I'd been sentenced to a life of name shame. A life of childhood teasing followed by inevitable, awkward introductions and endless spelling corrections.

Brooke Baldwin. Cheryl Strayed. Bob Dylan. Cher. These were the names that rose to the top. Note, please—no Fingershes or Shmeck-ledorfs or Snotgers among them. Could Neta-Lee Hershlag have become Natalie Portman with her real name? How about Stefani Joanne Germanotta (Lady Gaga)? Jonathan Leibowitz (Jon Stewart)?

Right. *No.*

How different would my life be, I wondered, if I had a sexy, beautiful name, strong but feminine, filled with grace and mystery? Hi, I'm Jules Lansing. I'm Chase Winters. Just call me Blake.

But no. I was Julie Fingersh. And the experience I'd had earlier in the day when I checked in my car with Brandon, the hotel valet, was typical.

"Last name, ma'am?"

Brandon was one of those valets who you imagined was part of an army of young, wholesome-looking men and women working just for the season at the resort hotel. They were ski bums. They were waitstaff on the side. Their parents were trying not to be worried about their futures.

"Fingersh," I said, and watched his eyes flash with the tiny burst of disorientation, which is what usually happens when people first hear my last name.

I imagined it was one of Brandon's first days on the job. He was nervous. He wanted to impress his boss. He wanted to look good in front of Keira, the cute redheaded valet next to him.

I knew what came next. Either he'd ask me to repeat my name or he'd be too embarrassed and decide to wing it, which meant he would mislabel my valet tag to say *Fingers* or *Singers* or *Ringrish*, so that when I came back that afternoon for my little Toyota rental it would be lost in the hilly field of cars behind the hotel. I would be nice about it, sure, but I would be a little pissed, because I'd dealt with mislabeled tickets and tags and reservations a million times.

Back at the retreat, I was two people away from introducing myself. Besides the unpleasant job of having to package one's entire life in sixty seconds for all to judge, I braced for the reaction to my name, which would reliably trigger a minor case of PTSD.

"Hi, my name is Julie Fingersh and—"

"Sorry, what's your last name?" Candace cut in, her feather earrings waving at me.

"Yeah," I laugh-muttered, "I know, it's kind of weird . . . um, Fingersh?"

"Fing-rish?" Even Candace was confused and tentative, saying my name like it was a bad word. An uncomfortable pause followed.

Laura, our retreat leader, put up her index finger. "I try to think of fingerling potatoes and then drop the 'ling' and add 'sh'!" she said cheerfully, as if that weren't an even worse word.

"See?" I said. "Julie Fingersh. Doesn't sound as good as Anna Quindlen, does it? That's who I was hoping to eventually become, but so far, no luck." Self-deprecation had grown around my bad last name like a birthmark.

"Oh, forget Anna Quindlen," Laura said. "*You* are Julie Fingersh, and *you* are awesome!"

I knew Laura was just doing her job, but this was the saddest thing I'd ever heard, basically like saying, *You have a horrible name that I am likening to fingerling potatoes, and now we're all going to pretend that despite or perhaps because of this misfortune, you are awesome.*

"That's very nice of you, Laura, but let's be honest . . . it's the worst." With that I started talking a hundred miles an hour, mainlining my name shame. "When my husband's grandmother met me after we first got engaged, the first thing she said to me was 'What's your last name?' I told her it was Fingersh, and she said, with her face all screwed up, '*It's what???*' And I said, '*Fingersh.*' And she waved her hand at me and said, 'Jesus. Well, don't worry, you'll be rid of that name soon!'" (Much to Grandma Lil's chagrin, despite my ambivalence about my name, I did not change it when I got married. Personal principle—though it didn't hurt that my husband's name was no better.)

Mercifully, the group laughed at Grandma Lil's exclamation, and I rushed through my introduction about where I was on my creative journey and how I wanted to recover my voice and blah blah blah.

One by one, we met the group. Everyone had a background in writing. Everyone was there on a search, looking to fix something a little bit broken inside.

After everyone had said her piece, Laura held up a rock. "Over four hundred people have held this heart-shaped rock in their hands."

She leaned toward me. "Julie?" Somberly she put the cold, gray stone into my hand with both of hers. "Julie. I want you to hold this rock to your heart and close your eyes. Then I want you to put your intention in it."

Having lived in California for nearly two decades, hearing the word *intention* had become an almost everyday occurrence. In Kansas City, you could go your whole life without *putting your intention* into anything. But in California, the land of meditation and vegan cat food and turbo self-hood, intention was like water, like chakras, like dogs with Patagonia vests.

I held the rock to my chest. I looked at the women around me, forcing my eyes to close rather than roll out the back of my head.

That's when the Committee broke in. *C'mon now, are we really pretending that a rock can help you here? Are you really going to believe that a freakin' rock is going to break through decades of blockage and psychic fog?*

Just fucking go with it! I silently hissed back into the black void of my mind.

Then I sat there for a few breaths. I closed my eyes and tried to imagine all the hands that had held the rock. Hands that, like mine, had spent collective decades searching for the things we all search for—love, constancy, the feeling that we matter.

A part of me—a teeny, hopeful part of me—felt something: gratitude. Gratitude to be getting a new chance. Gratitude to be holding this rock, a timeless rock that had come before and would last long after me and everyone in this room, in my hands. Gratitude that I got the chance to spend the next four days in the company of women and possibilities and the chance to claw through, swim through, cry through, breathe through layers of time and scars and heartbreak and blessings to reach some part of ourselves we'd lost.

I opened my eyes to the sort-of-heart-shaped rock in my hand. Maybe it could be magic if I let it be.

Sixteen

Turns out, if you give yourself over to things, sometimes they work. For four days, our writing group huddled over our notebooks and laptops and went inside ourselves, peeling away layer after layer.

Like pure magic, my fingers flew across a real page with an ease I hadn't felt in years. Oh, my God. Look at this. *Handwriting!* I was still in there. Maybe the writer in me really did still exist!

By the second day of the retreat, I felt the pure joy of writing as I had when I was my younger self, when writing felt free and filled with possibility, like a great friend who promised to stay with me forever. If only I could keep writing—if only I could hold myself to committing to that purpose and achievement—I felt certain I would be at peace. The thin tendril of hope I'd felt on the plane rose in me like a determined green shoot.

As the days passed, I experienced a self I hadn't known for decades: a person in the world, alone and free. Not a mother, not a wife, not a caregiver. Just another student. The feeling transported me. I felt filled with exhilaration and freedom.

It occurred to me that maybe my recent envy of Jesse's beaming ambition and success was just a message from my deepest soul reminding me that I, too, had a fire inside, and it was time to feed it. Maybe there *was* still time to become the writer I'd always thought I'd be. Maybe Montana was the blank slate I needed in order to recover this part of my life and myself again.

The days flew by and, before we knew it, our circle was gathering one last time. We looked around the room at each other, quiet, connected to one another, full of giddy hope. It was time to get ready for the solo portion of my retreat. I would spend three extra days at a nearby hotel so

I could continue writing on my own, take my training wheels off, and seal my commitment.

No sooner had we said our goodbyes and I'd packed my bags than panic set in. The tiny shoot of hope that felt so rooted just hours earlier was suddenly thrown under the weight of decades of proof that it couldn't survive.

It was one thing to break free at a structured retreat, but it was fully another to build a new writer's life alone with my thoughts—and the Committee who would surely start their yawping campaign the moment I left the safety of this space.

I rolled my suitcase up to the massive, wooden front desk of the Lodge at Whitefish Lake, schlepping with me the familiar mix of excitement and alarm.

"Welcome!" said a woman who introduced herself as Lauralee. She extended her hand and grasped mine with a warm, iron grip. She looked to be in her thirties, with short brown bangs; plump, rosy cheeks; and wire-rimmed spectacles.

I told her my name and she didn't even flinch. I loved this woman already. Then she announced joyfully, as if I were a dear friend whose happiness was her greatest concern, "We've got you in the lodge with us for four nights. You're just going to *love* your room, I guarantee it!"

"Okay, super!" Like a good middle child, I aimed to please.

I looked around. The lodge was massive but cozy; giant stone fireplaces sat at both ends of the lobby, each one encircled with oversized red leather chairs.

I'd been psyching myself up for this moment since that first day at the retreat. I'd whipped up all kinds of Oprah to convince myself that I would use these next days to build on the momentum and forge a path to my next chapter. But now that I was here, I was losing confidence. Who did I think I was, racking up all kinds of expenses for no purpose other than to write? I had no book contract, no guarantee of getting published. Suddenly the scope of this experiment I'd created felt intolerable.

Then I thought about my neighbor back home. Ruth was a talented and prolific artist. She spent her days in her sunny studio, surrounded by colors and oils and canvases. She painted for the sheer joy of painting, without contract or gallery shows or guarantee of any kind of income.

From where did she summon the confidence, let alone the stamina, to work on her art, day after day, just for its own sake? I was in awe of the unapologetic value she placed on her own creative expression. She held her art making in such high esteem that she didn't need a specific outcome. No ambivalence. No angst. She created simply because she wished to, with no external proof of success. How? *How?*

I slid my room key into the slot and the dark wood door clicked open. The room was spacious and clean, and it was filled with natural light from the large windows overlooking the lake. The little table and chairs on the balcony called to me.

All at once a rush of freedom and joy washed over me. Maybe I could do this after all. Maybe if I could just make good on my promise to stay put and write, I could nurture the green shoot inside me into something strong and rooted.

Suddenly, Jesse's face appeared in my mind's eye. *How is she? Where is she?*

I sat down on the couch and looked out the window. Look at me, bathing in my ruminations of transformation when I had every reason to believe that, right at this moment, my daughter was huddled in her bed, getting worse. What if the steroids had stopped working? What if she was already on her way out of remission, on her way to losing touch with her old, healthy life and the person she'd always been?

I shook my head at myself. I knew I was catastrophizing. *Right?* But it was so easy to speed down a perilous path in my mind, imagining the worst. It was a well-worn habit, born from years of perseverating about Danny.

It was impossible not to see the parallels between them. The old Danny had been so much like Jesse. Smart, loving, handsome, and skilled, the world had been wide open to him. He'd had everything going for him until mental illness came for him. And after it did, he was never the same. *We* were never the same. In what felt like the blink of an eye, we'd gone from being a happy, healthy family to being lost in a secret and ex-cruciating odyssey. And there was the timing, too. I'd been close to Jesse's current age when Danny began to spiral.

Now here I was, decades later, trying to regain my footing in my own life, only to have another loved one's life suddenly torn apart. While my daughter was ailing, how could I sit here in my sunny hotel room and just . . . write? *For my own pleasure?*

I shook my head. No good could come of going down this road. All I could do, I decided, was what I had learned through years of practice with Danny: force myself to look at what was in front of me and step into it, even if only for a little while. For this one moment, I had three whole days ahead of me to be alone, all alone, to write, think, and try to reconnect with that clear-eyed girl I used to be.

I didn't know if it was the serenely appointed hotel room at the Whitefish Lodge, the utter silence, or just the pure fear of failure, but I woke up on the first morning of my solo retreat and found not fear but freedom in the silence. Words flew from my brain to the page in a way that seemed fully out of reach in the circus of my daily life at home. The tendril!

After a full morning of writing, I looked out the window and remembered: I was in Whitefish, Montana, one of the most beautiful places in America! I'd yet to see beyond the four walls first of the retreat center and now the hotel. Shouldn't I make time for a bike ride? Wasn't that what normal people would do on a beautiful afternoon? Why else did the lodge have fifty bikes lined up outside its entrance?

The Committee filed in. *You came here to work! Look at you, already wanting a break. Wasting time! Weakening your resolve!*

I thought back to the summer I spent going to school in a seaside town in France. Every day, each member of my host family would come home for lunch. They'd sit down to a two-hour meal with wine, after which they'd have a two-hour siesta before going back to work or to school for a few (very few) hours. They showed not a trace of guilt or conflict about their leisure-loving ways. They seemed, in fact, perfectly happy and wholly oblivious of any level of obsession with busyness and productivity. Was it just Americans?

But then I thought about my in-laws, for whom bike rides were utterly natural and non-risky. I loved my in-laws. They were warm, loving people, much like my own parents; they'd felt like family right from the start. But there was one thing about them that was completely foreign to me, and that was their unabashed practice of indulging in leisurely pleasures.

You know the montage part of rom-com movies when couples are just starting to fall in love and within five minutes are swept into a marathon of romantic activities, all the while shaking their heads, agog at *how amazing they are together* and *how amazing life is*? Those were my in-laws. They seemed to live in that movie montage full time, making the rest of us feel like we were living in a much less festive movie. Every time I called Sue and Jeff, they were out doing something that I could easily go my entire life without doing.

"Hi, honey!" Sue would say. "Papa and I are out taking a nice ride in the country!" Or "Oh, hi, honey, we're antiquing!" They were always strolling in some impossibly quaint New England town with names like Cranwell, Lenox, or Manchester-by-the-Sea. ("We'll call you back! We're having a lovely lunch at the Red Lion Inn. Papa and I are sharing a nice grilled cheese and a cup of coffee. Delicious!")

Most summer nights after dinner, they'd jump in their car and go out for ice cream. Although my family took wonderful vacations at appropriate times, my parents were as likely to go out for ice cream on a random night as they were to run naked through a shopping mall chanting the Koran. This was just basic law.

And so unless the break I was contemplating would involve a workout in which I would burn a minimum of ten thousand calories, in my mind, a "bike ride" was just shorthand for "moral and creative collapse."

I shut my laptop and walked to the window to survey the scenery and clear my head. The Montana trees waved their auburn leaves. Banks of fleecy, white clouds sailed overhead. Whitefish Lake glittered in the distance, making a mockery of the squabbling in my head.

In a moment of genetic transcendence, I stripped off my sweatpants and threw on my shorts. Evolution!

Down at the front desk, Lauralee thought nothing of my indulgent behavior. She just pulled a bike helmet and some pepper spray from behind her desk and started explaining how to use it.

"If you come up on a bear, you'll want to keep at least a car length between the two of you. Then, see, you pull this release real quick and just spray real hard into its face."

Sorry, come again?

Brandon, the valet, piped up with his two cents. "Also, you don't really want to be downwind when you spray, because that stuff is really strong."

I squinted. The truth was, I hadn't ridden a bike in years, in no small part because of the maniacal bike culture where I live in Marin County, where hordes of bikers constantly zoomed by in self-righteous packs, threatening to flatten every person, dog, or vehicle in their path. Said bikers also seemed bound by law to wear shiny, skintight bike pants that bulged in all kinds of upsetting places. Together, these facts were enough to keep me away from bikes, if only by threat of association.

So to find out—after working up the will to overrule the Committee and go on this bike ride—that I was risking being mauled by a bear all because I was trying to be like my in-laws seemed kind of ridiculous.

But what the hell . . . I went anyway.

Somehow I managed to bike into town clutching the bottle of bear spray under the handlebars without spraying myself blind.

When I made it to the town center, I hopped off my bike and locked it to a traffic pole.

In that moment, Whitefish, Montana, looked adorable. Despite its unappetizing name, which immediately evoked bar mitzvah buffets with their bagels and whitefish salads and little old ladies slipping pastries into their purses, Whitefish was one of those towns that gave the impression that everyone who lived and worked there existed in a permanent state of festivity.

The streets were lined with quaint restaurants and artisan galleries. People everywhere nodded and smiled and opened doors for one another. The whole thing made me feel like I wanted to ship in my family and stay forever.

After wandering around for a while, I pushed myself into the illicit and uncomfortable territory of eating ice cream *in the middle of the day.* As I sat down on a bench with my kiddy-sized, mint-chip cone, my thoughts turned to Jesse.

When we'd said goodbye a few days earlier, I'd resolved in my mind to let her have space, to wait for her to reach out to me. Sitting there on the bench, though, I felt guilty again. I'd gone almost the whole day without thinking about her once. How could I?

I realized that despite my excitement over how productive I'd been at the retreat, I wasn't going to be able to permanently escape my usual angst. It was like a repetitive loop I could escape only for small increments of time. I could live in the present moment temporarily—attend a meeting, go to the movies, sit on a park bench eating ice cream—but inevitably, all of a sudden, I would remember that someone I loved deeply was struggling, alone, while I was not.

I looked at the children playing in front of me on the grass. I thought about the privilege of my Montana retreat and the days ahead. Again I wondered, how could I allow myself to be immersed in this exciting new phase of my life while Jesse was struggling in hers?

I tossed my cone in the garbage next to me and thought about Danny. I strained to remember the sound of his voice, but I couldn't anymore. It was one of the things I was afraid of most when he died—that one day I wouldn't remember the sound of his voice—and now, sure enough, it had happened. It had slipped away from my memory without me even realizing it, without knowing when. Now it was just gone.

As if on cue, my phone sounded its jazzy voice with a call from my mother, the other woman who loved Danny most.

"Hi, Lulabelle!"

My mother's voice sounded light and balmy, which meant she was calling me from her daily walk.

"Hi, Mama," I said. Even all these years after losing Danny, it felt like a miracle to hear her sounding happy. She had survived.

"How are you, Lulu? How was the retreat?"

"Great. So great."

"That's so fabulous."

"It really was. And now I've been on my own and it feels like I've finally broken through something. I don't know, Mama. I'm afraid to say it, but I think I may be able to stick with it this time."

My mother couldn't have a conversation without offering advice, usually packaged in long, eloquent monologues. It was a habit that I'd developed a toxic response to—*Don't you think I know?!*—but the older I got, the more I listened.

"You know, Lulu, you're so porous. The world so easily seeps into you and you get diverted to other things. But underneath, there's a deep spring in you. In Hebrew, it's called *ma'ayan b'adama.*"

"What does that mean?" I asked.

"It's like a rushing spring underneath the earth. When you dig down, you find it, because the water is always there. The water is life. Lulu, you need to dig down to reach your underground spring. And I see that you keep trying. Every time you put in even a little effort, you find success. But then you don't nurture it."

"Yeah," I said quietly, "that's true."

"It's like you start to have success and it satisfies the top 10 percent of the topsoil, but it doesn't connect with the spring that's rushing be-low. It's like a spurt, and then it goes away. It doesn't last. Why don't you pursue it? Why is that your pattern?"

I swallowed. I had no answer, except that she was right. She was giving language, as only she could, to the last many decades of my life. So many strong starts, ultimately aborted: my bright and laser-focused start in journalism, abandoned; my success as an executive director, cut short; my freelance writing career, which started with a regular post with a na-tional media outlet, scattered against the tide of the more immediate calls of children and community work and relationships. My mother saw it all.

"When you don't tend to that well," she continued, "there's a sense of loss that diminishes everything else you do that *is* great. In a sense, I wonder if somehow you feel that you don't deserve it."

A lump rose in my throat. I listened as she went on.

"You know, you tend to other people's gardens all the time. Do you see that, Lulu? It makes you feel nice, picking other people's flowers. It gives you immediate pleasure. But inside you, you have an underground spring. The *ma'ayan*. You have to dig down deep to connect to the spring, Lulu. And that will take focus. A lot of space and a lot of focus."

Focus. The elusive element that seemed to always speed in front of me, beyond reach.

"Lulabelle," my mother said.

"Yeah, Mama," I said quietly, wiping tears with my sleeve.

"Start tending your own garden."

After hanging up the phone, I thought about how far my mother had come since Danny's death. I remembered reading about how peo-ple coping with the trauma of having lost a loved one to a devastating illness fell into two categories. One group took their grief and learned to savor life in a new way. Their grief and loss deepened their capacity for love and gratitude. The other group internalized the trauma. It lodged into their being and arrested their lives on some level, often without their realizing it.

I looked out across the hulking gray mountains before me. I remembered all those years I'd lived in fear that Danny would take his life. It had been a constant thought, always followed by the horrific dread of what would happen to my family in the aftermath. How would my parents go on? Who would our family become?

I tried to remember when my fear that his life would end in tragedy first took hold of my psyche, when it was that I understood for the first time that the trajectory of Danny's life—of all our lives—had taken a course that would never be reversed.

Seventeen

It's been three months since Danny was admitted to the hospital after leaving University of Kansas. After initially expressing feelings of relief at being in a place where he finally felt that his struggle was understood, Danny has grappled with the series of treatments he's undergone there—and their side effects—all the while coming to terms with the fact that he's left society because he can no longer function in it.

When he was first admitted, we hoped out loud for the panacea: *This time, we'll figure it out. They'll come up with the right diagnosis and treatment.* But after a few weeks, it began to sink in . . . Danny's treatment at Menninger will most likely be just another milestone in a journey whose end is no longer in sight. My parents, Red, and I don't discuss this realization. We don't say it out loud. But I can feel each of us falling prey to our own imaginations. I can feel the gradual reality of the situation settling into our family's core.

I can't wait for spring break to come, when I will go back to Kansas City, see my parents, sleep in my childhood bed, see my old friends. I had resolved to visit Danny at Menninger. Tucked away behind my excitement is a dread that is tinged with hope—hope that he is improving for real.

The day before I visit, I sit up in my room and write him a letter to bring with me and leave with him, words to help inspire and cheer him on. I know that I occupy a place in Danny's world that no one else does. He long ago stopped telling his friends the truth about his life. And we, my parents and Red and I, have stopped sharing much about Danny with other people too, including extended family. He's having a tough time, we say. He's taking a break from school, we say. We are uncomfortable enough and vague enough to make it clear to whomever's asking about Danny: *Stop asking.* We say it without saying it.

Mental illness is a term that is, at this time, avoided in mainstream society. It is a word reserved for the crazies who walk the streets talking to themselves. It is a word we have not yet accepted as one that could refer to a member of our family. Even with Danny living at Menninger Psychiatric Hospital, we somehow still can't comprehend that he—and we—have all joined this club.

To the extent that Danny understands what is happening to him, he still feels comfortable confiding only in my mother and me. But my mother's anxiety makes him wary of sharing too much. And despite the deep well of love that exists between Danny and my father and Red, his shame regarding his place in our family keeps their communication limited.

And so, fantastically, I imagine that I alone carry the only real chance of helping Danny find his way out of the shadows of his mind. My absolute belief that I have the power to accomplish this task has stretched into my everyday life like an invisible quicksand.

Today, it's: *if I can just write him the right letter, I will give him the resolve he needs to get to the other side.*

Suddenly I have an idea. Taking our red shag-carpeted stairs—the same stairs that Danny and I used to race down—two steps at a time, I go to my parents' room, where the family albums are kept. I open the cabinet to shelves of photo albums that span all the years of our lives as a young family, each one carefully labeled and numbered—one to thirty-one—in my mother's large script.

I sit on my parents' bed and flip through the yellowed pages, looking for pictures of the brother who was once as known to me as myself. I look at the pictures of our family, formerly so whole. There we are with our dog, Alfie, playing hide-and-seek. There's Red with his arms around Danny and me at the beach.

I look at the pictures of my parents. How is their relationship weathering this situation with Danny, I wonder, when they cope so differently? It is a mystery to me, and I am sure there is some conflict behind closed doors, but the strength of their love is a certainty. I feel it all the time—like the sun, like the air. After almost fifty years together, still, they hold hands. Still, they make each other laugh. Their marriage is the rock on which we all sit, even now.

Carefully, I choose and peel away photos from the album of Danny as a little boy. There he is on one of our family fishing trips—bright-orange bucket hat upon his head, arms spread as he splashes water at the camera with a wide-open laugh. There he is laughing at the Thanksgiving table, showing off a little Rice Krispies Treats turkey decoration. There we are, the two of us, mid-laugh, holding our pet rabbit together. I sort the photos and lay them out into a collage.

Maybe when he sees himself, he will remember. Maybe remembering who he used to be will help him find his way back.

I drive the forty minutes to Topeka, Kansas, following highway signs with names on them that, despite all my years of growing up in the area, are foreign to me. My heart drops at the sight of the last one: *Menninger Psychiatric Hospital.*

I turn into the parking lot. *Visitors' Parking.* I stare at the enormous compound of white buildings. *I am here as a visitor. My little brother is inside. My little brother is in a locked psychiatric ward.*

I push a button at the entrance, and the large metal door buzzes, clicks, unlocks. After I pass through, it slams behind me.

"Hi," I say to the receptionist, who sits behind a wall of glass. She looks to be in her fifties, the beginnings of crow's feet framing the corners of her face.

"Hello," she says matter-of-factly. She is like a clerk at a post office. She is a vacant face with eyes. She is a wall. "Who are you here to see?"

"Danny Fingersh," I say.

"Eating disorder? Addiction? Psychiatric?" the wall says.

"Psychiatric." My stomach is turning.

"Please empty the contents of your purse."

"I'm sorry?"

"We need to make sure you're not bringing anything in that could be unsafe for the patient," the wall says.

The patient.

I dump out my purse: wallet, random receipts, gum, a plastic container of toothpicks.

The wall picks up the toothpicks and drops them in a tray. "I'll keep these until you leave."

I look at her. *Toothpicks?*

"What's that?" She points to the photo collage under my arm.

My stomach sinks. "It's something I made for my brother." I don't move. I don't want to show it to her.

Her dark eyes flicker.

"Go ahead," she says, motioning toward another large steel door. "Stand in front of the door on the black square."

I stand on the square and the door buzzes.

"Now. Push now!"

I walk through a gray hallway. I am walking. I am floating. I am trying not to stare at the patients.

They are men; they are boys. They sit in chairs. Some are writing in notebooks. Some are sitting at smooth wood tables, looking out the window. They look at me. I smile like we're at a county fair.

The nurse shows me to Danny's room, which he shares, he's told me, with a sheikh's son from Saudi Arabia.

I knock on the door and hear my brother's voice behind it. I turn the knob and open it. Danny is lying on a narrow bed with a dark-gray duvet. Pink Floyd is playing.

"Hey, Jules," he says, getting up. He moves stiffly, in slow motion. Instantly, I see the medication in his eyes.

I try to seem casual and light—desperate to hide my fear from him, wanting to reassure him that I feel good about him being here, that I understand that him being here is a positive step forward. Still, I can't help but take it in: the skinny, tan boy who could never gain weight no matter what he ate is now heavy and bloated; his angular features are now spread across a blank, puffy face. His eyes are distant. He smells like days' worth of cigarettes.

I hug him and try not to cry. *Get a grip, Julie, get a fucking grip.*

"Stiggy, it's so good to see you!"

"You too."

"Wow, you put on some weight, huh?"

"Yeah, like twenty-five pounds. It's all the meds."

Immediately I see the tics. Every ten or fifteen seconds, Danny's eyes squeeze together, like he's trying to wake up, over and over again.

"So, how's the sheikh?" I listen to the words coming out of my mouth. *Good for me. I can act.*

"Jesus, Jules, you can't believe how rich this kid is," he says. He is up now, a bit animated; a wisp of my mischievous little brother is coming through. "He has his own personal servant at home. Like a butler. It's total poppycock!"

Poppycock. Danny.

"Wow, that's crazy," I say.

"Yeah, but now look at him. In a fucking psych ward. All that dough didn't help him none." The old Danny again. The steel block on my chest.

"Hey," I say, fake casual, "I have something for you."

"Yeah?"

I reach into my purse and take out the photo collage, which is curled up sideways now. As I flip it over, I watch Danny take in the photos of himself as a little boy. I watch the movie on his face: recognition, pain, withdrawal.

Fuck. I start talking fast, as if this will help. "Well, I was just looking through the family albums and thought maybe it'd be nice for you to remember the good old days. Because it's still you, you know, Stiggy? *It's still you.* That's who you really are inside. You know that, right?"

"Thanks, Jules," he says, and puts it up on his shelf on display. "That was really nice of you."

I know that he will take it down when I leave and put it out of his sight. *Fuck. How could I be so stupid?*

"This is also for you," and I hand him the letter I wrote for him.

As he takes it from me, I can see the expression dawning on his face. Danny is on to my rescue mission. He unwraps the blue-lined notebook paper in slow motion.

After reading the first few lines, he folds it up, and his face closes like a fan. "Is it okay if I read this later?"

"Sure, Stiggy," I say. *Too much, too heavy. How could I not get it? You idiot! Did he really need reminding that he's a psych-ward patient, need his sister to point out just how far gone he is?*

"Hey, want me to give you the grand tour of the loony bin?"

Somewhere in there, Danny is still Danny. He's trying to make me feel better. My heart hurts and hurts and hurts.

We walk the grounds of the facility, stopping to sit by the reflection pool, visiting the art studio and Serenity Room.

I greet Danny's fellow patients. "Hey, how's it going?" I say, and, "Oh, so nice to meet you." They are a mix of ages, mostly men, and the energy feels like a weirdly sedate summer camp. They could be students, lawyers, CVS clerks.

Danny gives me the scoop. "Jim. Twenty-three. Clinical depression. Told him he'd be out in thirty days, but he's been here for six months. James. Nice guy. I think he transferred from the eating disorder unit. That's Ken from Nebraska. Not sure of his deal except apparently he was sent here because he randomly cuts himself all over his body—says it feels good. He says it's a relief and stops his mental pain or something."

I shake my head. *How do people break like this? Will any of them make it back to regular life?*

I look at Danny as he checks the clock on the white wall.

"Sis, you have to go. Visiting hours end at four. We have group now."

"Yeah, okay, Stiggy. That's good that you've got a group of people you can talk to."

"Like any of them are in a position to give advice, Jesus."

I force a laugh.

We get to the steel door and hug for a long time. Even puffy and medicated, he's still my little brother, and I bury my head in his soft chest and try not to cry. I flash on our picnics in the park, on our neighbors coming to buy five cups of lemonade at our little stand. My heart rises in my throat, but I swallow it back down.

When Danny pulls away, he avoids my gaze.

"Love you, Stiggy."

"Love you, too, Sister Julie. Thanks for visiting me. Try not to get involved in any poppycock." Though he breaks into a crooked smile, his eyes are brown glass.

He looks at me, and, for a moment, I see all of him. I am cracking. He is breaking.

"We'll talk when I get back to school, okay?"

"Okay."

The door clicks behind me and I walk to my car quickly, feeling his eyes on my back, hoping that he can't see my shaking shoulders, the tears pouring down my face.

As I turn out of the parking lot, I look back to the entrance, under the blue *Menninger* sign. Danny is standing there, his dark silhouette framed by the massive, double-paneled steel door. He's holding my letter, watching me leave. It's an image I will carry to my grave.

Three days later, I open his letter to me:

Menninger
Topeka, KS
Dear Julie,
Thanx for coming all the way up here from K.C. you could probably think of better ways to spend your Sundays. It means very much a lot, infinite amount to me that you were here—I love you and hope <u>always</u>, <u>always</u>, to be a part of your life till the day I die. Even through pain, arguments or whatever.

I wish you luck in your job search for Esquire or whatever makes you feel comfortable, happy or where you feel a sense of belonging (maybe work has nothing to do with this equation, I don't know). Family is the only support system I can count on through all my pain and through all the pain between relationships for the family. I'm going to a seder on Tuesday.

The people at Menninger's are great, helpful and they even have nice looking nurses. I feel close to you, as I <u>hope</u>? you feel close to me. I feel lonely out here—physically close to home. But millions of miles mentally away from my Hebrew Academy roots which I find to be a goal I wish to achieve.

Well, have a safe way back home to K.C. and my spirit will be at Passover dinner and that's enough for now. I love you and appreciate your concern for me more than anything
Dan

Eighteen

The morning after my bike ride into Whitefish, I had an appointment with Willow, the horse whisperer.

Laura, our writing retreat leader, had raved about her and promised that everyone who entered her spiritual horse world learned something new about themselves and what was holding them back in their lives.

Why the hell not? I figured. I'd already been to a psychic and put my faith in a heart-shaped rock, so what did I have to lose? Also, maybe Willow would have something to say about the Meaning of Life.

Willow lived about fifteen miles outside of Whitefish in an area with no cell service. Because I've always had a chip in my brain that gives me 100 percent confidence to go in the wrong direction 100 percent of the time, I clung to every word of Willow's directions.

By some act of God, I arrived at the Medicine Horse Center, which looked like it was having a garage sale but wasn't. Benches and pails and tools were scattered in the sun. Two rusted red wheelbarrows were tipped over. Metal boxes were stacked high against a shed.

Goats bleated and roosters bobbed their heads through a burned-out field of grass, picking what they could find. A little girl with Down syndrome darted out from behind a shed, ran across the yard, and crouched behind a bush to watch me get out of my car.

A tall man in overalls with a stick in his mouth passed me without a word, shooting me a hard side-glance. I felt like I was in a movie, maybe an ABC Afterschool Special, right at the part when things are about to go south. Tiny alarms sounded in my head—until a small, strong-looking woman appeared from the entrance of an alarmingly leaned-over barn, her warm smile melting my concern.

Willow had cropped silver hair and hazel, almond-shaped eyes. She crossed the space between us in big strides and took both my hands in hers.

"Welcome, Julie!" she said with a squeeze. "Come on into the barn!"

I followed Willow through the double wooden doors, and they shut behind us with a metal clack. Before me, standing in a dirt horse ring, an enormous chestnut horse swished its creamy white mane and stomped in the dust.

Willow waved for me to sit at a little table at the entrance of the horse ring.

My work, Willow explained, was to approach Chester and *be* with him. *Understand* him. *Respect* him. And then try to lead him around the ring. If I had trust or self-esteem issues, he wouldn't respond. If my boundaries were firm and warm, he'd follow my lead. As we got to know one another, he would tell me things. I would learn about myself. I would grow. I sure hoped so, since I was paying a lot of money to learn from a horse.

"So, Willow?" I said, trying not to sound suspicious. "Who exactly is this for? Like, who are your clients?"

"Oh, it's for anyone," she said in her golden voice, massaging the knuckles of her right hand, tanned and freckled from a life of work. "Arthritis," she explained. "Yes, so really, anybody. It even helps people who are bipolar. You put 'em on backward, and the energy of the horse actually starts affecting them. It affects the vagus nerve, which is connected to the reptilian part of our brain, the fight-or-flight response. That nerve runs all the way down the front of our spine, so when we lay them down on that horse, the energy is being affected. It works on them."

The Committee balked: *Bullshit!* I beat the voices back by doubling down on my enthusiasm for Willow. "I bet it works for depression, too."

"It does. People have a hard time understanding it and believing it, but science is finally starting to catch up with what horses can really do."

I looked at Willow. She was so sincere. In the deep map of her face, I could see that she'd been through something harder than anyone would ever know, just like my mother had. Just like I had. I thought about all the signs from Danny that my mother was always talking about, and what she often said to explain the world we cannot see. *Who says we know everything?*

Willow slapped her thigh. "Now let's get you in there with Chester. But remember, you won't be riding him. This is about you both being on the ground, communicating eye to eye, soul to soul."

Soul to soul. *That* I understood.

I walked into the dusty ring toward the chestnut stallion.

"Hi, sweet boy," I said softly.

Chester swung his long, graceful head back at me, gave me a quick glance, and then swung it back away, his creamy white mane following with a swish.

He was a giant and I was a dwarf. He could crush me.

"He's saying hello," Willow said.

"Okay," I replied. "Um, hi, Chester. Now what do I do again?"

"Stay with him for a little bit, and then, when you're ready, lead him around the circle. See if he'll let you take the lead."

Chester didn't budge.

"I don't think you've properly acknowledged him yet," Willow said.

"Hi, Chester," I whispered again, standing next to him. My head came up to the middle of his and we were about eye level now.

He snorted, turned, and fixed me with his right eye—and then, for no reason I could see, I was suddenly walking Chester around the circle. Or, rather, Chester was walking me around the circle.

"You gotta let him know that you're in charge," Willow called out from the corner of the stable, because Chester was pulling me along like I was a toddler.

I pulled on his reins and stopped. He stopped, too, and stared ahead. "Chester, I'm going to lead you," I said with fake authority.

I stroked his head and ran my hands beneath his soft muzzle, and he turned to face me.

"Hi, baby," I said, and I was struck by how quiet it felt around us. How still.

I leaned in and put my cheek on his. His coat smelled like the earth. I pulled away and looked at him again. He was looking at me now, taking me in.

His eyes were dark and deep and endless. I recognized something in them.

We stood there for a long time, looking at each other. A strange sense of serenity and calm enveloped me. *Is it the vagus nerve? What is the vagus nerve again? Am I insane?*

Danny's name rose in my mind, as it so often did. He'd been alongside me in so many countless ways over the years. A silent companion. I looked into Chester's eyes, dark and certain, looking right back at me. I thought about the dragonflies. So many dragonflies on the windows, so many dragonflies hovering over our lives.

I didn't know whether Danny was just in my thoughts or whether he was somehow looking at me from behind Chester's enormous brown eyes. I only knew that tears were streaming down my face because I knew that he was here with me now and that his presence in my life was a microcosm of life itself. Love and loss. Mystery and beauty. Magic and hope and a recurring sense of homecoming.

I looked back at Willow, leaning against the corral gate.

She had stopped giving directions. She just stood, nodding at me, smiling with a deep empathy in her eyes. I wiped my tears and nodded back.

Nineteen

The morning after my date with Willow, I started the day with breakfast at a local diner.

For some reason I felt entitled to the "Number 1": one egg, one huckleberry pancake, and three strips of bacon. It was the huckleberry pancakes that made me do it.

I'm not sure anyone knows what huckleberries are, but when you arrive in Montana, suddenly, you simply must eat them in every possible form available. You might start out reasonably, by buying a little cellophane package of huckleberry taffy tied with a nice purple ribbon. You'll probably stay within bounds for a while, ordering huckleberry ice cream or buying bars of huckleberry dark chocolate. But before you know it, you'll be in line with the other human sheep, ordering and buying anything that happens to crop up with the word "huckleberry" in it.

Pretty soon, you'll be scarfing down huckleberry hot sauce, cocktails, and who knows what, all without actually knowing what huckleberries are or paying attention to the fact that they don't really taste any different from blueberries.

But it was all part of the Montana experience, and I was all in.

Now that I had a purely recreational bike ride and a horse whisperer session under my belt, it seemed criminal not to visit one of the most famous national parks in the world: Glacier National Park, a mere forty-five minutes from Whitefish.

As I pulled into the visitor center, I came upon my first awe-inspiring sight: a park ranger, dressed head to toe in a snappy green uniform, who appeared to be as old as the park. The man was walking toward his car as if to leave, bent at the hip so that his head bowed to the necks of the people walking toward him.

I needed to know this man's story immediately. I walked over and, after the briefest exchange of pleasantries, Ranger Doug offered to show me his favorite place in the park down the road. Instantly I said yes. True, I was getting into a car with a man I'd known for only five minutes, but Ranger Doug was a government employee in uniform whose job was to play host. The man had time on his hands and (theoretically) a valid driver's license. I was on an ontological search. How could I refuse?

Ranger Doug, of course, knew nothing of my obsession with old people, who I believed knew more about the Meaning of Life than anyone else. What else could explain the fact that old people always seemed to be sitting on park benches in utter contentment, watching birds and taking in the view? How else did they sit in large circles around outdoor tables at Peet's, chatting and laughing without a care in the world?

To me, older people exuded an aura of *Yep, I know how this all works.* This is why I worked myself into conversations with them as often as possible while they sat on those benches or waited in movie lines or sat at my table at bar mitzvah brunches, and then I moved swiftly from "So, how are you?" to "So, have you figured out the Meaning of Life yet?"

I looked at Ranger Doug. He had to be close to one hundred years old. Wouldn't he *have* to know the Meaning of Life by now?

I watched from the other side of the car as Ranger Doug lowered himself very slowly onto the torn upholstery of his Buick and then fished a keychain out of his frayed pocket with his gnarled, veiny hand. He studied his hand as he separated the keys until he found the right one, and then he aimed his hand toward the ignition in slow motion.

I tried not to ask myself whether Ranger Doug should still be driving and whether I should be driving with him. I batted away the headline in my head: *Ranger Doug and Middle-Aged Writer Seeking Meaning of Life Drive Off Cliff.*

The car started with a wheeze and we made our way slowly, loudly, over the gravelly lot. Ranger Doug unfurled his story like a well-worn map. "Born and bred in the area. Married, four kids. Served in the Air Force and was all packed up to go to war. Never had to, but if Harry hadn't dropped the bomb, I might've been in on the invasion of Japan.

I've been in the Department of the Interior for about sixty-seven years now. Just wrapping up my fiftieth season at Glacier."

"Fiftieth?" I gasped. "Good Lord, what's kept you here so long?"

"The people. I was born into this stuff, so I get to take the scenery for granted. I couldn't afford to see the rest of the world, but I'm in Glacier, so the rest of the world comes to see me! Well, they don't really come to see me, but I'm standing in the way." He chuckled at this statement.

I looked at Ranger Doug's face. He was so old. So beautiful, like an ancient, wizened Willem Dafoe with his chiseled cheekbones, square jaw, and sheer-blue eyes. I imagined him as a young man, and I felt my heart bow to his humanity.

I asked Ranger Doug what he'd learned on the job.

"Well, I've learned that people feel like their national parks are kind of a religion to them. It's like the national parks are our cathedrals. And the people in the big hats, like me, are the high priests who've been given the responsibility to protect these sacred lands and trusts. I'm not sure our political leaders appreciate it quite enough. . . ."

Ranger Doug was Oprah, I realized.

"Well, let's go over and see the lake," he said. "You'll see why."

The narrow road was hugged by a thousand trees and shone charcoal from a fresh rain. We turned into a clearing that stretched before us like a silent miracle, a biblical mirage. At the end of the empty parking lot was a glimmering sheet of water that extended for miles. It offered itself up like a giant, light-filled mirror.

The massive range of the Glacier Mountains towered silently across the lake in all directions, casting its huge, blue, shadowy figure into the water. Rings and rings of pines and aspens whispered with their autumn canopies in the wind.

"Oh . . . My . . . God," was all I could say.

Ranger Doug nodded. "This is a moment, see. These are moments. Look! You couldn't improve on it if you lived forever. It's a moment of color. It's clear. Not foggy or smoky. And in the fall, the sun is at an angle, and the shadows emphasize all the pieces of the mountain. You see galleys and valleys you didn't even know were there. Because of the angle of the sun. It's a moment."

It *was* a moment. Ranger Doug took in the sight of the lake, and I took in the sight of Ranger Doug in his sacred vestment—a straight-brimmed ranger hat ringed with a USNPS-stamped, chocolate-brown leather strap. He *was* a high priest of the United States National Park Service. His handsome, strong profile was all angles and bones under his almost transparent skin. His face beamed at the sight before him.

That's what being present looks like, I thought. Then I couldn't help it. I couldn't help but look at Ranger Doug and imagine him waking up in the morning trying to get out of bed. I imagined that he wore briefs without a shirt. I imagined his body, skin hanging off the bones, just trying to go on. My heart clenched at the vulnerability and dearness of this old man.

". . . And this is why we have to watch the public lands. Because there are predators out there who would peddle them off to the highest bidders. So we need to make a fuss over our national parks and make damn sure politicians understand that the guillotine may not be out of fashion for people who don't appreciate their public lands."

Yes, but I wasn't really listening anymore. I lobbed the question I'd been wanting to ask from the moment I saw him.

Ranger Doug felt along the brim of his hat as he considered it.

"Well, I can't tell you exactly what the Meaning of Life is, but I would say: Get your plan. Make sure you know where you're going. So when it's over, you can say, 'I feel pretty good about it.' Otherwise, you look back on forty years and say, 'Oh crap, I did the wrong things.'"

I had to admit, as much as I was in love with Ranger Doug . . . that was *it*? I felt a familiar disappointment.

The Buick wheezed back into the visitor center, and we pulled up to my car. Ranger Doug looked at me with a soft, wrinkly smile. "Well, you'll have to come back and see me again!"

"Okay, I'll look forward to that," I said lightly, knowing that the chances of us ever seeing one another again were slim to none. I looked into Ranger Doug's deep-blue eyes. It seemed like we both wanted to enjoy the thought of meeting again, and, in service of that thought, we'd help ourselves past a truth that didn't want to be known.

The moment was a variation on how things worked between my mother and me. How when we ended a conversation we'd say, "Let's talk tomorrow," although we both knew it would almost certainly be days before we'd talk again, prone as we were to getting lost in our respective worlds.

But the truth didn't matter, because behind our dance of words was the comforting idea that we *could* talk tomorrow, that there would *always* be tomorrow, even if somewhere inside we both understood that one day our lives together would end.

I helped Ranger Doug out of his seat and hugged him tight before he slowly lowered himself back down.

Then I shut his squeaky door, and we gave each other one last wave. My heart stung a little as I watched him drive slowly over the gravel in his Buick, headed into one of the rest of his days.

Twenty

As I drove back to the hotel, I thought about Jesse and how much she would have loved Ranger Doug. I wondered how she was, and I felt another pang. Here I was, still on my big, fun adventure, with no idea how she was adjusting physically and emotionally to her new world. I had called Dave that morning to see whether he'd heard from her, but he hadn't. It took all I had in me not to break my word to myself that I would leave communication in her court. It seemed like an eternity since we'd spoken.

Funny how the tables had turned. I thought about all those bittersweet moments in parenthood when we separate from our kids for the first time. We drop them off at preschool, kindergarten, high school, maybe summer camp. One day, we give them keys to the car. They leave for parties and outings and experiences that we will never know anything about. After what feels like a lifetime of sharing everything, we know our children—both their inner and their outer lives—less and less.

I was set to fly home the next day, so I got an early start on packing that night. While I folded my clothes, a thought arose: during this week, I had felt freer and happier than I had for as long as I could remember. I had felt like my pure self—the self I used to be. Being away in Montana had loosened something inside, given me the presence of mind to create and write freely for the first time in years. The dark force that had been plaguing me had, at least for the moment, taken a leave of absence.

But the fact that the block could disappear just like that seemed all too simple. There had to be a catch. What had been different this week?

When I was at home in California, my consciousness blinked and pumped with an endless list of people to get back to, satisfy, check up on, help. There, my head noise was like air—all I breathed.

Here in Montana, I'd been severed from the cycle of call-and-response, separated from the driving whip of technology and its relentless, shrill call to respond and serve. All the hundreds of emails, texts, and notifications waiting—like crack. All those people waiting to be attended to, dopamine to follow.

After days of quiet, I heard only one voice. *Mine*. Words floated around me, and I could hear them asking to be written down.

But what did it mean? Was it just a dumb and obvious conclusion that I could focus when on vacation? Was that really all? Or was this something deeper? Something to do with my identity? That I could not access myself in the company of the needs of others?

As I packed my things, I spotted an unopened bottle of wine I'd bought a couple of days earlier that was sitting on the mantle. I decided to give it to Lauralee, who seemed to live at the front desk and whose sole mission was to make everyone feel good about themselves.

I took the stairs by two.

Lauralee wasn't at her desk, but a big family of all generations was gathered around the roaring fire, smiling, with mugs and glasses of wine in hand.

"Wow, that looks cozy!" I said, because we were all friends at the Whitefish Lodge.

"Yup!" a large man in a navy cable-knit sweater said.

"You guys here for a special occasion?" I asked.

The woman sitting next to him perked up and rocked in her rocking chair.

"My whole family met here to celebrate my birthday!"

My heart warmed. "That's so wonderful. Happy birthday!"

"Why, thank you, sweetheart. I'm eighty-seven!" Her bright blue eyes sparkled in the light of the flames.

"Wow," I said. "Eighty-seven years. How does it feel?"

She smiled and closed her eyes for a moment. "I've had a good time with my life," she said, raising her mug. "I've had a real good time."

The silence that followed her words held the beauty of that idea: *the value of having a good time with your life.* As badly as I wanted to interview the birthday girl about the Meaning of Life, I figured I should spare her my existential interrogation during her party.

Just then, Lauralee walked by with a happy wave and went to her desk, where she opened a large hardback book. Lovely Lauralee with her spectacles and rosy cheeks and freckles on her nose. It was hard not to hug her on sight.

"What are you doing, Lauralee?" I asked as I walked up to her desk.

"Oh, I'm studying Esperanto," she said brightly.

"Really? Esperanto? You mean, like . . ." I couldn't remember what that was.

"Oh, you know, it's the international language. It's not really used, but it's based on all European languages and was created to try to unite all nations with one language."

"Wow. That's amazing! Are you going somewhere?"

"Nope!" she said cheerfully. "I've never been much out of Whitefish and Glacier. Actually, I've never even been on a plane."

Wow. *Wow.*

"Well, that's amazing," I told her. "That's amazing that you're just learning for the sake of knowing it."

And I nearly choked on the poignancy of that, and the beauty of people and their dreams, and that here was Lauralee learning a language meant to unite all nations. Lauralee, who had never been on a plane and had no plans to get on one.

I handed her the bottle of wine. "I never got to this, but I hope you will."

Lauralee's face lit up and her cheeks reddened. "Oh, my gosh, thank you," she said, looking up at me, eyes shining. "Really, thank you. That's the nicest thing."

I thought of Lauralee. Ranger Doug. Willow. The birthday girl by the fire. Their humanity washed over me. I was going to miss Montana.

Twenty-One

As my plane took off in the early Bozeman light, I looked out the window at the blue-gray clouds sailing by and thought about my time in Montana. Had I really arrived only last week?

I thought about my wish that the writing retreat would be my answer. A rehab of the soul that would deliver me from my head prison of paralysis and dread. It remained to be seen what the long-term outcome would be. But one thing was certain: the retreat gave me a glimpse of who I used to be. If only one week could spark a reconnection to the clarity and ambition of my younger self, surely there was some hope?

I thought about my mother and the underground spring she spoke of, the *ma'ayan b'adama*. If only I could dig down deep enough to hit the rushing stream of my whole self. If only I could stay the course.

The moment I arrived back at home, though, I knew I would be confronted with my relentless urge to jump into the endless cycle of tending to other people's gardens. Just as the thought occurred to me, the Committee barreled in, waving their gavels wildly in the air, chanting, *Nothing works! Nothing works! Why do you think this one week away is going to work when nothing works?!*

Their voices were so loud. Those two words—*nothing works*—seemed to encompass the story that had kept me hostage in the airless back room of my own life for so many years.

I thought back to Nadine, the psychic, who had reported to me that I had built an identity around my block. Was she right? Had I built a block not only between me and my ability to enjoy the blessings of my life but also between me and my ability to fulfill my potential as a writer?

But why? All I knew was that, whether I had created it or not, there was a voice lodged within the operating system of my soul. And it always said, *Stop.*

I thought about Danny and wondered at what point my entire makeup as a person started to change.

His stay at Menninger had turned from weeks to months, and every new month brought new treatments, new trials. It felt like he was floating away. As time passed, I could feel myself slowly splitting apart, like a glacier breaking into three pieces that slowly drift away from one another. One part of me was an aspiring journalist with stars in my eyes, striking out on my own; one was the sister of a brother who was free-falling into darkness; one was the daughter of parents whose hearts were breaking, all fifteen hundred miles away.

Danny was like a storm flowing through my veins. His struggle churned through my days. My psyche grew increasingly tethered to him. Each day began with two questions: *Is Danny okay? Is Mom okay?*

I looked out the window at the Montana wilderness below and my mind returned to home and the voices that called me there. They were the yawning voices of expectation. They appeared as voices of the people in my life now—friends, colleagues, family. I wondered, in that moment, whether I recognized the urgency of a girl trying to save a drowning brother.

Danny's been at Menninger for eight months by the time I move to New York after graduation to take a job as an editorial assistant at *Business-Week*. I learn that the routines of adult life are a buffer against the uncertainty of what is going on in my family. It's a relief to be in the real world.

But my double life comes with me. At some point each day, the red alert sounds in my head—an emergent impulse to reach for the phone. It can be in the middle of an interview, a staff meeting, a deadline. As soon as I can, I run to my desk, pick up the phone, and dial the 1-800 number to Menninger.

"Hi, Stiggy!" I say one day with manic enthusiasm, as if enthusiasm might cheer him out of clinical depression. "What's happening over there?"

"Hey, Sister."

I can feel him trying to act like everything is okay, as if he isn't getting worse, as if he isn't in a mental hospital.

"Nothing."

"Nothing? Really? How's the sheikh?"

"Fine. He's in isolation for a couple days because he attacked one of the nurses, but he'll be back tomorrow, waking me up in the middle of the night with his vicious snoring."

I try to laugh. Then I try to find out how he really is. Does he feel any different? Is he able to eat? Is he making friends? What do the doctors have to say? Is—

My colleague motions to me.

"Oh, shoot. Hey, Stiggy, our staff meeting is starting. I should probably go."

"Okay," he says, and I hear the slight drop in his voice. Dread seeps into my gut as it does at the end of every conversation. I am afraid that once we hang up, Danny will again be at large, mental destination unknown. Anxiety squeezes my chest. We talk a few minutes more. I feel us both delaying our goodbye.

"So just tell me," I say, looking up at the clock, "what's on tap for the rest of the day?"

"Group. Meds appointment with Dr. Barnacle. Art therapy."

"Really? You have art today? That's fun."

"Yeah, we're making vision boards for our future. It's like a teenage girl party but depressing. They're just trying to keep people from being suicidal."

His voice is becoming flatter. We are blending together now. I understand that his link to my voice, my regular life, is a salve.

"But it's fun," he says, and I can feel that he is lying for me. Even in the midst of his intractable depression, he wants to protect me.

"Hey," I say, "you should call Mom."

He understands. This means he should call and show our mother that he is doing okay, try to ease her constant anxiety about him.

"Yeah, okay, Sis, I will. You've got to go."

"Okay, yeah, Stiggy, I should." I try to make myself numb.

"Love you, Sis."

"Love *you*, Stiggy," and I hang up.

I look at the conference room door, my colleagues sitting at the table, waiting for me. I feel the steel block crushing my chest.

Dear Julie,

I just wanted to tell you how proud I am to have you as a sister. This is so incredible how you're a writer for BusinessWeek *at age 24. Most people still have their heads up their asses at that age. So if you don't get enough congratulations from others, here's mine to you. I love you, your brother, Dan*

The trip back to Marin, door to door, took six hours, and before I knew it, I was walking back into the familiarity of home.

But my happiness at being back was tinged by the ambivalence of leaving behind who I'd been for the past week—a student, a writer, a person in and of myself.

Unbelievably, in the span of hours, I was back to the full psyche and baggage claim of the now: mother, wife, neighbor, house manager, carpool driver, and social/emotional life management consultant.

Slowly, reliably, the sweet rewards of home drowned out my inner conflict for a while. There was Sam, standing at the door waiting for me, wanting to go out for smoothies together and to check out the guitars at the music store. There was Scotch, who trotted up to accept my shower of love for about ten seconds before breaking away and shooting out his doggie door to sniff a stick. And there was Dave, smiling and watching my homecoming with that lined, beautiful face I adored. The silo was nowhere in sight, a sign that all was well. And at least for the moment, the demons, the dark animal force, the Committee, were all being held at bay.

Meanwhile, it had been more than a week since I'd left Jesse on the street outside her dorm, ready to start her new life. Now that the initial storm of her illness had passed, it finally hit me: *Jesse is at college.*

We were *in*—fully in—the next chapter: hers, a new freshman in a new world; ours, with everything (at least physically) as it had been, except her bedroom, which was so empty that it echoed. An image of Jesse as a little girl flashed in my mind—red curls bouncing, eyes looking up at me brightly. "Mama! Mama!" As a little girl, she was always calling for us, always wanting more of her parents: *Come play, come read, come sit with me, come cuddle me!*

Here we were now, tables turned. I waited until I couldn't stand it. I'd barely talked to her in more than a week. *Fuck it*, I thought, *that's enough restraint*. I sat down at our kitchen island and started texting.

Any chance you can FaceTime for a few minutes?

The little dots floated up and down.

Sure, give me a minute.

Suddenly there she was, shining red hair pulled back, walking across campus, wearing her mirrored Ray-Bans, glancing at me every few steps.

"Hi, Mama!" she said. "Where's Scotch? Let me see him."

Saying goodbye to Scotch was one of the hardest parts about leaving home for Jesse. All calls from her began with my looking through the house for Scotch so she could talk to him while he looked away, bored, his little cropped tail wagging slowly back and forth, until he eventually got up and walked away. Even fifteen hundred miles away, Jesse could not break free from the chains of canine emotional pursuit.

This time, I found Scotch curled into a tight dog crescent in Jesse's bedroom, head resting on her pillow.

"Hi, Scotchie! Hi, good bad boy!" Jess cheered into the phone.

He opened his eyes for a moment and then closed them again.

"Well, that's it for Scotch," I said, and our laughter collided across the miles.

I walked back to the kitchen and poured myself a glass of iced tea.

"So? What's the report?" Jesse asked.

I looked at her on the tiny screen. She looked good. She looked *well*. I wanted so much to cut in with my own questions: How was she feeling? Was she having cramps? Were there any traces of blood in the toilet?

But I stopped myself. It was part of the agreement: Jesse had expressly told us she did not want to be asked how she was feeling—ever. If she was having a problem, she would tell us.

It was torture.

"Mom?"

The report, yes, the report. Suddenly I felt put on the spot, clear about the need to serve up a fun summary that would not push any wrong buttons, that would not make her miss home or regret calling on any level. The goal, I figured, was to deliver a tap dance that would simply entertain Jesse and leave her happy so that she'd want to talk to us again soon.

But the truth was, I didn't have much to say. I worked up some local news, weather, and sports. *Uh-huh, uh-huh,* she said. Then I remembered seeing her friend Jake at Target and that he asked about her. She broke into a wide grin on hearing it.

"Oh, really?" she said, suddenly animated. "That's so nice that he asked about me! He's such a sweetheart! How *is* Jake?"

After I'd answered and I went back to the report, my radar picked up her flagging attention.

"Okay, Jess, go," I said preemptively.

"Yeah, sorry, I have to go."

"Oh, no problem!" I said with false cheer.

I flashed back to that sweet talk next to our firepit we'd had just a few short weeks earlier.

Like, Mama, how's it going to work? Like, are we going to talk every day? Oh, however you want it to work, baby.

I'd been the freaking Dalai Lama back then. Now, without warning or discussion, we had moved to a new stage. Jesse wasn't asking for my advice anymore.

We said our goodbyes and "love yous," and I put the phone down and swallowed.

"She sounds so flat and uninterested," I said to Sam, who sat across the kitchen island from me, studying his laptop screen and clicking away—at Minecraft, I presumed.

"Maybe that's just a coping mechanism," he said without looking up. "She doesn't sound that way when she's talking to me."

This was supposed to make me feel better?

Just then, Scotch trotted into the kitchen and lasered his eyes into me, imploringly, as if he hadn't been fed for days. But hadn't I already fed him dinner? I shook my head at him. He was almost certainly lying. He *knew* that his stare was convincing enough to make me question my memory—which was, in fact, questionable. How often did I end up feeding him twice because of his lies, lies, lies? Although, truth be told, another reason to give into the bed of lies was that feeding him was my whorish way of winning his affection. Which I wasn't above.

I chuckled as a new thought occurred to me—Jesse was like the new Scotch in our family. Basically, she was like a new boyfriend whom I was trying to win over by playing hard to get. Instinctively, I felt it necessary to impart the vibe of "Yeah, sure, I *love* you, but I don't *need* you. If you call, sure, I'll be happy, but . . . you know, *whatever.*"

I thought about it more. Yes, in this version of the boyfriend dance, my two-step also said, "Oh, we're great over here! No need for you to worry that I'm hanging on your every word, because I'm having a *great* time without you. We all are!"

The intended effect was to make calling home a pleasant and fun affair for Jesse, so she would want to stay connected.

Suddenly, I felt a pang. I thought about my mother, who was hyper-conscious about not imposing on my space. My empathy for her started growing as soon as I became a mother myself, but it was only once Jesse hit adolescence that I fully understood the tightrope she'd always felt she had to walk.

Now it was me who was trying to navigate my desire for connec-tion with my daughter, feeling that same fear of showing up where I wasn't wanted. Now I was the one thrown into a never-ending session of tea-leaf reading. *Is Jesse just answering the phone out of a feeling of obliga-tion, or does she actually want to talk to me? Is that impatience in her voice? Is it time to hang up?*

Sure, I wanted to know everything about her new life, but I knew that my job as a parent was to keep my distance so that she could grow her agency and voice in the world, free of the noise and distraction of my voice and influence. I knew that her ability to truly individuate depended on my being able to keep my own needs and wishes for connection with her in check. And now we'd all won the shit lottery with her chronic illness, making that tightrope even thinner and higher off the ground.

As the weeks passed, our conversations settled into a new pattern. I became adept at translating Jesse's "hello" when she answered my calls. Was it a *yay-I-love-my-mama* hello? Or was it an *ugh-this-is-annoying-but-I-feel-guilty-screening-your-call* hello? If it was the latter, my instant response was "Okay, you sound like you're busy! Let's talk later!"

Some days I became weak and dropped my boyfriend facade altogether.

I need to FaceTime you! I texted shamelessly. *I'm craving your face!*

How were parents supposed to endure this—going from living with their children, knowing how their scalps smelled, knowing what they ate for every meal, falling asleep with them in bed, to exchanging one- to five-word texts a day, saying things like *How's it going?* and *Good!*

How exhausting. Where was the Nobel Prize for this hellish job?

I refrained from sharing that last question. When I was at my boyfriend best, which was most of the time, I ignored my own wishes and wrote, as breezily as I could manage, *Hey, Jess. FaceTime sometime?*

Then one day, finally, Jesse gave me her Truth.

"Mom, I don't really want to FaceTime or talk every day. I need time for things to build up so that I have stuff to tell you."

Should I tell her *my* Truth? Which was: *Sure, it's nice to hear what you're up to, but frankly, I don't give a remote shit about a report. All I want is to be able to look into your eyes every day, to have you in my life again beyond a few fucking tiny words on a tiny screen.*

No, I shouldn't. So I didn't. And at least for the moment, the show went on.

"Oh, okay," I said—casually, like I was barely paying attention. "Sure. Whenever works for you."

Twenty-Two

Meanwhile, one week after my homecoming from Montana, the demons were back. In no time at all, I slipped back into the lists, the calls, the endless tasks that made me numb to that green shoot of peace and promise.

I summoned some advice I'd learned during our retreat. I downloaded an app called *Freedom*, a program designed to facilitate focus on one's work by blocking Internet service.

The first time I used it, I was amazed by how much it helped.

But on my next writing session, every time I started typing on the keyboard, a message popped up on my screen announcing: Freedom *wants to make changes. Type your password to allow this.*

I typed in my password and it was rejected again and again, until my screen made another announcement: "Freedom *is not working.*"

The Committee was right on the case, laughing like hyenas, pounding their bony fists on the floor of my mind. *Now even your* Freedom *app doesn't believe in you! Get it? You don't know your password to* Freedom! *Bahahahahaha.*

But my malfunctioning app was just part of my failing strategy to beat back the block.

I had come home with all kinds of new tricks of the trade, the first of which was the writing desk shrine. At the retreat, everyone had talked about how magical her writing desk was. They swore that these writing shrines, festooned with little Buddhas and candles and voodoo dolls, were 100 percent nonnegotiables in seducing the Muse into long, languorous visits.

Although the whole thing sounded like a hoax, I figured I had nothing to lose.

First, I put on my desk a glass vase of fresh tulips, a floral burst of purple and yellow that offered a little prayer to nature's glory. Then I added a little figurine that Sam had made for me by taking a spool of black wire and wrapping it around and around until it formed a tiny black bandit figurine—a perfect manifestation of what creating something could be.

Actually, Sam *himself* was a skinny, redheaded manifestation of what creative could be. No matter what, he was always making something with his hands. He did not need shrines, candles, or meditations. The creating didn't have to *mean* anything or accomplish anything. It didn't have to prove he was worthy. It was just for fun.

This was why Sam spent many of his waking hours scrolling through endless feeds of websites and YouTube channels, finding something that interested him and then learning to do it. Last month it had been little wire guys. The month before, he'd made sculptures using plastic guns that spurted colorful spools of wax.

One recent morning, I'd walked into his bedroom and there he was with a balisong (butterfly) knife, practicing terrifying tricks that he'd been learning from a guy online in Singapore. He'd say, "Watch this!" and then the blades would come within centimeters of cutting off two fingers. Training myself to trust Sam's uncanny skill and good judgment was one of my proudest parenting feats.

"Want me to teach you, Mama?" he asked with great enthusiasm, swooping the multibladed knife my way. "No thanks!" I said, and the fact that my fourteen-year-old son wanted to teach his middle-aged mother knife tricks tugged at my heart.

But back to my writing shrine: next to Sam's black wire bandit, I laid down a yellow leaf I had picked up off the ground at the Whitefish Lodge. I decided it meant growth.

Next, I fished out of my purse the glorious Claudia Coral, a little figurine I'd bought at the Glacier National Park gift shop. Claudia Coral was a teeny piece of rock coral from the ocean that had been made into a little lady with googly eyes that rattled crazily when you picked her up. On the bottom of her case, it said: *Made in Indonesia and Malaysia. Sold from China.*

To me, Claudia Coral's origin story was pure inspiration. Who, I wanted to know, had the idea of taking a teeny-tiny sea rock and making it into a Claudia Coral? Who'd had the fortitude and persistence to forge a path of production through *three countries* and then managed to get the result—an army of Claudias—on the shelves of a gift shop in the middle of nowhere in Montana? Who was hired to harvest the coral? Who glued each set of googly eyes onto the Claudias? Were they old grandmothers perched on straw stools? Factory workers with gloves? Who was tracking the sales of each $4.50 Claudia Coral on some random spreadsheet somewhere in the world?

And if Claudia and all her coral friends could be brought to life through the vision of who-knew-how-many people, could I not stay committed to writing *a few fucking pages*? Was it really *so fucking hard*? (Newsflash: The shrine one builds for one's writing desk is not supposed to make one feel bad about oneself, but, surprise, mine did.)

I put Claudia next to the leaf and gave her a nod.

Last came the rock I'd picked out of Glacier Lake during my visit to the park to remind me of the exercise we did the first night of our retreat, when we all put our intentions into that sort-of-heart-shaped rock. I had walked the shores of Glacier Lake for a long time before finally choosing this rock—a whiteish, heartish-shaped lump that seemed like it might have magical properties.

I was so pleased with my rock that it felt suddenly necessary that I show Dave and Sam before I put it on my shrine. I found them both in the kitchen, trying to make Scotch cuddle with them on the beanbag chair. I presented my rock.

"Nice, hon," Dave said, kindly mustering up a little enthusiasm.

"Isn't it cool?" I said to Sam. "It's right from the lake at Glacier National Park. It's part of my new writing shrine."

I looked at my son, who couldn't even begin to pretend to like my rock.

"What?" I demanded. "You don't think it's cool?"

Sam gave up on Scotch and walked over to the refrigerator to get his fourth can of sparkling water of the day, which would almost certainly end up abandoned—half-full, on a side table, not on a coaster.

"I mean, *it's a rock*," he said. "Sorry, Mama—I love you, but you were at Glacier National Park. It seems like you could have found a lot cooler rock than that."

Aha! I smiled. "True, *and!*" And then I went into my new philosophy about writing shrines and intention and blah blah blah, which I was trying hard to believe in.

When I finished my rant, he just said, "Okay, Mama. I'm happy for you and your rock."

I went back into my room and put my rock down gently next to Claudia Coral. And then I lit my white linen candle, which was so imbued with special powers that it had two wicks, and I tried to bang something out on my laptop just a few inches away from Sam's little wire man, who was pumping his fist at me in either support or protest, I couldn't tell which.

Twenty-Three

Besides learning how to swing knives around and do explosive chemistry experiments in our kitchen sink, Sam was growing up and away. More and more, we occupied the same space but lived in parallel, each tending to our outer and inner lives.

Eventually my anxiety about our slow drift apart would kick up enough of a storm to cross my consciousness.

"Sam?" I'd call with sudden urgency from the kitchen.

"Yeah?" he'd call back, and I'd hear the tone—*ugh*.

"Can we talk?" I'd ask, fake nonchalant.

"About what?" he'd ask, always kind Sam, trying to be nice.

"Um . . . anything?" I'd say, trying to dress up my longing for the good old days with sad humor.

"C'mon, Mom," he'd say, irritated by my immaturity but guilty about the truth it implied.

There was no going back. My role in Sam's life had shifted from primary to pastel, and the reality seeped into my psyche like ice water in a hot bath. The days of being the emotional center of his world had all but vanished. Conversations and outings and long-held routines of walking together in the hood or going out for a treat had been washed away by YouTube, *Family Guy*, friends, and homework.

It was hard not to yearn for all those years of *Mama, come cuddle me; Mama, do you want to play with me?*; *Mama, look!* You never really think that one day your kid is going to stop asking for you. And then they just do. After all those years of me saying, *Just one minute!* I felt the sting of time and how it had reversed our roles with a cruel irony. *Just a minute!* he always said to me now when I called for him.

I knew that our growing irrelevance in our children's lives was a sign of a solid foundation. I knew Dave and I were supposed to be happy and proud, and we were.

But also, just as it had with Jesse at this age, the passage of time moved the three of us into a space where the rules changed by the day. There were no stormy fights and no declarations of independence. Instead, sheer instinct propelled us into a slow, invisible march through a training ground for less intimacy, less ease, and less connection. It all made me profoundly, heart-hurtingly sad. The increasing shift also underscored the importance of me getting my own shit together so I would not end up like one of those needy mothers who endlessly pined for their kids' attention.

Meanwhile, I'd been home from Montana for two weeks now and it was clear: my writing shrine was not working. I thought about the *ma'ayan b'adama*, the underground spring inside of me that my mother had spoken of, the stream of my life force and true potential.

Here I was once again, stopping short after a strong start.

I shook my head. I could not let it happen this time. Not after investing so much time, so much money, and so much hope into my time in Montana.

And so I did two things.

First, I called and set up an appointment with Sheila, a psychologist I'd met a few months before at a lecture called "Seven Ways to Take Control of Your Life." Sheila had offered her service to anyone interested in continuing the conversation. Now seemed like the perfect time to be interested. Would Sheila be a good therapist? Unclear. But given how hard a time I was having digging my well, I had a feeling that just seeing her face on my computer screen each week might be medicinal.

Second, I decided to take full advantage of the virtual writer's retreat reunion coming up by bringing in my own private agenda: finding out how my fellow writers were following through with their writing goals.

How do real writers write? was the question at hand, a question that seemed to hold the key to my future. It was no joke. I had spent a lifetime trying to figure it out. Despite years of reading interviews with writers and going to book readings to interrogate authors about their writing process, no one had fessed up the truth of how to actually get it done.

It was time to nail it down, once and for all.

My main motivation, going into the reunion call, was desperation. What if after pouring all this effort and energy into my reboot, I simply failed to follow through? It seemed frighteningly possible.

As I waited for the call to begin, I had to chuckle at myself. Yep, I was still that kid toting around a legal pad, interviewing everyone in my path for the Meaning of Life. And just like that kid, I still harbored hope that someone was going to give me the singular right Answer, as if one existed.

The call began and we said our hellos. When my time came to check in, I didn't hold back.

"Okay," I launched in, "so I'm failing miserably over here. I just can't seem to stick with it. I need to know, you guys, how are you not being hijacked by your lives? How are you actually moving forward with your writing?"

"Sorry, what do you mean?" Candace asked, her feather earrings welcoming me back to the circle. Clearly she had no idea what I was talking about.

"I mean, how is it going to actually *happen*?" I clarified. "How are you actually forcing yourselves to sit down and write? To follow through? To find the will to go on?"

One by one, my fellow writers chimed in.

I light a candle.

I start by listening to Bach's cello suites.

I go to my kitchen and sit in the same chair.

I put on my special writing scarf.

I reserve every Saturday for writing.

I depend on my writing shrine.

The freaking writing shrine. A lot of good mine had done.

Then Molly chimed in.

"I just put it in my schedule," she said cheerfully. "This is my writing time."

"And then?" I asked impatiently. "Then what do you do?"

"What do you mean?"

"I mean, what do you do *exactly*? You just sit down at your desk and you *start writing*?"

Molly laughed. "Yeah, I just turn on my computer and . . . I write."

I stared at her in disgust. *What was wrong with her?*

The call went on and my writing friends whipped up all kinds of tips and tricks, but I hung up the phone feeling defeated. The familiar dread had settled back in.

Why did everyone else seem to be able to write so easily? Was I the only one who was struck with panic every time I sat down in front of my laptop?

Maybe Sheila would be my ticket to finally breaking through.

The next day, I sat down and looked at my watch: 12:59 p.m. One minute until my FaceTime appointment with Sheila.

My computer buzzed and I clicked on Sheila's number.

"Sheila!"

"Julie!"

Sheila looked to be in her sixties. She had a head of shiny, thick, blonde hair, the kind of hair that I, having spent my life as a frizzy redhead, envied. Her vibe, I'd remembered from her lecture, was somewhere between a concerned aunt and a hired professional. Her presentation had involved a mix of hyperconcern for her audience members, questionably personal anecdotes, and PowerPoint slides on the latest in productivity research.

After a few pleasantries, Sheila suddenly bowed her face close to the screen; her Hollywood-perfect hair followed a split-second later.

"Julie, I can't help but notice that you're clenching your fists. How are you doing? I mean, really?"

"That's perceptive of you," I said. Could she even see my hands? "Actually, yes, I guess I am clenching my fists, and that's the reason I reached out to you. I am having a bit of a breakdown."

I imagined Sheila lived for moments like these. She looked at me with wild intensity as she pushed her ultra-magnified, horn-rimmed glasses up the bridge of her nose, making her look like a blonde owl.

"Tell me."

"Well, I came back a few weeks ago from a writing retreat and I loved it so much."

"How wonderful!"

"It really was," I said. "I came back feeling like I was finally going to become the writer I always thought I'd be. But after only a few weeks, I'm back to feeling paralyzed and hopeless."

"So, you've been feeling like that about writing for a long time?" Sheila asked.

"Yeah, you could say that. Like, fifty years. I still can't figure it out."

Sheila laid both hands on her desk and got down to business.

"So, tell me, Julie, what is your writing cue?"

"Writing cue?"

"Yes. You know you *can* write and that you *want* to write. But now you need to build a habit, starting with finding a daily cue so your mind knows it's time to write. So, what's your cue?"

"A sudden rush of anxiety followed by depression?"

Sheila chuckled. "No, something else!" Seeming to have missed that I was only sort of kidding, she smiled and rested her chin on her palm, her French manicure framing her face.

Something else, I thought. "I have no idea."

"Well," she said, "what happens when you try?"

That was easy. "Every time I finally force myself to sit down and write, I'm flooded with anxiety and the thought that if I haven't gotten anywhere by now, why do I think I ever will?"

"But I remember you telling me you were a journalist—so doesn't that make you a real writer?" Sheila asked.

"Not the kind I wanted to be. I wanted to be a columnist, to write about life. And then—before I could get anywhere with that, for some reason I still don't really understand—I switched careers to something that came much more easily to me. And every time I try to go back to it, I just can't seem to follow through."

She looked at me, waiting for me to go on.

"And then there's the Committee," I continued, "which is like a chorus of old white men living inside my head that comes banging in with gavels, shouting its agreement that I'm hopeless, along with the fifty things on my list that are waiting to be done that are more urgent than my self-indulgent writing fantasies."

Sheila's eyes widened. "What kind of things are on that list?" She looked at me intently.

"You know, just all the stuff that has to get done." I paused and thought about it more. "My list is like a drug. It's like an endless dopamine cycle of checking boxes."

Sheila waited in silence. I studied her face and thought how thera-
pists must go through a lot of training to just sit there while other people
floundered around trying to figure out what the hell was going on.

"So that's it," I said quickly. "I keep getting diverted. I never allow
myself to focus on what would mean more than anything else. I never
seem to get traction."

The truth of those words echoed in my head. *Never allow myself.*
Never get traction. I never could stick with digging down to the *ma'ayan*
b'adama, the underground spring rushing with so much life and possibility beneath the surface of my locked-up self. But why?

What happened next was that weird therapy thing when the truth
ambushes you and, embarrassingly, tears spring to your eyes without
invitation.

In hopes of willing them back down their ducts, I looked out the
window. For a moment, my eyes got lost on our big oak tree and its massive canopy. I wiped my eyes on my sleeve.

Sheila didn't seem to realize that this was *her* cue. Her cue to give
me *the freaking Answer.* Instead, she just looked at me. I looked back
and waited.

Finally, after what felt like way too much silence, I had an idea. "You
know what, Sheila?"

"What?" she asked, apparently rapt.

"Maybe we can figure out how I learned to make exercise such a
nonnegotiable part of my life and use that to help me write."

She straightened up. "Go on."

"Well, I spent most of my life never being able to consistently exercise. It was a never-ending cycle of falling off track, of resistance and
avoidance, just like with my writing. It was really only about ten years
ago that I finally locked it in as a habit that I know I'll never let go."

Sheila was at 150 percent attention. A different quality of attention
than before. Hmmmm. My mind clicked on why.

During her lecture, Sheila had revealed that even though she had a
PhD and had authored a book on how to develop habits for life, she still
couldn't get herself to exercise regularly.

"Yes," I remembered her saying, hanging her head in front of her
fuchsia-pink-and-orange PowerPoint presentation, "I even bought one
of those Pelotons. Well, unfortunately, it's become my towel rack."

Although Sheila was theoretically acting as my therapist, as soon as I mentioned my exercise habit, I could *feel* her personal agenda through the screen.

Yep, upsettingly, it looked like she was no better off than me: a fellow seeker of the Answer to her own angst.

"So how did you finally get committed to exercise?" she asked eagerly.

Instantly, the power dynamic shifted. I knew how hard it was to get over the exercise hurdle, and I couldn't resist my own impulse. So, just like that, I jumped into playing the role I knew best: helper-fixer-rescuer.

"Well," I said, awash in the low-level adrenaline of helping to solve someone else's problem, "here's how it happened. For years, I said, 'I don't run. I hate running. That's just me.' But then my friend Lucy changed everything."

"Yes?" Sheila urged me on. "*And?*"

"Well, here's the thing. Most runners I know are type A. Like, not relatable. Lucy's different."

Recounting this story, I realized it was exactly like my reunion call, when I demanded to know how my fellow writers actually wrote.

"Okay," I remembered prodding Lucy, "explain it to me. How do you stick to it day after day after day when it's hell?"

"Because I just *do* it. I feel really good when it's done."

"Yeah, but so what? I feel really good, too, but that doesn't mean I'm going to do it."

One day, Lucy forced me to come with her.

"But Luce," I insisted, "I can't. I don't run. I *hate* running."

"Okay," she said, "but you *could* run."

"Yeah, but why *would* I, when it's hell?"

"Just try it. Come on, just come and see."

I went, and it *was* hellish, but not as hellish as I thought it would be (except for the part where the insides of my thighs both hurt and itched, making me scratch them constantly like I had mites *and* herpes, leaving raised scratches on the insides of my thighs for days).

In fact, it wasn't terrible at all, and what I noticed was that it was great to be outside and actually *in* the emerald-green Marin County hills that I usually just saw from my car. It felt good to run on a dirt trail, to quiet my usually racing mind with the task of simply dodging rocks and jumping over little streams, to lay my eyes on the grass that carpeted the hills—lily-green velvet—to smell the eucalyptus trees, and to see the sky for a whole hour. Running became the one time of day when my mind rested.

"Just come with me tomorrow," Lucy said every day. And on it went, until, without noticing, I became a runner. And once I got into the habit, the full benefits embraced me in so many ways that even I, a serial exerciser burnout, could not help myself. I kept doing it.

Sheila was positively riveted. Her giant owl eyes were taking it all in, drinking in my every word as if I had the magic elixir.

"So now," I told Sheila, who was bent so close to the screen that I was leaning back in my chair, "it's just so much part of my life and identity. I'm a runner. I run most days. I love it and need it and feel grateful that my body can do it."

"Wow!" Sheila said. "*Really*, wow, that's impressive." And I could see the longing in her eyes.

"Sheila," I said, thinking about her Peloton, "really, once you get into the habit, you won't want to give it up."

I looked into her hopeful eyes, and I felt a rush of pleasure. *I'm so good! I'm so smart! Look how I'm helping her.*

The Committee banged their gavels and shouted their verdict in unison.

Shmuuuuuckk! You're paying her to help you!

Fuuuuuuccccckkk. I heaved a sigh. As Jesse would have phrased it drolly, *they weren't wrong.* How quickly I had jumped back into my rescuer saddle with Sheila. Why did I feel such a burning need to be of use to others? Even at my own cost? Literally and emotionally. It felt like I was getting pulled into the usual undertow in my life.

I sat up straight and leaned forward. *Not this time,* I thought. This time, the Committee had to prevail.

"So, Sheila," I said, a little too loudly, "back to the writing quandary. What do you think? How can I apply the exercise-habit experience to writing?"

"Well," Sheila chirped as she tried to check her watch inconspicuously, "we're going to have to pick this up next time."

The Committee raised its collective hand to point out that Sheila should have given me extra time since I'd just spent the last fifteen minutes "therapizing" her, but it was too late.

"Well, Julie, this was great," Sheila said. "I think we've made some strides and I'll look forward to seeing you next week!"

"Okay," I smiled weakly. "Thanks, Sheila. Don't forget your Peloton!"

I shut my laptop and sighed as I looked out the window at the golden hills beyond. The reunion call had yielded no answers, and Sheila had been no help either. I could see the parallels so clearly between my struggle to make exercise a habit and my struggle to write, but with writing, I couldn't see how to get from Point A to Point B.

With running, Lucy had been my catalyst for transforming my struggle to success. But what could be the catalyst for my writing? I'd hoped it would be the retreat, but already my focus was waning. Why couldn't I just *do it* when I knew it was my heart's true desire? Why, whenever I sat down to write, was I compelled to distract myself, get off track, and give up? I could not understand my block.

It would take a long time before I'd realize there was a much deeper-seated reason for my inability to keep my promises to myself. Writing shrines and candles would not help to crack this code. The answers lay in wait in the events of the days ahead.

Later that afternoon, my phone buzzed. I pulled it out of my pocket and answered.

"Hi, Beauty!"

"Hi, Mama!"

I ran Jesse's voice through my soundcheck, and the data was good—all-out positive.

Jesse charged into a full and enthusiastic report. She'd gotten an *A* in her social policy class, had been recruited to be a producer for a theater production, and had just rushed a great new sorority. "I love my school," she gushed. "It makes me so happy."

It was a relief to hear her voice so light. It had been a long time. As I listened to her go on, it occurred to me that it might be time to think about shifting our blueprint a little bit.

As I see it, we parents unwittingly create blueprints for our relationships with our children. The blueprints are formed by all the tiny and big choices we make that shape our connections. There are things we talk about and there are things we don't. There are things we always do together and things we never do together.

When I was growing up, the blueprint in our house was clear. My father took my brothers on hunting and fishing trips. My mother and I never took trips alone together. We didn't hunt or fish, so why would we? My friends would tell me about going to lunch with one of their parents, and I would stare at them. Why did you have to go out to lunch together when you lived in the same house?

When I left home for college, my mother and I spoke almost every day and had conversations that could go on for hours. My father and I spoke maybe once a week for ten minutes.

We often don't see our blueprints until we choose to examine them. They're so baked into our family dynamics that we don't realize that they drive how we relate to and behave with our loved ones, and therefore we rarely think to question them.

Years after I was married, I asked my father why he and I had never taken trips together. He shrugged. He'd never thought about it. I suggested that we start taking an annual father-daughter trip to Las Vegas, where he'd been a regular for sixty years and whose guilty pleasures I'd also come to love.

At first it felt strange, almost awkward, to be alone together for three days. But by the end of our first weekend together of great eating, drinking, hitting the casinos, and reading and watching TV together, we'd deepened our relationship in ways I couldn't have imagined.

Now that Jesse seemed to be getting grounded, I wanted to be sure that our blueprint evolved. Historically, our conversations had been one way. She was the talker; I was the listener. When she was young, this arrangement was natural. I was her mother, and my role was to mirror and nurture her. Ultimately, though, I knew that if our relationship was going to mature along with her, I needed to become part of the equation.

"So, want to hear what's going on over here?" I asked.

"Oh, right, yeah. How's it to be back from the retreat?"

It felt strange to say words I'd never said to her before. "Well, I'm kind of struggling with some stuff, actually."

She cocked her head. "Really? Like what kind of stuff?"

I took a breath. "I'm going to tell you this, but I don't want you to worry," I said. "I'm fine, but I might as well just tell you what's going on."

"Um, okay," she said, and her apprehension at this new twist in the conversation was clear.

I shared with her how things had been lately. I told her how, during her senior year of high school, I'd been overcome by not just sadness at the prospect of her leaving but also a jarring reminder of who I was at her age.

"What do you mean?" she asked.

"Well, you just reminded me so much of myself back then, so driven and ambitious."

"You were like *me*?" she asked, taken aback. "Really?"

I laughed, but her surprise stung. I knew that to her I was basically "just a mom," someone whose role was restricted to attending to everyone's needs, taking care of the house, and having great friends. Sure, I had written a few freelance stories and worked as a writing coach to college-bound students, but most of my time had disappeared into the sinkhole of womanhood in the most traditional sense: the fraught province of nurturing others.

"Yeah, I was exactly like you, actually. And seeing myself in you was hard, to be honest, because it was such a stark reminder of how far I've drifted from that part of myself."

Jesse was quiet. I could feel her integrating this new information.

I thought about the blueprint and pushed on.

"It really haunts me that I never became the writer that I always assumed I would be. I was just your age when my future—especially as a writer—was so alive and clear and without question."

"I've never heard you talk about any of this before," she said softly.

My heart stopped for a second. I worried that I'd dropped too much of the veil.

I imagined the weight Jesse might be feeling on learning for the first time that I harbored real regrets about my life. I imagined her ambivalence at knowing this. And I remembered my own struggle about having carried my own mother's worries and fears and sadness for so many years.

"What do you think happened?" she asked, her voice low. "Why did you change so much?"

I told her I knew it sounded crazy, but I really didn't know. It made no sense to me, and, truthfully, I hadn't even allowed myself to know what I'd lost in myself until she had grown up to be so much like me.

"Wow, Mama," Jesse said. "That's really sad."

I could hear her hesitate before she asked, "Do you think you've sort of been giving that part of yourself up for us all these years? Do you think it's because you had us?"

I breathed in. I had not expected the conversation to move so quickly and easily into the rawest, most complicated territory of my heart. I didn't want to sound like I needed my nineteen-year-old daughter's emotional support. But in this new chapter of our relationship, I *did* want her to know me as a whole person, regrets and all. So I told her part of the truth. "I was exactly the kind of mother I wanted to be for you. I wanted to give you and Sam my full attention. The problem was that in the process, I sort of blocked myself out of any chance to hold on to that part of who I had always been—but I think it all started before that." As I said the next words, I recognized them as the whole truth. "Motherhood was a convenient way to keep myself blocked out, and the mystery I'm trying to uncover now is why."

Jesse was quiet again.

I flashed back to my own sense of disorientation when my mother was in pain—how helpless I felt, how much it absorbed me. *It was too much*, I thought. *Too much.*

"But you know what, baby?" I said cheerfully. "I'm figuring it out! And you see how I'm really trying to get back to writing again. So don't worry, okay?"

"Okay, good, Mama, because you deserve to have your dreams too, besides being a great mom," she said. And with that, we went back to talking about her and her life. Enough work on our blueprint for one day.

Twenty-Four

A few months later, the phone on my nightstand buzzed at 6:00 a.m., sending my heart pounding.

"Jess? Everything okay?"

"Yeah, hi, Mama." Her voice was barely audible.

"How's it going?"

"Eh."

"What do you mean? What is it?"

"I don't feel good."

I don't feel good. Danny's words all those years ago.

"What do you mean? What's going on?"

"I've been going to the bathroom. A lot."

"Really? Like how often?"

"Like probably ten times in the last few hours."

"Oh my God." The adrenaline entered my system. "Is there blood in the toilet?"

"Yeah."

I breathed and tried not to sound afraid. "Uh-huh. So, like, a lot of blood?"

"Yeah, today for the first time, there's been a lot," she said, and now she was crying softly.

"How long has this been going on?"

There was a pause.

"How long, Jess? Tell me."

"A few weeks, but not like it is today."

My heart stopped.

She'd been losing blood for a few *weeks*. There it was. Horrible proof that we'd made an awful mistake.

For the past several months, at her request, we'd tried not to raise the issue of her health with her. Instead, we'd immersed ourselves in the new rhythms of a three-person household. Sam was getting used to high school, Dave was slogging through the middle age of his medical practice, and I was trying to move forward with my writing.

Of course, Dave and I had talked about Jesse constantly during this time—worrying, wondering how she was feeling and doing. But we'd held our tongues, and the few times we'd felt compelled to ask how she was doing, she'd answered resolutely, "I'm fine. I'm *okay*. Again, please don't ask me. I'll tell you if I need you."

And, much too late, here we were.

"Jess," I whispered.

"I'm so tired, Mama." It was the first time she'd let her guard down since I could remember.

The steel block pressed on my chest.

"And I'm scared, Mama. It won't stop."

It won't stop.

"I can't stop going to the bathroom, and now there's just a lot of blood."

Panic rose in my throat. I knew what this meant. She needed to go to the hospital.

"Jess, I can take the next flight out and be there by this evening. We'll go to the ER. They need to see what's going on. And I'm sure with going to the bathroom so much, you're dehydrated, which is making you even worse."

"No, Mom, you don't have to come. *Really.* I can go by myself. Or maybe Leila will come with me."

OMG, no. Even now we were going to do the freaking parent-child dance? Yes, apparently we were. It went like this: As much as I felt I should go, I didn't want to push myself on her. I wanted her to know that I thought she could handle this situation herself, if that was what she truly wanted. I didn't want to lunge into action with my Pavlovian need to come to the rescue. I'd done enough therapy to know that this impulse came from my need to quell my own anxiety, to feel in control, and—most difficult of all to admit—the siren call of my need to be needed.

But she was *bleeding.* How could I stay? Had I lost all perspective?

I danced. "Jess, I know I don't have to. But wouldn't it make you feel better if I came?"

"I want you to do what you want," she said.

How do we help our children at this tender age, when they're walking the narrow path between childhood and adulthood?

How do we treat them like adults when they still feel like kids?

Ulcerative colitis made the quandary especially fraught. It's a disease with a wide range of symptoms: stomach pain, diarrhea, fatigue, and bowel urgency. All miserable, none fun to share, let alone discuss.

But this was too much. Enough with treading lightly.

"Jess, sorry. Maybe I'm coming for my own selfish need, but I'm coming."

"Okay, Mama, okay." We sighed loudly at the same time and then laughed.

Thank God. At least this time, I danced it right.

But my relief that I'd be on the next flight out was short-lived. As I shared the news with Dave, the weight of our inaction began to sink in. Jesse had been spiraling for weeks without us having a clue, and now who knew what the consequences would be?

"Hon," I said, "we've both been in total denial. Our job was to protect her. We didn't protect her."

Once the words were out, the truth in them sent tears down my face.

Dave was quiet. I knew he agreed.

In our desire to let go and give her space, we had been unwitting accomplices. We didn't want the illness to ruin her plans, waste her time, or derail her future.

And clearly that was Jesse's plan, too, no matter the cost. She never missed a class. She produced theater productions. She rose to the leadership of club after club. Her hunger to achieve drove her on and on and on.

For months now, she'd carried out our family legacy of pursuing, prevailing, achieving.

But the family legacy had failed to win this one. And a new teacher, the teacher of illness, was about to prevail.

Twenty-Five

I caught the next flight to Chicago. As my Uber sped through the dark city night, once again I marveled at how easy it was to traverse fifteen hundred miles in the span of just a few hours.

The next thing I knew, I was in Jesse's tiny dorm room, where she was curled beneath her quilted duvet. She looked small and pale, and the pain on her face was plain.

"Where's Leila?" I asked.

"In the library," she said hoarsely. "But only because she knew you were coming. She wanted to give us space. She's so great."

I lay down on the bed and pulled her head to my chest.

"Mama," she said. "Mama, Mama."

"I love you so much, baby," I whispered, trying to stave off my tears. "I'm so sorry you've been so alone with this. I'm so sorry we didn't push more to know how you were really doing. We thought it was what you wanted; we thought it was the right thing to do."

"It's okay, Mama," she said gently. "You didn't know."

I shook my head and looked at her. When we'd dropped Jesse off at school five months earlier, she'd worn her sickness like a windbreaker, a thin outer layer she threw on once in a while. But now, after weeks of suffering, I saw how the illness had started to claim her spirit. Her whole energy had changed. She was withering from the inside. She looked small and vulnerable, so different from the strong, swaggering girl we'd always known.

I pushed away thoughts of Danny and his metamorphosis from my happy, funny brother to the version of him that emerged in those four haunting words: *I don't feel good.*

I looked at Jesse under the covers and fought back my tears. "Let's get you to the hospital and get some fluids into you," I urged her. "You'll feel better."

"Okay," she said, pulling herself up.

She dropped clothes into her backpack while I called Dave to tell him that we were ready to go. This time we would not go to the local hospital in Evanston. Instead, Dave had arranged for Jesse to be admitted to the University of Chicago, known for its team of doctors and researchers who were dedicated to cracking the code of irritable bowel syndrome. It was time for the big guns.

The double doors of the ER lurched open, and we walked through.

It's an odd thing, what happens upon admission to a hospital. You walk in as yourself, dressed in your clothes, holding all the things you need in the world—your purse, your wallet, your backpack, your jacket. But as soon as you're led to your hospital room, you're stripped down naked and handed a hospital gown with a flimsy tie at the neck, and suddenly you change from person to patient. A room number, a case, a treatment plan.

Instantly, our world shrank to tiny and clear: When is the IV coming? Can we get someone good to give it? Where is the ice machine? Are there crackers in the patient kitchen down the hall?

Jesse knew the drill. She got into bed, pulled the stiff white sheets up across her chest, and immediately glued her eyes to her phone. Her phone was her bridge to normal, allowing her to text up a storm like she was at home, like she was anywhere.

My phone buzzed. It was Dave.

"How is she?"

"Okay. Waiting to get the IV."

"Has the doctor been by?"

"No, we just got here. They said sometime later."

"Okay."

Dave was calm, but I could feel past his doctor voice to his anxiety. He did not talk to me about all that could go wrong—how it could all keep spiraling, where the spiral could lead. But I knew that was where his head was.

My role was optimist. "She'll be okay, hon. The care here is so good."

But we both understood that the quality of care was only part of the equation; there was so much more to consider—like how badly things had actually been going for Jesse and how in the dark we had been about it. We now knew that Jesse had been experiencing regular bouts of searing abdominal pain and had been running to the bathroom twenty to thirty times a day for weeks now. She'd been struggling with chronic urgency and accidents—a toxic brew of discomfort, humiliation, and severe pain.

That first night, we both slept fitfully—Jesse in her bed, me once again in the foldout chair next to her. What we thought would be an overnight stay stretched into a second long day. That afternoon, Jesse's lab work showed that she was anemic and her C-reactive protein—an indicator of disease activity—was high.

Later that evening, less than twenty-four hours after being given a higher dose of steroids, Jesse began to have what we learned was a rare dystonic reaction of paranoia and anxiety.

She looked at me with wild eyes. "Mama," she said. "Mama. Something's happening. Something's happening inside me and I'm scared. Stop it, please, Mama, help me."

I got into bed with her and squeezed her hand, trying to shut down the fluttering in my chest. "I'm right here, baby. Just breathe with me, just breathe."

The episode passed and the doctors reluctantly reduced her dosage, knowing that doing so pushed us further down a risky path.

Four more days passed as the team tried to regulate her system and get control of her blood loss and rising C-reactive protein. We filled the days with a hyperfocus on little activities: watching episodes of *Friday Night Lights*, FaceTiming with friends and family, and walking slow laps around the hospital floor, while Jesse dragged her IV pole behind her.

I lived out of my carry-on suitcase and showered in the tiny hospital room bathroom. I cycled through time by tidying the room, clearing away the constant collection of water cups, snack wrappers, and food trays. Each night before going to sleep, our heads inches away from each other, we'd squeeze hands and say good night.

At the end of the fifth day, we got word from the nurse that the team did not plan to discharge Jesse for at least two more days.

Dave, Sam, and I had planned to meet Red's family in Wyoming for Sam's fifteenth birthday that coming weekend. After a flurry of calls, Dave and I arranged to switch places: Dave would fly to Chicago and take my place in the hospital, and I would fly to Wyoming to celebrate Sam with Red's family.

As I hung up on a call with the airlines, Dr. Ben Bronstein walked into our room. It was the end of the day, the time when one of the doctors always checked in with us. But Dr. Bronstein was not just head of the team; he was head of gastroenterology at the University of Chicago, and we'd seen him only once, briefly, since we'd been there. This was not a good sign.

As Jesse and I registered who he was, we sat up abruptly.

He sat down in the chair next to us. "Hi there," he said, his cool, blue eyes trained on Jesse. "I wanted to let you know what was going on and why you need to stay with us for a while. Jesse, your condition is concerning. Your flare isn't responding to the steroids, which is unusual at this stage."

"What does that mean?" I asked, trying to hide my alarm.

Dr. Bronstein didn't look at me or respond to my question. My irritation at being ignored was tempered by the comfort of his authority. And I couldn't help but appreciate his treating Jesse like an adult.

"Our next step is to start you on cyclosporine," he continued. "It's a very strong medicine that's typically used for kidney transplant patients but has shown results under these circumstances. But there's a chance it will fail, and we need to talk about a backup plan."

"What do you mean?" I asked sharply. As much as I wanted Jesse to have agency, I also didn't want to repeat my mistake of allowing myself to be in the dark or putting too much on her shoulders. I wanted her to know that we would not fail at parenting, at least in that way, again.

This time he met my gaze. "It means that there's one option that will end this problem," Dr. Bronstein said. "Jesse's colon is highly ulcerated, and her C-reactive protein is climbing to dangerous levels. If we remove the colon, she will be out of danger."

Jesse and I stared at him.

"It's called a colectomy," Dr. Bronstein went on. "It's actually a very simple procedure."

"Sorry," I said, shaking my head. "Can we back up? You're suggesting that we consider removing Jesse's *entire* colon?"

He looked at Jesse. "I'm suggesting that if this next course of treatment does not take, we may not have a choice."

With a colectomy, Dr. Bronstein explained, the colon was cut out and the lower intestine was brought up through the skin of the abdomen in a nodule called a stoma, which was then kept attached to an ileostomy bag.

The body would digest food normally through the intestines, but instead of solid waste being processed through the colon, it would be brought up through the stoma and into the bag, which would need to be emptied every few hours.

There would be times, Dr. Bronstein said, when things would go wrong. The bag could leak. If the adhesive failed, the bag could detach without warning, spilling its contents.

After a certain amount of time, Dr. Bronstein said, if Jesse decided that she did not want to live with a bag, she could elect to have two more surgeries, in which an artificial colon, called a J-pouch, would be made from the lower intestine and then connected back to the rectum, allowing waste to be eliminated without a bag.

But results were variable with the J-pouch. Some people did well; others had chronic infections or leakage. Those for whom the J-pouch failed would have a fourth surgery, in which the patient's pouch was removed and they returned to life with a bag permanently.

Dr. Bronstein finished talking and put his hands on his knees. "Any questions?"

"No, thanks," Jesse said quietly.

Dr. Bronstein nodded, thanked us, and left the room.

I looked at Jesse. Her eyes were wide and filling with tears.

We sat in silence, looking in front of us, trying to absorb the words. Permanent removal of the colon. An ileostomy. A stoma. Potential leakage. Three surgeries.

Jesse was holding the hospital blanket from underneath in a tight fist. An ancient dread gripped my heart and I felt the flush of Danny, the reeling turns of his illness.

I looked into Jesse's face and felt in my gut, for the first time, the real possibility that the future could follow the same slow-motion descent. It flowed over me like a high, foaming wave: the constant uncertainty, the ache of being utterly powerless, never knowing how to help, what to do, and where it would end.

Dear Julie,

I don't have much to say because I talk to you on the phone and tell you all. But I want to say that I'm lonely and craving family, at the same time realizing the emotional and physical space needed for me to deal with my problem. I miss you and wish you were here. I look forward to the next time you get to see me in person—and I get to see you.

I feel close to you now like I did when I was six and we used to hang out together, trust each other and understand each other.

My depression is getting better—loosening—I know this because I'm more talkative and am laughing at jokes. The desipramine level in my body is high and good—where it needs to be.

I just met with the rabbi from Topeka. I plan on going to Friday night services and maybe from there do volunteer work or work at the religious school. The rabbi was familiar with the Jewish scene in KC. When I feel depressed I think of times in my life when I felt understood and it gradually gets me out of the sadness.

I want to be close to you, to be able to turn to you when I have problems.

Trjei Al-saud (the prince) put on his relapse prevention sheet when he feels vulnerable he calls his sister in Saudi Arabia—you're just in NYC.

My relationship with mom and dad has improved 100 percent with me getting out of the depression, and working on my issues and then coming up and showing the effort to work and talk at social worker meetings.

I'm talking to the people on the unit and it feels good to small talk as well as learn from the intelligent patients about spirituality, religion. The people on the unit are very well read. On Sunday night me and Emily (22 year old heroin addict from Seattle) went to the coffee shop and drank mineral water and listened to blues music and poems and had a nice, fun, light time. She was sensitive to my needs and told me to tell her when I felt I wanted to cave due to anxiety.

Hope all is well with Dave and your work.

I love you and think about you much.

Dan Fing

Twenty-Six

After almost a full year at Menninger, even with periodic moments of hope and progress, the team of doctors has still not landed on a clear diagnosis for Danny. There seems to be no label for his struggle beyond an extreme, intractable depression.

They try one drug after another. Each time we talk, I sense in Danny a deepening layer of disassociation, which rises in proportion to my anxiety. He is slipping into a blank unknown, words slurring from the medication. His voice is hollow, like the inside of a shell, a vacuum. It's an emptiness that strains against my heart. We are boats bobbing in a vast ocean, and the tide is taking us.

At his one-year anniversary, the Menninger team suggests electro-convulsive therapy, a last-resort treatment. I can feel the disbelief and grief blooming inside my mother, blooming, blooming.

"No, Mom," I cry into the phone. "They can't. They're going to give him electric shock to *his brain?*"

"Lulu"—and she is crying too, trying to get the words out—"nothing is working. *Nothing is working.* They have to try something different. They said it's different now than it used to be; they said they work gently and can be very exact with it. We consented to one treatment they'll do tomorrow."

As my mother's words trail off, I look out the window of my tiny New York City studio at the canyon of gray and white buildings stretching for miles below. In my mind, all I can envision is Jack Nicholson in *One Flew Over the Cuckoo's Nest*, staggering down the hallway of the psychiatric hospital like a zombie, his brain electrified, his personality obliterated, his spirit erased.

The next day, I wait until I get home from work to call him. I need to be alone. I need my own walls to hold me up, to metabolize what comes next.

I dial the phone and ask to be connected to his hospital floor. The receptionist puts me on hold, and I scan the patches of gray sky out my window, looking for birds paddling through the sky, anything normal.

"Hello?" Danny asks in wonder.

"Hi, Stiggy!" I say with a hysterical cheerfulness. "How do you feel?"

My radar is desperate, searching for Danny on the other end of the line, seeing whether he's still really him.

"It's weird but I actually kind of feel better. Just like lighter, I guess."

I'm breathing, breathing. "But"—I am trying to find the right words—"but do you still feel like . . . yourself?"

"Yeah." He chuckles. "Don't worry, Sister, they didn't fry my brain too much. I'm still here. Unfortunately."

Sickness and relief. Still Danny, thank you God, still Danny, and yes, maybe lighter. But he is joking about not wanting to be alive. Isn't that one of the signs of being suicidal?

A week later, I get a letter from him.

Dear Julie Fing,

I've been thinking about you and wish you were here with me. You are my sister, friend and a supportive person. Are you just listening to my gripes or do you have problems too? You will never ever realize how I feel you are in my corner. Thanks for traveling down my Mental Highway. I appreciate your patience in letting me psychobabble you to death. You're Mrs. Sigmund Freud and I'm her patient but you listen to me but don't charge me. I will reciprocate to you in the future.

Thanks for listening to me. I feel good I have someone to talk to and I know I don't let you reciprocate, I just talk over you. You're such a great person I love you so much. I feel appreciative because "real" relationships go two ways and last night's cries were crying sessions for me and listening sessions for you. The Navone (major tranquilizer) has thwarted my efforts to write any more. Thanks for being there for Dan Fingersh in my hard times.

Ta Ta, Julie F. Love, Your brother, Dan Fing

I put down the letter and sit on my couch. The tears come slowly as I reread his words, which are choppy and disjointed. He is lost in a world without the order of punctuation or sequence. I wonder whether his thought process has been literally shocked by the electroconvulsive therapy. My eyes blink back the tears as it dawns on me that whatever those doctors did to the architecture of Danny's brain, they did not blunt his wry sense of humor. They could not touch the pureness of his love, the rawness of his pain.

Seeing pieces of him there in the black, jagged scrawl of handwriting, I am undone. I fold the letter and drop my head onto the couch. Powerlessness and grief give rise to uncontrollable sobs. *Danny, Danny. My beautiful little brother. You are so sick.*

Two weeks later, I can't reach him at the hospital. The nurse tells me she is not at liberty to say where he is. The familiar dread flushes through my body. My heart hammers as I dial my mother and she picks up.

"Lulu," she says in a wooden voice.

"Mom, where's Danny? *Where's Danny?*"

She tells me he's at Research Hospital. That they've moved him. My mother is trying to get the words out through her tears. "He was doing so much better that he came home from Menninger for a trial week to see how he did on his own here." *How could I not know this?*

"And then what?" I want to climb through the phone.

"And the head nurse there had given him his medication for the week. As soon as he got home, he took the whole bottle."

"Mom," I hear myself say, "is he going to die?"

"No, Lulu. He was trying to overdose, but then he got scared and came downstairs to tell me...." My mother's voice breaks into jagged sobs.

"Oh God," I whisper.

"No, he's going to be okay, Lulu," my mother cries.

"Is he?" I am trying not to yell. *Is he?*

Danny stays at Research Psychiatric Hospital for the maximum days allowed and is then discharged to come home.

We fear for Danny to be in the house unsupervised but are running out of options. After two years and the latest nurse's indiscretion, discharging him with a bottle of pills, my parents no longer trust the care at Menninger.

By now, my parents are well versed in the mental health care system, and eventually they find a father in the area who has converted his home into a halfway house for his own troubled son to live in with professional supervision. My mother arranges for Danny to move into the house.

I am desperate to get on a plane back to Kansas City so I can lay my eyes on Danny and be with my parents. I board the plane with a mixture of apprehension and relief, filled with anxiety about what Danny will be like since I last saw him, since the electroconvulsive therapy, since his suicide attempt.

It is 10:00 at night when my taxi pulls around our circular driveway in the dark. I spot a shadowy figure standing on the side of our house, a tiny orange light moving up and down. Instantly I recognize Danny, smoking a cigarette, its bright orange point moving in his hands. I feel a chill go through me as dread turns my stomach.

I pay the taxi driver and slam the door shut.

"Stiggy?" I call into the dark, my heart beating fast against my chest. "Is that you?"

"Yeah." His voice is flat, and he registers neither surprise nor happiness at seeing me.

My eyes fall on him as he comes into the light. He looks both familiar and strange.

His big, brown eyes are veiled and hollowed. I am startled by how much more weight he's gained. How could he be twenty-four? He has the carriage of a middle-aged man, hunched over in a white button-down shirt, wearing steel-rimmed glasses. He could be a librarian or the guy behind the desk at Barnes & Noble.

"Hi, Jules."

"Hey, Stiggy."

We step toward each other for a hug. I feel his coarse hair against my cheek. His body is thick and warm, and he smells of cigarettes.

"What's up?" he asks with a little rise in his voice. He is trying.

"Oh, I don't know. Everything's okay. I'm still dating that guy, Dave. I think you'll like him."

"Yeah? Good, Julie F. I'm happy for you. You deserve to be happy."

"So do you, Stiggy," I say quietly. "You know that, right? So do *you*."

"Yeah, well. I'm going to this new place next week."

"I know. Mom told me all about it. It sounds good, right?"

"Yeah, I hope it will be."

The sound of his hope makes my heart ache. All the false starts, all the dead ends, how does he have the will to keep going?

The following week, the doorbell rings in the early morning. Two men arrive to pick up Danny, to take him away to the halfway house.

My parents and I stand in the doorway as Danny gathers the rest of his things upstairs in his room. Danny's face is puffy and pale and blinking as he walks down the stairs carrying his duffel bag. He walks over and hugs each of us. He holds himself with a quiet dignity.

"Okay, bye, Mom and Dad—bye, Jules," he says softly, his eyes darting at us and then past us.

As my father closes the door, my mother and I reach out for him. The three of us fall into a hug and then pull away before any of us breaks down.

One week later, Danny is in the ER. He shaved his eyebrows and cut himself up and down his arms. They are stitching him up and he will be okay, but his bedroom is stained with blood and the owner of the house will not take him back. He is too much of a liability.

My memory lets in Danny's words from months ago when I visited him at Menninger. *Ken from Nebraska. Randomly cuts himself all over his body. He says it's a relief and stops his mental pain or something.* At the time, both of us grimaced at the thought. Why would someone cut himself for relief? Now it's Danny. He's learned.

"Oh my God, Mom. I'm so sorry."

Something inside me is withering. Something is dying for all of us now—for Danny, for my parents, for Red, for me. I think it's hope.

"Danny is so sick, Lulu. We just don't know what to do anymore."

Danny is taken to University of Kansas Psychiatric Hospital, a short-term hospital where they can evaluate what should be done next.

The doctor meets with my parents and the message is simple: "Danny is very, very smart," Dr. Groton says. "But he is fighting a war, and this level of depression is something the medical community just doesn't have an answer for. The only thing we can all do now, until we have more treatment options, is just try to keep him alive."

My parents research the next option: Timberlawn Psychiatric Hospital in Dallas, a facility that is, once again, supposed to be *The Best.*

Danny is admitted into the psychiatric ward until he is stable enough to transition to their halfway house program. The days pass and there seems to be progress. Danny reports that the people are kind, and the new cocktail of medications seems to be working.

"I like it here," Danny calls to tell me. "Maybe this will be the answer, Jules."

"I hope so, Stiggy," I say, "that's what you deserve."

But I can't stop thinking about the doctor's words. *All we can do is just try to keep him alive.*

I hear something catch in his voice. "What else, Stiggy?"

Silence.

"Stiggy? Tell me."

"Now that I feel a little better, I can see more clearly."

"But isn't that good?"

His voice is deep and forceful. "I've been in these fucking places for so long now, *how will I ever go back to a normal life?*"

There is a foreboding in the space between us. A new level of understanding of his larger situation and the enormity of the road ahead.

I catch my breath.

"What would I say I've been doing for the last three years? How am I going to live a regular life when my big accomplishment is not being depressed enough to be in a psych hospital?"

"Stiggy? You just will. You'll take it, like they say, one day at a time. You're in a good place and you'll just build yourself up, brick by brick."

"Yeah," he says quietly, but his words are followed by a silence that sends chills up my spine. I am afraid he is placating me. I am afraid that now that the fog of depression has eased enough to clarify anew the crushing distance between where he is now and a functioning life, his center will no longer hold.

But I cling to my hope as I hear his words. "Yeah, okay, Jules. Okay."

Twenty-Seven

I tried to be light and happy for Sam's birthday weekend at Red's family cabin, but I wasn't very successful.

Every few hours, I'd duck into the bathroom to call Dave at the hospital, only to find that nothing much was happening. They'd begun Jesse on the cyclosporine and were waiting to see whether it would bring her blood work back to normal.

On the second night, I texted Dave while everyone was doing a puzzle in the other room.

Hon? What's happening? Is it working?

Not really, not so far.

The words were flat, distant. The silo.

Okay, and so?

So, nothing. We just have to wait.

The weekend dragged on, and all I wanted was to get back to that hospital room in Chicago. I had no illusion of control, just a desire to be there, to walk this road with her.

Finally the end of the weekend came, and Sam and I drove our rental car to the airport. He was flying back to California alone on his birthday.

"I'm sorry, Sam," I said, looking over at him as he looked out the window. "I know it was kind of a shitty birthday weekend with Jess sick and everyone preoccupied."

"It's okay, Mama." He looked back at me and put his big hand on my shoulder. I thought I picked up troublesome signals with my radar and peripheral vision. Then I heard him swallow hard. "I just want Jesse to be okay," his voice breaking.

I just want Jesse to be okay.

In that moment, it hit me. How could I be so dense? Of all people, I knew what it was like to make yourself the good child, the one who didn't need too much, so that your parents could focus on the kid who was in pain. Now here we were on Sam's birthday, with him thinking about his sister.

I closed my eyes and shook my head. It was not Sam's job to process this problem with me. The last thing he needed was to have to help me assuage my guilt. No, I just needed to do better. And project reassurance, no matter how shaky I felt.

"I think she'll be okay, Sam," I said firmly. "She's got great care, and, as we know, she's a badass. I mean, they better watch out that they don't get on her bad side over there."

He smiled and nodded.

An hour later, I walked him to his gate and took him in my arms for a long hug.

"I need to hurry to my gate, baby."

"Love you, Mama," he said to me, working up a smile. "Tell Jess I love her, okay? Will you remember to tell her?"

"I will, baby. I promise I will. Happy birthday, my beautiful boy. I love you so much. Have a safe flight."

Wistfully, I watched Sam walk down the Jetway, his oversize backpack sagging from his narrow shoulders. My heart jumped into my throat. For the first time, I feared the road ahead for Sam and the toll it was certain to take on him.

I rolled my bag to my gate in a daze and waited for the boarding call. I walked down the narrow aisle, squeezed into my window seat, and closed my eyes.

I fell asleep in the few minutes before takeoff, until my phone buzzed in my hand.

I jolted awake and looked down. It was a text from Dave. I stared at it.

She has to have the surgery.

My heart froze.

I typed back furiously. *What do you mean?*

The colectomy.

I stared at the screen. I remembered Dr. Bronstein's words. It would end her problems. She would be out of danger. But it was also a traumatic and permanent surgery, almost always a last resort. It might alleviate the symptoms of her ulcerative colitis, but it also meant the lifelong consequences of living without a major organ.

I tapped away. *What about waiting to see if the cyclosporine works?*

I watched the three dots dance as Dave texted back.

Finally: *C-reactive protein is so high that her colon is at risk of perforating.*

So that's it? No choice?!!!!??? I typed back stupidly.

If her colon perforates, it could be fatal.

I looked at my watch. *I get in at four. What time is the surgery?*

Now. Rolling her into the operating room now.

Dave was far, far into the silo. I stared at the words.

Hon, but—

"Ma'am? Ma'am?"

Startling at the sharp voice coming at me from the aisle, I looked up into a big, red-lipsticked face.

"You need to turn your phone off now. *Now.* I've been asking you."

I nodded dumbly and turned it off.

I opened the window shade and looked out through my tears. I tried to regulate my breathing. In, out. In, out. No choice. It was happening. This was happening. It was one of those moments that divide one's life into a "before" and "after."

I closed my eyes and prayed.

I'd been here before.

Dear Julie F.

Happy Birthday, I love you very much

You have helped me more than you know

You're right I am a survivor—a Big Survivor

I wish there was a magic plane that could take me to you.

You better be turning 29 because I don't want to

make the mistake of wishing the wrong age.

To my one and only sister.

I love you

Forever, always

No matter what

The call comes on May 15, 1996. I am twenty-eight, Danny, twenty-six.

I am in bed, waiting for Dave to get home from work at the hospital. I am talking to a friend when a call beeps in from Red. My heart pounds when I see his number on the screen and realize that it is 1:00 in the morning his time.

"Julie," Red says in a voice I've never heard.

My heart drops. Adrenaline starts its flood. "What happened?" I hear my voice say. "What did he do?"

Without thinking, before Red says a word, my hand shoots out to my nightstand, where I keep one of Danny's letters, a good-luck charm by my bed.

I will look at this letter while Red talks to me. Danny's handwriting will make whatever this is go away.

Dear Julie, My one and only
Sister—On your wedding day, I just want to say
How much I love you.
I know your wedding day
is probably your most important
day on earth

"What, Red, what?"

He doesn't speak.

I am floating now. Somewhere near the ceiling.

My voice is climbing. "What did he do? Just tell me!"

In the yawning silence, I begin to know. I begin to know in my chest, know in the marrow of my bones. Hot tears rise and fall down my face.

"He's going to die," Red says in a hoarse whisper.

I am whirling. I am not there.

"*He's going to die.*"

I am not there.

Red struggles to get the words out in between jagged silences. "He was using a lighter to light the fumes of an aerosol spray on fire. The can exploded."

Finally my voice screams. "No, no, no, it's not true!"

"*Julie!!!* Stop it!"

"Where are Mom and Dad?" I cry from the ceiling.

"I don't know."

"Where is Danny?"

"At Dallas Memorial Hospital in the burn ward."

We hang up, and I watch my hand dial Dave's number at the hospital.

"Mass General, operator speaking."

Dear Dave, I know I just met
you recently. . . .

"I'm calling for Dr. David Rudnick, my husband. It's an emergency."

I am detached now, calmly taking note that this is the call I've envisioned for years.

I know that as soon as David hears the word "emergency" from home, he will know what happened. He has also envisioned it, I am sure of it.

Dave, you are nice, smart and
honest. I hope you and Julie live
the rest of your lives in
harmony and loving of each other.

The call clicks through.

"Hon?" I hear the panic in his forced, calm voice.

I hope to visit you and Julie soon

"Danny's going to die," I say flatly. "He caught on fire and he's going to die."

I do not absorb the words. Now I am oddly numb.

My ears hear my words, and my mind asks me dumbly, *So this is how Danny is going to die?*

I blink and I stare at the wall as Dave says he's going to hang up and come home.

Twenty minutes later, he runs through the door. The sight of him breaks my trance.

His heaving shoulders and the tears streaming down his face tell me that what I have told him is true. I run to him and wail into his chest.

As I try to catch my breath, I ask him to call the doctor in Dallas who is treating Danny, as if that matters now. But I feel urgently we need to do it. Right now, right now.

Within minutes, Dave is put through to the ICU. I imagine the phone is just a few feet from Danny, who must be wrapped in bandages. His body, his face, like a mummy taped alive. I can see him, lying there. I can't get the image out of my head.

Somewhere in the distance, I hear Dave put on his doctor voice, calm and detached.

"Mass General," Dave answers woodenly, and I come down from the ceiling and go from disembodied to enraged as I realize that the doctor, having given the update on Danny, is now chatting, asking where Dave is training. *How could that doctor? What a fucking monster.*

"Stop it," I hiss. "Tell him to stop."

Dave puts his hand on my shoulder and hangs up the phone.

"What is *wrong* with that man? Fuck, I don't care, what did he say?" I ask. "Just tell me everything. I need to know everything."

Dave tells me the story that was relayed through the head nurse by Rodney, the head of Danny's halfway house at Timberlawn.

Danny had just gotten home from work. The guys in the halfway house were making dinner, and Danny said he'd shower first and then come down. He went upstairs and into the bathroom. From what the firefighters could tell, he picked up a lighter in the bathroom, picked up an aerosol can of deodorant, and started to light the fumes on fire—a trick they use in movies and on TV shows. The fire reversed its course and exploded the can.

The firefighters did not think Danny's death was intentional. They'd said they doubted that he'd know that the can could explode.

"Was there anything else?" I asked.

"Yeah. The doctor said that another indication that he'd not meant to harm himself was that as the ambulance workers carried him out of the house on the stretcher, Danny called out to his housemates, 'See you soon.'"

This last detail undoes me.

Danny, who had just lit himself on fire and had begun the process of dying, was so conscious of his impact on others that he would think to say "so long" as a kind of apology, an assurance that he would be back.

I will learn later that my parents got the first word of the news by way of a message left on their answering machine, asking them to call the hospital immediately.

They had spent the evening with old friends at a monthly lobster dinner at their country club. From that carefree and ordinary evening, they drove home and walked into their kitchen to find the red light flashing on their answering machine, signaling a message, like a terrible winking genie about to release them into the after of their lives.

Sister, I would like to be there for you and
give you the love and support which you
have given me.

I love you and wish you tons of happiness in your life and Marriage. —
Love, D.F.

P.S. my phone in Topeka will be welcoming any calls by you—24 hours
a day.

Twenty-Eight

I walked into the hospital room at University of Chicago to find Jesse lying in bed, eyes half closed, plugged into an IV machine and a catheter.

Dave crossed the room to hug me for a few long seconds, and I pulled away before I could lose my composure. Sadness and relief mixed in his eyes. The surgery had been successful. He was back with me now, ready to draw near.

"Hi, Beauty." I bent to kiss Jesse and hid my face in her hair.

"Oh no," she said weakly. "Please don't cry, Mama. Also, just a heads-up: don't make me laugh, because it hurts."

I pulled back and took her in. She was white—scary white. I looked down at the blanket that covered her and braced myself to see the stoma rising from her belly with a bag securely attached to capture waste.

I had only heard of ileostomy bags like this one. I'd always thought they were for old people, infirm people. Jesse was eighteen.

"It's okay, Mama," she said, looking at me. "I'm okay."

"Can I see?" I said, gently touching her abdomen.

She looked at me and nodded, her eyes wide and sad.

For a girl who couldn't sit next to a jar of mayonnaise because she found it repulsive, it was hard to envision how she was going to handle living with a bag of poop attached to her.

I lifted the covers and my eyes fell to the transparent plastic bag sagging from her stomach.

I moved my gaze back to Jesse's face; she was looking blankly ahead.

"I can't even look at it," she whispered. "It's revolting."

Just then, a woman in her fifties with short, cropped, brown hair entered the room.

"Jesse?" She looked up from her clipboard with a trained, happy smile.

"Yeah."

Michelle introduced herself as Jesse's ostomy nurse, whose job it was to help people learn how to manage life with an ileostomy bag.

"How we doing?"

"I mean . . ." and now Jess had her droll voice on, a comfort to hear.

"Right. Not lots of fun."

"Yeah, no."

"Can I take a look?"

Michelle pulled up a chair to the hospital bed, lifted Jesse's gown, and, squinting her eyes, examined the bag, running her index finger around Jesse's skin around the bag.

"Looking good!"

"Uh-huh," Jesse said without looking down.

Michelle launched into her tutorial.

"So, we don't want to let it fill up too much," she started.

Jesse's lip curled in disgust.

Michelle sat back and took in her face. "Jesse, I know this is pretty gross stuff. But you're going to learn to take care of this, and it's going to be okay. It's going to become part of your life, and after a while it'll just become normal."

"I know," Jesse said quietly as her eyes pooled. She looked up at the ceiling to stop the tears from falling.

After Michelle left, Dave and I moved to opposite sides of the bed and held Jesse's hands.

It was a lot to take in. We lived in a society where anything to do with bowels was unmentionable—an acceptable topic of conversation only when babies were in diapers. Now, suddenly, it was the main thing on our minds.

We looked through the brochure that Michelle had left us, which featured Jesse's new world: ostomy land. We learned that there was a whole science of living with an ostomy—a process for finding the right model of bag, the right adhesive, the right kind of powder to soothe the irritated skin around the bag that would be permanently covered in adhesive. It was like wearing a thick Band-Aid that never came off. There were websites like Ostomy Mates and Ostomy Secrets, filled with models with ostomies wearing swimsuits and dresses. Having an ostomy doesn't have to change your personal style! Fashionable Living with an Ostomy—It's Here!

"It's just so hard to believe this is happening." Jesse looked from me to Dave.

Dave leaned over and rested his head on her shoulder. "I know it is, Beauty. It sucks. But you'll get through it."

I climbed into the bed and turned on my side so my back was against the hospital bed rails. "Maybe we need to look at this bag differently. Thank God there was a solution. You have no more pain, Jess. You have to be grateful to your body for adapting to a whole new way of functioning. It's pretty miraculous."

I tried hard to believe my own words. I was making it up as I went along, feeling my way to a new narrative that we could both hold on to.

"Yeah," Jesse said quietly, trying to believe it too.

I looked at Jesse in her hospital bed, holding a stuffed animal to her face that a friend had sent. In this moment, illness had taken our swaggering college theater producer, president of this, director of that, and turned her back into a vulnerable little girl. A vulnerable girl she'd never been when she was young, a girl we'd never known before now.

After she fell asleep, Dave and I went into the hallway. His face had fallen.

"What is it, hon?"

He shrugged. "It's just . . ."

I hugged him and tried to keep my voice steady. "She'll be okay," I whispered. "She'll come back. She just needs to go through this."

"Yeah."

In the white fluorescent light of the hallway, we smothered our tears in one another's shoulders.

Our second week at the hospital suspended us in time. Besides checking in with Sam, who was staying home alone with Scotch, the world outside froze along with our former life. As the days passed, we sank into the hospital's rhythms and routines. Each morning at 6:00, the doctor came in for rounds, followed by a posse of underlings in white coats. He or she asked questions while the posse scribbled on pads, nodded, and hung on Jesse's every word like she was Moses.

The kindness of the nurses meant more than anything. They came, they took vitals, they made jokes. Angela became one of our favorites. She was pure light and kindness, and she wore a tiny dragonfly on her lapel. I took it as a wink from Danny.

The whiteboard in front of Jesse's bed had her name scrawled at the top in blue marker: Jesse Rudnick. Every morning the nurse came in and changed the day and date.

"Just because I lost my colon doesn't mean I have dementia," Jesse said to me as the nurse left the room the first day.

When a nurse came to check in and administer medicine, the conversation was always the same.

"Confirmation of name?"

"Jesse Rudnick."

"Pain level from one to ten?"

"I don't know."

"Guess."

"Four."

"Good."

Then they scanned her ID bracelet like she was a head of lettuce at Safeway.

Every day they injected her medicine into the IV, and every day I urged them to go slowly, because going fast made the medicine burn through her veins.

Little routines amassed themselves. Little jobs to be done—clear off the counters, keep her Styrofoam cup filled with fresh water. The day took shape with simple questions: Do you want to try a graham cracker and see how that feels? Are you tired? Do you want to watch an episode?

TV became a balm; each episode promised an escape from what was happening all around us.

"*FNL*, Jess?" I'd ask. Her eyes would light up and she'd say, "Yeah!" like a little kid. And then we'd watch another episode of *Friday Night Lights*, of which there were, mercifully, about one thousand.

We entertained ourselves by narrating each episode.

"Jason is such a cutie!" I said, working myself up into good cheer.

Jess obliged. "Ew, why would Lyla want to be with Riggins? He's such a dum-dum!"

"Yeah, but look at him. He's gorgeous."

"Who cares! What an idiot! No, Lyla, don't do it!"

I could never have imagined thinking about TV as a blessing, but I did now. It had become a respite, a sanctuary in which I could draw Jesse close to me in the crook of my arm, her head on my chest, golden hair splayed all around. In those moments, I felt at peace. I felt that everything might be okay.

Then the phlebotomists would inevitably come for her. We called them "vampires."

"Time for labs!" Drake, Jesse's most frequent and least favorite vampire, would say as he wheeled his horrible little cart into the room.

After ten days of blood draws, twice a day, Jesse finally lost her shit. "No! No! You were just here! You don't need more blood!"

From the look on his face, Drake had been here too many times before. He was just trying to do his job. Just hand over your fucking arm.

I called for Katherine, the nurse on duty. "Hi, Katherine, sorry," I said. "I need to talk to the doctor. I know this is protocol, but we just can't go through drawing blood again unless the doctors actually really need it."

Katherine (nice but not that nice) looked worn and tired. She looked at Drake, whose glare back to her said it all: her job was to support him.

"Sorry," she began.

"Okay, never mind." I waved at them both. "Drake, you can leave or you can stay, but you're not taking more blood from Jesse until you talk to my husband, who is a physician."

I didn't care if they thought I was a prima donna. Jesse's arms were bruised up and down, and she wasn't going to give blood again just so Drake could check off his box. Katherine left the room quickly while Drake stood in the corner of the room, holding his evil cart and pursing his thin, faded lips.

I called Dave, who was two floors down in the cafeteria. Less than five minutes later, he came through the door for the face-off.

"We're going to refuse blood work today, thanks," Dave said briskly in his doctor voice, leaving no room for negotiating.

"Okay then!" Drake said with an annoyed wave and rolled his cart out the door.

And then, suddenly, I became worried.

"Wait, should we have refused it? What if they really need it?"

He looked at me. "Hon, it's fine."

Right. Anxiety. I didn't go to medical school.

After two long weeks in the hospital, Dr. Bronstein signed Jesse's discharge papers. She'd come into the hospital to get more steroids. She was leaving it without a colon and with an ileostomy bag.

After one night of rest in a hotel next to the hospital, the three of us flew home.

It was a relief to be back in our little neighborhood in Marin County and to be back home with Sam, who had been staying at a friend's house while we were away.

Mercifully, we were just in time for Jesse's spring break. We had two weeks to help her regain her strength so she could go back to school without more absences.

If we'd ever questioned human resilience, no longer. Jesse, the kid who before had barely looked in the mirror before she left the house, learned over the course of just a few weeks to take care of her permanently altered body and digestive system.

Meticulously, she tracked her intake of food and her output of waste. Every few hours, she slipped away to the bathroom. Sometimes I would see her kneeling next to the toilet as she shut the door.

My stomach clenched, imagining how she had to carefully tilt her hurting body toward the toilet, empty and clean the bag, and make sure all attachments were secure so that there wouldn't be an accident—a prospect that held Jesse in a state of constant terror.

I imagined her having to do this again and again and again and again. There were no accidents in those early days, but we'd been warned that it was not a matter of *if* but *when* and *how often*.

Back at home, Sam rallied for Jesse. After all the years of feeling the weight of his overachieving big sister, the dynamic had flipped. Jesse was now shrunken and frail. Time and time again, I peeked into her room to find her sleeping with her head on Sam's broadening chest as he scrolled through his phone. There was a heightened level of intimacy among us all now—one of the gifts of illness.

"Mom," Sam said to me one night, "is Jess going to be okay? Like, actually, is she?"

I bit my lip. Sam was sinking deeper into worry about his sister. I knew better than to make promises.

"She's recovering really well now, and we've just got to think positive."

Sam nodded, but his eyes were lowered to the ground. I could feel the reality settling in for us both. There were no guarantees.

His question reverberated in my mind. *Is she going to be okay?*

I thought about his question. That word, "okay."

A dark, strange feeling seized my heart before I understood why.

Then I remembered.

Okay. The last word of the saddest story of our lives.

Twenty-Nine

The week Danny dies, the cicadas scream.

The humidity hangs a haze in the trees and colors the air greenish. The Midwestern heat has come early, and the cicadas must have been confused into coming out early, too.

It's a heat I will never feel again without being engulfed in sadness, an indelible, visceral memory woven into the images of a week that will forever be seared into my cells.

When we wake up the morning after Danny's funeral, the dragonflies are waiting for us at the windows. They come out of nowhere, slowly moving their long, iridescent wings against the screens.

"They're from Danny," my mother says.

I nod but can't find words. I just search her eyes and hope I will not lose her to another place.

That night, I clutch Dave in my blue-flowered childhood bed.

"I know this is a horrible thing to say, but I don't care about signs. Danny's dead. I don't care about dragonflies."

"It's not horrible," he says gently. "It's okay."

"Yeah, I guess," I say. My tears stream onto his chest as he holds me in the dark.

I can't stop thinking about Danny's last, single word. The doctor had given him a choice, we'd been told. His body had been too badly burned in the fire to survive. Either he could be kept alive long enough for my parents to fly to Dallas to say goodbye or he could die alone.

We can wait for your parents. Or, if you're ready, I can make you real comfortable.

This is the choice the doctor gave Danny. I imagine a long silence as Danny processed the question in the fog of his shock, in the twilight of his own death.

Okay, Danny said to the doctor.

Okay. A word he said to me a million times in our childhood to give me my way. *Okay, Julie*.

Now a final, quiet surrender. *Okay, make me comfortable. Okay*, he said. *Okay*.

I remember that surreal night when Red called me in Boston to give me the news. The doctor had called my parents to tell them of Danny's decision, which had sent them into a panic. They immediately decided to charter a plane so they'd get there within a few hours. Red urged me to call them and talk them out of it.

I will never forget that first moment when my father answered my call, that first moment we shared in the knowing of what had happened and that Danny was going to die.

I imagined the burns all over his body and his face. The bandages like a mummy ghost.

Dad, please, I begged him. *Please don't go to Dallas*.

I imagined my parents stepping into the hospital elevator, walking onto the floor of the ICU, hearing the beeping of the machines, entering the room, and seeing their beautiful boy wrapped in bandages, his face disfigured. Dying.

Mom won't survive seeing him like that, I whispered to my father. *Danny wants to go now. I beg you, Dad, don't go*.

Silence.

I can't let him die alone, my father answered me, breaking into a low cry I'd never heard before. *We can't let him die there all alone*.

But it was too late.

Danny's will prevailed. He did not live through the night.

We lost the long fight for Danny's life to a horrific and violent end. But I believe his last moments were an act of pure love. I believe he made his final choice thinking about my parents. Even in the haze of his own death and whatever fears he had of being alone, he wanted to spare them the sight of watching him die. Danny at his essence.

And that's how his brief life ended. That's how the weight of his suffering and all it entailed ended, the desperation to find the answer, the years of struggle, the brutal cycle of treatments, each bringing a ray of hope and then taking it away. This, finally, was the answer to his darkness.

All our love didn't save him. No more ideas. No more trials. No more hope. It was over. All over.

Danny died in the company of two strangers, the doctor and nurse at his side, recording his vital signs as they faded on the screen of the dark, blind monitors.

"Come sit with me under the tree, Lulu," my mother says to me two days after Danny is gone.

The big oak in the backyard of my childhood home has been a lifelong, silent witness to every chapter of our family's life.

As kids, we stood at the kitchen window for hours, watching the slanted blizzards fill our tree's branches with snow. In summer, the chipmunks raced across its broad boughs, trying in vain to reach the bird feeders that swung just out of reach.

Over the years, my parents have fallen into a ritual of sitting under the tree each night, rocking in their loungers, closing the day with glasses of wine and a Cuban cigar that they share between them—my mother's irreverent answer to kicking her cigarette habit of years past.

Now my mother wants me to come sit under the tree with her. Doing anything related to pleasure seems wrong in these bleached, early days, but the fact that my mother wants to resume her ritual seems a relieving sign of hope, signifying a wish for a normal future, even if it seemed impossible to imagine.

We rock in silence under the baking afternoon sun. The hot wind scrapes the dried leaves across the wooden deck.

"Lulu," my mother says, her voice in a trance, "do you hear the wind?"

"Yeah."

"Look up."

I look over to see her head tilted up toward the leafy, green canopy. "See how the branches are waving in the wind?"

"Yeah."

"I can hear Danny in the trees."

For all the years of Danny's struggle, I fought the gruesome images and memories and nightmares in my head, real and imagined. The cuts. The shaved eyebrows. Danny's heart-stopping calls to me in the middle of the night, begging for comfort. The image of him all alone, always alone, in his black tunnel.

My greatest, most terrifying fear was that Danny would end his own life and our family would go down with him. First we would lose Danny to his illness; then we would lose my mother to her grief. A deep, yawning chasm would swallow us all.

I look over at my mother and my heart fills with gratitude. She is here next to me, still here, still beautiful with her thick, red hair tucked behind her ears and her electric, sky-blue eyes resting their gaze in the trees.

It has been only a few days since our worst nightmare came to pass, but she is here.

I listen to the cicadas calling their loud, rhythmic, scratching call. Maybe this is a good sign. Maybe this is how my mother will find her way: finding light through the wind in the trees, sitting with my father, talking softly in the twilight of the days. Maybe this is her resolve to go on.

"That's so great that you can hear him in the trees, Mama," I say with glassy eyes. "That's so, so great."

I look over. My mother is rocking and rocking, eyes closed, wineglass in hand, her cheeks wet. She has a gentle smile on her face, and I imagine she is listening to the trees, listening for Danny.

I can see that she isn't listening to me anymore. She is off somewhere, far away.

She is flying, flying up into the trees alone, looking for Danny. And I am down below, waiting, sinking, slipping into the search for how to make her stay.

I close my eyes on hot tears. I try to push away Danny's voice.

Okay, he said. *Okay*.

I try to push away the heat, the haze, the screaming cicadas, the sadness, all the images that will embed themselves into the deepest corners of my soul.

Thirty

Two weeks after Jesse's emergency colectomy, she managed to return to college and finish her freshman year.

She learned to live with the complicated needs of the ileostomy bag, even in the confines of a tiny dorm room and a hall bathroom she shared with thirty other girls. She made the dean's list, worked in the theater, organized events for her sorority, and deepened a tight circle of friends who stood by her through all the ups and downs.

While her friends geared up for summer jobs and travel, Jesse prepared herself for her two remaining surgeries. By early summer, her body would presumably have healed from having her colon removed. Her second surgery would build the artificial colon, the J-pouch. Six weeks later, the J-pouch would be connected to the rest of her system, enabling her to get rid of the ileostomy bag and return to being able to use the toilet.

The J-pouch method was invented in the 1980s and had generally good results. The best part was that there would be no more ileostomy bag. The worst part was that Jesse would be susceptible to ongoing infections of the pouch that would bring on a host of painful symptoms and the need for frequent doses of antibiotics. No matter what, with the removal of her colon—the body's main absorber of water—Jesse would be engaged in a lifelong battle with dehydration and electrolyte balance.

A few weeks before Jesse's school year ended, I thrashed around in bed.

"What is it, hon?" Dave asked, rolling over.

"I'm just thinking about how Jesse's entire summer is going to be hospitals, surgeries, and recovery. It's so surreal and depressing."

"Yeah."

"We need to bring something joyful into our lives. Something new and exciting and ridiculously good." I could no longer keep it to myself. He needed to hear my plan, and then he needed to get on board, happily or not.

"Meaning?"

"Well, I think it's time."

"Oh, no. For what?"

I screwed up my face and braced for the blowback. "Another dog."

"Oh, Jesus."

I knew for Dave the mere mention of another dog conjured up the prospect of double the vet and dog-boarding bills, along with increased pressure on poop duty. Dave had already been forced into intimacy with our gravel courtyard and its poopy minefield. One of his terrible jobs was to painstakingly extract each pile of poop, usually encrusted with little rocks. One more dog: twice the poop.

I sat up in bed and made my case. After a full year of illness and trauma to her body, Jesse was facing a grim summer of hospitals and IVs, pain meds and nausea, weakness and endless trips to the bathroom— three months of adjusting to a whole new, and awful, way of life.

"She needs this, don't you think?" I said. "Some giddy joy to counterbalance the awfulness ahead. Plus, who knows—maybe it'll help keep you out of your silo."

He chuckled. "Yeah, maybe. And maybe it'll keep you from needing to constantly process."

I laughed. "Yeah, don't count on that."

I could feel Dave getting there.

I waited in the dark.

"Hmmm . . ." he said playfully.

Maybe he agreed with my perspective, or maybe he just didn't have the strength to put up a fight. Either way, I found his thrilling answer in the silence.

I jumped up. "We're getting a newwww dog!" I was like Bob Barker on the old game show *The Price Is Right*: "*It's a newwwwww car!*"

Dave slapped his forehead in the dark. I knew that slap. It was a sign that Dave was excited.

It was settled.

The next morning, I sat down at my laptop to try to write and again it happened—like a dark, animal force, dread filled my system and I was seized with panic. I needed to do something else, anything else.

It had been two months since Jesse's colectomy, and during that time I had barely gotten anything done on my writing project. The Committee greeted my panic with their customary support: *Still not working! Because nothing works!! You are a writer who never writes! Bahaha!*

I was still seeing Sheila every week, hoping I could shed some light on the issue now that I'd banned myself from using my therapy session to help her treat her exercise problem.

"What if I just can't do it?" I'd said to her in our last session, raking my hands through my hair.

"But you know you can," Sheila said, fixing me with her owl eyes.

"But I really don't, Sheila. It's been weeks, and I've barely puked up a page."

"First of all, your child just had her colon removed two months ago. Give yourself a break. But here's an idea . . . what if you didn't force it? What if you just committed to spending one hour a day simply feeding your imagination? Forget the rigid rules of writing a certain number of words a day. For now, just play."

It felt impossible. How could I play when I felt immobilized by dread? How could I woo the muse? Did my muse live only in Montana?

On the other hand, maybe Sheila was right. Maybe the problem was that I was too stuck on the idea that there was some mysterious, magical way to Be a Writer.

I thought about how routinely I tortured myself with my own thoughts. What if I started leaving myself alone? Stopped expecting anything and instead just allowed myself to be?

Clearly, I needed to find a way to mow down the Committee, which at that very moment was banging around my mind, yelling, *See? All that money down the drain! Accept that it's no use, you putz! You're a hopeless case!*

Then I thought about Sam and something he'd said at the pediatrician's office the week before.

Sam had a mild case of acne. Not terrible, but bad enough to be irritating to him.

"What are you doing for your skin?" Dr. Piel asked Sam. "Like, what's your skin-care routine?"

"Oh, not really anything," Sam said without a care in the world. "I'm not good at routines besides the really critical stuff," he said cheerfully, "like brushing my teeth and showering."

"Oh, well, it's good that you know that about yourself!" Dr. Piel said with complete sincerity. She did not lecture him, coach him on how to be different, or inform him that everything depended on him changing his very essence. No. Instead it was, *Okay, then, good. It's good that you know that about yourself.*

What if, like Sam, I was just not one of those creatives who followed a scripted schedule day after day? Was it really such a crime?

I thought about Dave and his Olympic-level, executive-function and organization skills. I was never going to be that person. But what if that was just fine? What if I stopped trying to beat myself into being something I wasn't and never would be?

Maybe it was okay that I could force myself to do laundry only when we all ran out of underwear. Maybe it was okay that the only way I did housework was while chewing gum, listening to podcasts, and talking on the phone all at once. Maybe it was okay that I had twenty thoughts at the same time, always remembered what I needed at Costco just as I was checking out, and always had to call back Dave thirty seconds after we'd hung up because that was exactly when my mind delivered into my consciousness what I had actually called to tell him.

So?

What if I could just be who I was—without bludgeoning myself?

It occurred to me slowly, like a dawning. *What if we could just all give in to the mess of who we are?* Maybe we were all born to a certain number of basic abilities so that we would eventually, after coming to peace with all we couldn't do, surrender to the things we were meant to do. And maybe that required a deep listening to no one but ourselves.

It was a thought.

The day after the come-to-Jesus conversation with myself, the dragonfly came to visit.

It started with the dumpster. Dave and I had been talking about cleaning out the garage for what felt like most of our adult lives. If a casual observer had come in and taken a look around, they might have wondered whether, just one or two millimeters under our sane family facade, we were hiding a raging, hoarding disorder. What else could explain the heaping piles of crap everywhere?

"Okay, hon," Dave said to me. "*Seriously.* It's time."

Once Dave made up his mind to clean, he turned into a maniac. He motored through like the Road Runner, hurling rejected items over his shoulder into the trash. I was right behind him, sorting through what he'd just tossed, saying, "Wait, you're throwing *that* away?"

After a few rounds of our ritual debate about recycling versus donating, we both got to work. Four hours later, we'd fallen in the grips of a complete and utter frenzy. *We would keep nothing.*

As always happened when I finally forced myself into a clutter-clearing marathon, I felt new, light, empowered.

"Hon," I called out from a pile of old luggage. "Don't you feel like you could do *anything* now? Isn't it crazy how cleaning like this feels like it unblocks you spiritually?"

"I mean . . . I don't know about 'spiritually,'" he said into a pile of sports equipment, courteously not wanting to pee on my parade.

"Okay, fine. Well, it does for me. Now if only it could help me break through my paralyzing writer's block that's such an old story I can barely stand myself."

Just as I uttered the words "writer's block," a dragonfly about the size of my palm landed six inches away from where I stood.

With its silvery wings and giant, staring eyes, it looked like a beautiful, prehistoric piece of flying art. It lay at my feet and its wings slowly opened and closed.

Suddenly I was seeing Danny on the bright-red swing set in the backyard; Danny racing me down the street, his brown, lean body glowing in the sun; Danny's loving eyes, his raspy voice. In my mind flashed his very last written words to me: *You are my one and only sister. Forever, always no matter what, I will always love you, Julie F.*

He was here with me again—that I knew. And it seemed like he kept showing up to give me a message. Maybe it was that he would always be with me. Maybe it was that he wanted me to be free.

I looked at the dragonfly on the ground and remembered the day they came to us, en masse, to drape the windows. Danny. *Danny.*

Thirty-One

I board the flight to Kansas City to begin a journey I've turned over in my mind for years. I'm going to Danny's funeral. Dave will join me later tonight.

I take my seat at the window next to an older woman, maybe in her late seventies. She is overweight and, with her silvery bun and soft hazel eyes, kindly looking.

As the plane takes off and the pilot announces our destination, the moment sinks in and the tears come. I turn toward the window to hide, but I can't help it, and soon I am heaving in my seat, then sobbing.

I feel a plump, warm hand on my arm. "Did you lose someone?" the woman asks me gently.

Her words force me to speak the words. "My little brother," I whisper. "My little brother is gone."

Without a word, the woman leans over and puts both of her big, warm arms around me. It is not awkward or strange. It is pure mercy and kindness as she holds me and strokes my arm for the next two hours and I do not stop crying. I will never forget her, though I don't know her name.

My father is waiting for me at the gate, his face gray, and I fly into his arms and dissolve.

"Okay, honey, okay," he says over and over. I can feel his heart beating fast beneath his shirt.

We drive to Red's house. Though it is only mid-May, the heat is yellow and blinding. As I cross the yard to his front door, I think, *It's just me and Red now. Two children in the family. Not three ever again. From now on, he's my only brother.*

At Red's house, we convince my father to let us be the ones to go to the funeral home and make the arrangements for Danny's burial and service.

Our parents are strong and independent and have always been the heads of our family. But this time it's clear to Red and me both that they should at least be spared this trial.

"Please let us do this for you," I say.

My father, pale and quiet, looks down and nods. "I'll go home to your mother," he says.

"Are you okay to drive?" Red asks.

"I'm fine." My father looks shrunken, already changed.

After he shuts the door, Red and I reach for each other. "Mom and Dad will be okay, right?" I whisper into his shoulder.

"Yeah," Red whispers back. "They'll be okay."

We drive to the Louis Memorial Chapel on Troost Avenue in silence.

Stan Durwood, the funeral director, greets us at the door with a Kleenex box in hand, and I know in an instant that he always greets his customers with a Kleenex box in hand. First good impression and all.

Stan towers over us in his cheap, gray-pinstripe suit. His black curly hair is greasy, and dandruff rings his collar like fake snow. His steel-gray eyes are wet stones.

Stan's funeral home is like a sausage factory, a convenience store, absent of anything but its own grim purpose. It's easy to see by Stan's practiced little bow, his stones for eyes, and the way he keeps checking his watch that this first part of the meeting with the bereaved is a snooze to him, like he's at a foreign movie where he can't bother to read the subtitles.

He ushers us into his dark-paneled office, where silver-framed photos of his family line his desk. Stan must have a heart, right? I study the pictures. He's much younger in all of them. His wife looks like a Macy's mannequin with painted red lips; his two daughters are dressed like Nutcracker ballerina dolls.

Red and I sit down in the faded, red-velvet chairs. I hand Stan a printed copy of Danny's obituary, which he requested so he could send it to the newspapers that afternoon.

"Okay, now," he says, looking at me with his stones. "So, you might want to add some more detail here." He points to something on the page.

I stare at his pale pink lips. Editorial feedback from a funeral director.

"Yeah, thank you," I say. "But this is what we will be saying." *Also, fuck you, Stan.*

But this party is just starting. After Stan gives us the rundown of the funeral agenda—when *the body* will be delivered, the fees for the grave-diggers, the sequence of the service—it's time to go casket shopping.

"Right this way," he says with a flourish, eye stones shining now. Red and I walk together behind Stan, and we are robots. We are tin men. I watch how our feet can walk toward a room of caskets for our little brother.

We come to a glossy wooden door with intricate carvings in it. It's the door from *Clue*. We are in a game.

Stan turns around with a proud little smile on his face. "Just upgraded our collection," he says, and then he gallantly swings open the door.

I suppose everyone who makes funeral arrangements for a loved one has to bear that moment when you are hustled into an actual show-room of coffins. Who knew there could be such variety, such choices? There are maybe thirty different caskets, displayed on carpeted shelving along the walls. *Here we've got your basic pine casket. This one here, it's a little pricier, that's because of the walnut inlay and all.*

Red and I walk around the room in a stupor. Red points to the plain pine casket and looks at me. I nod. It's a Jewish custom to be buried this way, for one's body to return to the earth in raw wood. Dust to dust.

Stan's brow furrows, his eye stones gone dim. We say our goodbyes and push as quickly as we can through the door.

As we step out into the bright light of the afternoon, I blink up at the sun. Red puts his arm around me, and I think about how our parents are at home, waiting for us.

My heart hurts at the thought of them. I wonder what they are do-ing, what they are saying. I wonder how they will make it through this nightmare. I wonder how we all will.

Thirty-Two

Dave and I finished our massive spring-cleaning project and called Jesse to check in. We needed to set the date for her next surgery and get her a ticket home from school for the summer.

It turned out that she'd made up her mind weeks before. She wanted to do the surgery the first available date after she got home.

"Don't you want some time to relax at home before the operation?" Dave asked.

"Dad, please," she said. She was worn down by the trauma to her body, worn down by the anxiety of taking care of the ileostomy bag in the confines of dorm life. "I just want to get this over with. I want this bag out of my life."

And so two days after she arrived home, we made the forty-minute drive to Mission Bay Hospital in San Francisco, our little roll-on suitcases in tow.

By now, we were hospital pros. As Jesse prepared for the operating room, I launched into action, seeing whether she could get a room with a window, scoping out the nurse situation, casing the penny-candy selection in the gift shop for room decorations and treats.

A few hours later, she was wheeled into surgery.

"Bye, Beauty," Dave called to her as they rolled her away. We blew her kisses and took our seats in the waiting room. We sat next to each other silently. Dave needed his silo now, and I needed my friends.

Four hours later, Jesse woke up from the anesthesia and turned her head to look for us.

"Hi," she said as we jumped up from our seats at the edge of her bed.

"Hi," we said back, bending down from either side, covering her face with kisses, tucking her stuffed animal under her neck. The gesture had become familiar.

"Surgery two, down," Dave said, smiling his everything-is-going-to-be-okay smile.

She put her hand to his face and closed her eyes.

The days after the second surgery went by like an endless C-SPAN hospital live stream. Eat, sleep, monitor bathroom visits, watch TV, accept visitors, repeat the stories, take a lap around the hospital floor, repeat.

Here are some things you learn when your kid spends a lot of time in a hospital:

1. Nurses rule your psyche. You swing from gratitude to fear to anger. If they're calm and happy, you're calm and happy. If they're nice to you, you are awash in gratitude. If they're gruff, they send you into a rage at their power.
2. Siblings rise to the occasion. After years of Dave and me standing on Sam's head and monitoring his homework like prison wardens, suddenly he was on his own. And probably not coincidentally, he was doing better than ever at taking care of himself. Lesson learned: When we over-function, they under-function. And when we under-function, they learn independence.
3. Marriage has endless layers. Dave and I were naturally compatible, but by now we'd turned into an efficiency machine. *Remember to let the dogs out before you come to the hospital. Did you get Sam a ride to martial arts? Do you think Jess needs more pain meds? Did you call your parents?* Every once in a while we'd look up and make eye contact. *Wow, this is really happening. We're real fucking adults now!* We learn how to cope together; we learn how to cope apart.

Once again, the world outside the hospital receded into the far distance. We fell into slow motion, transfixed only by watchfulness for Jesse's healing. All projects, quandaries, to-do lists, and social obligations fell away without a sound.

Life shrank to our little hospital room, our little family, the four of us in pure connection, wading through the primal waters of food, waste, sleep, and love.

Six days after her surgery, Jesse was discharged.

As the doctor had warned, recovery at home was rough. Jesse lay in bed for hours, glassy eyed, with energy only to scroll through her phone.

We stared down the summer. Six weeks until the next surgery, with one piece of good news: the arrival of our new puppy was just a few weeks away. Into the midst of this painful odyssey, we were about to throw into the mix something not just good but also thrilling, joyous. God willing, that little being would help Jesse through the weeks and months ahead.

While Dave took cover in his silo researching new therapies for Jesse's condition, I distracted Jesse with obsessing about our new dog.

There's something healing about following the lives of people who live in an alternate universe, and Jesse and I found delight in fixating on Beverly, the Napa-based Brittany spaniel breeder from whom we were procuring the newest member of our family.

For starters, we found it positively entertaining that Beverly was openly disdainful about our lack of ambition when it came to dogs. Breeders of certain kinds of dogs live to show their dogs in competitions, in search of a wall full of trophies and ribbons. Brittany breeders are a special kind of dog crazy, because they want their dogs to be both physically perfect *and* top-performing hunting dogs.

Inside of two minutes into our first conversation, Beverly discovered that we were not interested in showing our new dog.

"You don't hunt *or* show?"

"Well," I said, "I grew up with Brittanys and my dad did hunt, except I can't say he ever came home with much. And he only hunted for quail. Said he didn't want to hunt anything that could look him in the eye. We're just looking for a great family dog, which we know they are."

"Oh," Beverly said, barely containing her contempt.

Once Jesse and I connected with Beverly on Facebook, the larger picture snapped into focus. Her entire Facebook community had profile pictures not of themselves but of their dogs.

During those first days home from surgery, Jesse and I buried ourselves in posts with photos of dogs with snappy names standing on show benches with owners proudly holding up ribbons or trophies. Spencer. Hunter. Ace. Rex. Tanner. All winners. It was another universe, and for me and Jesse—lying in bed, waiting for her body to heal—diving into it was like medicine.

Finally, one week later, the news pinged into my inbox. I brought my phone into Jesse's bedroom, where she lay pale, looking at her phone. She looked at the message and broke into a huge smile.

Hello. Eight puppies. Two females. We're keeping one, but you've got the other one. Puppy Day is next Saturday.

Puppy Day seemed nothing short of a gift from God.

It had been a full two weeks since the surgery, and Jesse was now able to move with more ease. The days had been long and hard for her, with little relief from the nausea, weakness, and physical discomfort of a body adjusting to the trauma of having a huge chunk of her small intestine cut out and shaped into a makeshift organ.

Jesse, Dave, and I piled into the car and sped up the highway to Napa.

"Can you believe it?" I asked them. "A tiny little being will soon be running around our kitchen!"

"And pooping all over the house and biting us constantly," added Dave, but he was smiling above the steering wheel.

I noticed, with a rush of love, how his dimples were deepening with age. He was wearing the well-worn, green-and-gray flannel shirt that I loved. I put my hand on his shoulder and he looked at me and smiled.

"Oh, stop, who even cares," I said. "You know you'll be happy. We're so lucky!" I turned around to look at Jesse. "Right, Beauty?"

"*So* lucky," Jess smiled. She looked so small and tired in her seat, but behind the weariness was the distinct presence of what promised to be a new source of enduring happiness. For the moment, it was all we could ask for.

Thirty-Three

We parked our car on a shady street, walked up the driveway to Beverly's house, and went around the back alley, as instructed. When we arrived at a skinny, white door, we knocked.

The door swung open. There was Beverly—a mountain of a woman whose face was a web of deep wrinkles.

No hello, no smile, just "Step into the bleach bath, would you, please?"

Dave, Jesse, and I looked at each other quizzically and, one by one, stepped into the shallow tray of bleach, careful not to get it past the soles of our shoes.

We crossed the doorway into a converted garage, where ten other people sat on folding chairs talking in hushed tones. There was a bizarre split energy in the room between the somber circle of people and, at their feet, the playpen full of brown-and-white puppies with giant, floppy ears who were jumping, sneezing, peeing, and barking their tiny puppy heads off.

"What's the deal?" Jess whispered to Dave and me. "Why is everyone just sitting there?"

"No idea, but it's weird," I whispered back.

Dave leaned in. "Maybe because they're just looking for show dogs?"

I grabbed Jesse and Dave's arms and squeezed. "Guys, oh my God, will you look at them??"

I turned to Beverly, who was parked on an alarmingly flimsy beige folding chair, touching her helmet of brunette hair.

"Beverly, is it okay if we go in the playpen with them?"

"Yup." She waved a hand with no trace of emotion.

Jesse and I kicked off our shoes and climbed into the steel playpen.

Puppies! Along with the most delicious puppies on earth, the play-pen was filled with sawdust shavings—presumably there to soak up the pee, but who cared?

When the shit hit the fan, I'd found it was wise to scale back on humans and sink into the canines. We opened our arms and took them in, one by one. I looked at Jesse, who was giggling in bursts, kissing, and nuzzling her face into their soft, warm bellies. The light in her face was a balm. How is it that animals can so instantly take away our pain? Hospitals, blood tests, IVs—all so far away.

Dave pulled up a folding chair and sat right on the other side of the metal playpen fence. I smiled. Such a Dave move. He was right there with us, smiling and relishing the moment, but keeping his distance from the unsanitary floor and any errant face licking.

"So, Beverly?" I said. "Which are the two females?" I tried to sound adult, even though I was sitting with my legs stretched out in front of me in a wide *V* like a toddler in a gymnastics class, covered in wood shavings.

Beverly put down the can of Diet Coke she was drinking a bit too hard and walked over to where we were. She leaned over and poked the air with her index finger. "That one and that one. One's kind of a clown and the other's more of a lover."

A rush of joy coursed through my heart. *One of these two will be ours!* They had similar white-and-mahogany-brown bodies. But one of the puppies had perfectly symmetrical markings on her face, whereas the other female's markings were lopsided, like she'd been dipped into her colors sideways, so that only one side of her face was dark, solid brown, while the other side was only a little brown bordering a spray of light-brown freckles. Her little doggy face was fastened to Jesse's, licking and licking her cheeks.

Just then, the Committee walked in: *Better be the lover. You've already got one dog that couldn't give a crap.*

"And do you know which one you're going to keep?" I asked Beverly.

"Nope. We've got some testing to do. You'll find out when you come back, and then you can decide if you want the other one."

And with that she turned on her heels and said to one of the men standing nearby, low but loud enough to hear, "They're here for a pet."

Two weeks after Puppy Day and one month before Jesse's final surgery, we brought her home.

"*The lover!*" Jess opened her arms to the ceiling. "We got the lover!"

As we'd suspected, Beverly had chosen the conventional beauty for herself.

Lucked out! the Committee said.

Carefully, Sam put our tiny new dog down in front of Scotch's large and marginally interested face. The puppy bowed; she lunged. She jumped up to nip at his cheek and barked her tiny bark. Scotch took one doleful look at her, gave two brisk sniffs of her behind, and then walked through his doggie door to go lie in the sun.

We laughed and hugged our puppy and watched her prance around the house, sniffing furiously at the baseboards. Dave and I couldn't stop catching one another's gaze. In a universe that had swerved so far out of our control, we'd done something decidedly right.

"Oh my God!" Jesse said, cradling the puppy's little head, which was licking her chin at high speed.

Sam sat next to them both and gently cupped the puppy's head in his big hand. "God, she's so little!"

I looked at Sam and registered his calm pleasure. I thought about how all these months, he'd been through his own experience—quietly, without fanfare—and I felt a pang of remorse. I'd promised myself I'd do better about staying conscious of the burden he'd been carrying right along with us since Jesse's health issues began. But in my hyperfocus on Jesse, it had not occurred to me how much he needed this puppy too.

I leaned over to kiss his head. "I love you, Sam. I'm so happy that you get to have this new bundle of joy too. You deserve it. It's going to be such fun, right?"

Sam fixed his cool blue eyes on me, searching my eyes, as he often did, for what was behind my words. The puppy jumped in his lap, and he bent his head to hers.

"Yeah, Mama," he said into her little brown head. "It's great. I'm happy for all of us."

My heart squeezed.

The next task ahead of us was a big, big job: settling on her name. After months of deliberation, it was not going to be easy.

Our friends were so thrilled at the prospect of a puppy in their lives too that they tried to get in on the name game. For weeks, I got hopeful texts from various friends with ideas, all of which the family summarily rejected.

Lucy was determined to be the one who found the right name. Day in and day out, she texted me with lists of names—no greeting, no comment, just names:

Roxy?

Ricky?

Bailey?

Frankie?

Fifi?

Brigette?

Kayla? (I laughed especially hard at that one, since that was Lucy's daughter's name.)

Buttons?

But in the end, it was Jesse who came up with the perfect name.

"Hey, guys?" she said one night at dinner. "What do we think of naming her Scarlett?"

Scarlett. It was strong. It was beautiful. It evoked a woman of independent means who knew how to get what she wanted.

We called her by that name about ten times, until her nicknames started to unfold. Scarlett. Scarletto. Carly.

Scarlett walked around the yard, surveying the world, a sniff here, a sniff there. Pawing ants, chewing on branches. It was all hers.

"Look at her," Sam said. "She's like a tiny baroness out there, surveying her kingdom."

"The Baroness!" Jesse said. "She's the Baroness of Tinytown."

"Look at her," Dave said. "She's so little. She really is tiny!"

"She's our tiny, tiny girl," I said.

"Tiny Gurrrrllllll!" Jesse yelled to Scarlett, and she perked up her head.

Scarlett had worked her magic. And for the moment, all felt right with the world. Almost like normal again.

Thirty-Four

The day of Jesse's third and final surgery arrived.

"This last surgery should be the fastest of all," Dr. Patel told us. "All we're doing is reversing the ostomy and connecting the J-pouch to her system. It's basically a replumbing. Should take about forty-five minutes."

We had become so conditioned to our situation by this point that it seemed almost normal for Dave to take Jesse to the hospital alone while I dropped off Sam at a friend's before meeting them there.

An hour after Dave and Jesse left the house, my phone rang.

I grabbed it and answered. "Everything okay?"

"Yeah," said Dave, "but I need to report a mystical occurrence."

A mystical occurrence for Dave?

"Go on," I said.

"Well, you know how this hospital is in a total industrial wasteland, right?"

"Yeah." I did know, as I had been struck by the vast expanse of concrete, cranes, scaffolding, and throngs of men in bright-orange hard hats the last time we were there.

"No nature anywhere, right? Anyway, we were waiting in a line to register Jesse on the fourth floor and I kept hearing this little clicking sound."

"Yeah?"

"I realized it was coming from behind the nurse. And when I looked beyond her, I saw that it was a huge dragonfly bumping against the glass of the window, over and over again, like it was trying to get in."

"Danny," I said.

"Yeah," he said.

Two hours later, I parked in the hospital lot and looked at my watch. The surgery began in twenty minutes.

I ran through the maze of walkways, cutting through neat lines of bright green hedges. I looked both ways before running across the street toward the entrance.

When I was just a few strides away from the opening sliding doors, a huge dragonfly dove through the air and danced around me.

I stopped and looked up. "Thank you, Stiggy," I whispered through glassy eyes. "Thank you."

An hour and a half later, Dave and I sat in the waiting room in chairs with half desks, like we were in a high school classroom.

"It's been way longer than forty-five minutes," I said.

Dave looked at his watch and nodded.

"Is it weird that there's been no message for us?"

"A little bit," he said in his fake-casual, definitely anxious voice. "But it's fine. Let's just sit tight."

Instantly, my mind was off, zooming crazily down dark, jagged roads.

After two hours passed, I went up to the desk.

The receptionist was in his twenties, with long hair pulled back into a ponytail and a butterfly tattoo on his neck. He looked at me brightly, with the determination of someone who coped with anxious people all day. "Hi!"

"Hi. So our daughter, Jesse Rudnick, is in surgery with Dr. Patel; she said it should only take forty-five minutes, and it's been two hours."

He typed at warp speed and looked at the screen before shifting in his chair. "Hmmmm . . . let's see if we can find out what's happening. You can take a seat."

Dave and I waited in a thick silence.

Finally, the receptionist waved me back over.

"Yes, they're still in surgery. The nurse said there was just a lot of scar tissue and it shouldn't be long."

I thanked him and sat down. Scar tissue. Scar tissue from all the ulcerations in her intestines, all the bleeding.

It had been three hours total when the doctor finally came into the waiting room in her blue scrubs, her thick, black hair matted from the surgical cap. She walked toward us with an expression that was placid, practiced, and inscrutable.

"Okay, all done. The ileostomy is closed, and the new J-pouch is working fine. Just a lot more scar tissue than we expected."

I'd heard Dave's stories about the secret life of operating rooms. I knew the moment the words were out of Dr. Patel's mouth that we would never know what really went on in that room—how well the surgery was performed or what the impact of whatever had or hadn't happened would be on Jesse's future.

All we could do was be grateful that it was over and hope for the best.

In the recovery room, we stood on either side of Jesse, holding her hands, as she came to consciousness.

"Mama, Da." She looked up at us. Her gaze was unfocused, but there was light in her eyes. "It's gone. The bag is gone."

Dave and I bent and buried our faces in her neck at the same time, our routine now, and the enormity of the truth washed over us. We'd gotten through all three surgeries. We were done.

A few hours later, Dr. Patel came in and sat down on the stool beside Jesse's bed. She was warm but all business.

"You did great, Jesse! How are you feeling?"

"Good." Jesse smiled.

"Great, that's great. So we've talked about this before, but I want to review everything now. Here's the deal: this is not a real colon, and as wonderful an advance as it is, it's by no means perfect."

Jesse nodded.

"Remember, real colons absorb water. Your J-pouch, because it's made out of your small intestine, can't be nearly as efficient. That means that from now on, your stool is always going to be very loose, which means that you need to try to thicken it with a lot of carbs, or else you're going to need to go to the bathroom constantly."

Jesse's eyes widened slightly. "Can you remind me, like, how constantly?"

"If you don't stay vigilant, you could be going anywhere from ten to fifteen times a day. You should be trying to shoot for six to eight times a day and another two times at night. Remember, the more often you go, the rawer your skin gets in those areas, which is painful and makes it more prone to infection."

Jesse straightened up in her bed. "Dr. Patel, how will I sleep if I have to get up that much?"

"Well, you've got to stay on top of what you eat, make sure you get plenty of protein and bind it with a lot of carbs like bread and pasta to try to slow your system down. Also, you should take Imodium a couple of hours before every meal."

"Wait. Take Imodium before every single meal? Like . . . forever?"

We had been so focused on the end of the surgeries that none of us had had a chance to understand the impact of the final outcome of the J-pouch on her eventual everyday life. I watched Jesse trying to absorb it all.

"Well, let's not talk about forever right now," Dr. Patel said, getting up. "Let's just get through the next few months and see how you do, okay? I'll be back tomorrow to check on you."

She left the room and we all looked at each other. No one could speak. Each of us was privately trying to absorb the magnitude of this new reality. Jesse would need to calculate everything she ate. She would not be able to sleep through one night for the rest of her life.

"Well," Jess finally said quietly, "at least there's no more bag."

We nodded.

Two hours later, we were on our way home. For the next ten days, Jesse barely had the strength to leave her bed. Her body was traumatized, struggling to adjust to a new, handmade organ and plumbing system.

Walking the twenty feet from her bedroom to the kitchen was an event—slow and fragile, painstaking. She couldn't be more than a few feet from the bathroom because her need to go was urgent and constant.

Thank God for Scarlett, who became Jesse's constant companion and confirmed 100 percent that puppies have healing superpowers. The mere sight of our new puppy altered everyone's brain chemistry on the spot, and Jesse and I busied ourselves with inventing a whole new world around the new Scotch and Scarlett duo, whose antics provided a constant respite.

"Tiny Gurrrrl!" we'd shriek, alternately, as Scarlett play-bowed to Scotch, ran maniacally back and forth across the room, and lunged at us to play.

"Look at her! No, really, look at her now!"

Every time we walked in the room, Scarlett raced up as if she hadn't seen us five minutes ago, pulling her lips back.

"Look! Look!" we'd cry. "She's smiling!"

It was like pure mercy, and it never got old.

Even Scotch seemed to have temporarily tuned in. While he still largely ignored Scarlett, he clearly sensed Jesse's compromised state. He took to following Jesse back and forth to the bathroom, walking with his head hung low, and waiting outside the door. When she got back into bed, he'd jump up and stare at her and then curl up next to her and lay his head on her stomach. Most shocking of all, he periodically—unsolicited—offered her a paw to hold while looking the other way.

It was Scotch's version of a Shakespearean love sonnet. We were overcome.

Thirty-Five

Three weeks after her third and final surgery, Jesse could be found most days on the couch, coloring and watching TV.

One night, Dave came home to find her with Scarlett on her lap, leaning over to color an intricate mosaic.

"Look at this ball of dog!" Dave said, throwing himself on the couch next to her and burying his face in Scarlett's furry neck. He looked up. "Hi, beautiful girl! Isn't this where I left you when I went to work this morning?"

Jesse shrugged. "Yeah."

Dave sat up and looked at her. "Jess?" he started in the self-effacing "dad" tone he used when trying to be delicate in making a sensitive point. "I'm afraid to ask, but have you left the couch today?"

Jesse shrugged again. "Not really, no. Because I love this Tiny Girl, and what better thing to do than color and love her all day?"

I stood at the door and watched Dave register Jesse's message: she was not taking his bait.

He threw his hands in the air in surrender, leaned into Scarlett's belly, and nuzzled her into the zoomies, sweeping the subject away.

That night, as we got into bed, I turned to Dave. "Dr. Patel said Jesse should be increasing her activity a little each day. She's barely moved off the couch since she came home. Shouldn't she be trying to gain her strength back? Like, how is she going to go from sitting on the couch all day to being back at school in two weeks?"

It was hard to tell whether Dave was truly unconcerned or just trying to make me feel better. "I really think she's going to be fine," he said in his most convincing, comforting, doctor voice, putting his hand on mine. "She'll figure it out."

I wanted to believe he was right.

But when Jesse planted herself back on the couch at nine the next morning and didn't get up for the next four hours, I couldn't help myself. I walked into the living room and sat down on the couch.

"Jess," I said—trying and immediately failing to be measured— "don't you think you should get up and try to *do something*? Also, I'm sorry, but I really don't get the idea of coloring for hours on end. Like, seriously, explain to me, what's the point?"

I knew those words coming out of my mouth were straight from the graves of my ancestors who deemed wasting time the ultimate sin, but they were moving my mouth and it wasn't my fault.

"I don't know. I just like it," Jesse said brightly, finishing off the dizzyingly detailed mosaic with a block of magenta.

"Okay, baby," I said, trying to put on Dave's cheery nonchalance and springing up from the couch to get myself out of the room before I said something I regretted. "Well, I'm going out for a run with Lucy now. See you later!"

As I walked out the garage door and got into my car, my thoughts unraveled. How was I going to keep pretending that this situation was okay when inside I was worried that Jesse might be caught in an inertia spiral, jeopardizing her chance of successfully returning to school?

But the key words were *might be*. Because maybe she was doing just what she should be doing. Who knew? By now Dave and I were lost in the land of *When Your Adult Child Has a Chronic Illness*. In this land, all terms have changed. Your child is no longer healthy and is, therefore, although the same person, also not the same person.

Your child is instead someone dealing with a life with new rules, a life no one imagined. A life whose territory was entirely uncharted. In this new land, there is no manual for your child, and there is no manual for you.

Before, you knew your job was to let go. Now? There's no telling how to navigate the borders of your child's independence. How much do you leave them to their own devices? In parenting adult children with chronic illness, where's the line between responsibility and codependence? Between support and enabling? Between respecting boundaries and not being there when they need you most because you didn't know the difference?

Start the parent-child dance. Do the two-step, the do-si-do.

Understand it will not end, possibly, um . . . forever?

By the time I got to the trailhead to meet Lucy, I was worked up and hell-bent on finding answers. Thank God I had her to chew it over with.

"Lucy!" I yelled from a few steps behind her as we ran up a hill. "It feels like Jesse's completely lost her initiative! She used to be the most driven person on the planet. Now all she does is color and watch TV— literally, and I mean *literally*, all day long! What if this is it, her new life forever, just sitting on the couch talking to Scarlett, coloring and binge-watching Netflix? Shouldn't we be having an intervention?"

"She just had surgery a few weeks ago!" Lucy called over her shoulder.

"Yeah, but still, she's supposed to be building her stamina a little each day, and she isn't even *trying* to do anything. Like, she doesn't even feel guilty about it!"

Lucy stopped midway up the hill and turned around. "Julie, c'mon. I know it's hard to watch her sit around all day, but coloring is so healing. It's what she needs to do. It's *good* for her."

I winced. "*It's good for her?* It's so upsetting to just see her whiling away hour after hour."

Lucy put her hand on my shoulder. "It shouldn't be upsetting, Julie. It's what she needs."

She seemed so sure, but I wasn't. Yes, Jesse had had surgery only three weeks before. But in just two weeks, she was going to get thrown back, full speed, into academic and campus life. How would she go from zero to one hundred that fast?

But maybe she just would. Maybe this was my own sickness. Maybe I just needed to shut up and get on board with the program.

Where was the Committee when I needed them?

Silence.

When I got home, I made a beeline to the couch, where Jesse was still coloring and Scarlett was now sound asleep beside her, flat on her back with her four little legs folded in the air.

"So, can I try a page?" I asked, trying to sound nonchalant.

Jesse shot me a suspicious glance. "Really, Mama? Is something going on? You've literally *never* wanted to color once, like, I mean, *ever*."

"I just want to try it. Plus, I want to be with you."

She cocked her head, her eyebrows raised, indicating her mistrust of the situation. Then she tore out a page and handed it over without breaking eye contact with *The Office*.

I chose my colors and started to fill in the tiny black compartments of a giant sunflower. Instantly, the Committee joined me, screeching, downright offended: *What the . . . ? What are you doing now? Coloring?? Coloring a flower in a coloring book? What a goddamned waste of time! What the hell for?*

I bit my lip and forced myself to sit there. I forced myself to sit and feel what it felt like to do something without a clear outcome, something done for the pure (theoretical) enjoyment of it rather than as something to check off a list. Meanwhile, I felt like jumping out of my skin.

I flashed back to high school English class, listening to Mr. Atkins, who would sit cross-legged on top of his desk and smoke his pipe while he pontificated about Southern literature. "I enjoy . . ." he would often say in his Tennessee drawl.

I don't remember exactly what he enjoyed, but he was always enjoying something. Even all those years ago, I'd felt discomfort with his use of the word, even the sound of it: "I enjoyyyy."

"I hate when Atkins says 'enjoy,'" I said to my best friend, Katie, as we walked out of class one day.

"Okay, that's weird. Why?"

"I don't know. It just bugs me. Can't he just say he 'likes' or something? It's so much less indulgent."

While I colored the bright yellow petals of my sunflower, I thought about all the years I'd both recoiled from and admired people who had the nerve to claim their preferences. There was something about the space around the words "I enjoy" that always seemed too self-centered, too self-serving.

As I colored the center of the flower with a chocolate-brown pencil, it dawned on me: Maybe my resistance to being still wasn't just a holdover from my ancestors or the Committee. Maybe it had to do with not allowing myself to enjoy life when Danny—someone I loved so much, someone whose life was being lived right there along with mine—couldn't enjoy *his*. I was almost ashamed of the idea of "I," of putting myself in the equation. How could there be room for me when he was falling down the abyss?

I flashed back to the image of Danny standing at the steel door at Menninger and watching me walk away. I felt the weight of leaving him. All that mattered then was figuring out how to make him feel better—to help him wake up out of his depression and deliver us all back to being the happy family we had once been.

I looked at Jesse. She was okay. She didn't need me to make things okay, to make *her* okay. She was here, coloring right through her own slow-motion trauma, handling it with grace and acceptance.

I reached out to put a wisp of golden-red hair behind her ear.

Maybe it was I who needed to learn from her.

Thirty-Six

W e arrived back on campus one week before fall classes began, feeling a mix of hope and trepidation.

As Dave had predicted, Jesse was ready to go back to school, and I was joining her for the week before its official start to help her get oriented for her new, postsurgical life with a J-pouch.

Saying goodbye to our household earlier that morning had been hard. "Tiny Girl, Tiny Girl," she had whispered into the soft fur of Scarlett's neck, holding back tears. Sam had stood behind them both, head bent, glassy eyes cast downward, his hand on Jesse's shoulder. The summer had gathered them into a new intimacy. Sam had changed from Jesse's little brother to her ally and witness. They'd spent hours lounging on the couch, lying on her bed, passing the time of her long and difficult recovery together. Now he was saying goodbye to her again.

Back on campus, the university felt both familiar and dauntingly new. After having the refuge of Leila and their tiny freshman dorm room, now Jesse was moving into her sorority house across campus. It would have been a tough transition under any circumstances, but especially so given that Jesse was returning as a citizen of a new world.

Her freshman year had been a survival course. She'd had neither the bandwidth nor the psychological readiness to acknowledge or ask for accommodations for her illness. Now, as a sophomore, she was coming back as a new version of herself.

After a lifetime of blending into the society of the healthy, she was ready to face becoming a member of the chronically ill community. Beyond grappling with this shift in identity, her illness had progressed and forced her into a need for ongoing and special accommodations. Her J-pouch meant being forever on guard. "Eating" no longer meant what it once had. Jesse had always eaten like a frat boy in the movies: scarfing down cold pizza for breakfast, a burger and fries for lunch, lasagna for dinner. Ice cream, bagels, burgers—these had all been food groups for her.

Now she was charged with wielding a warlike vigilance over everything she put in her mouth.

"Think of your J-pouch as a pipe," Dr. Patel had said at her last appointment. "First you eat a protein bound with a low-fiber carbohydrate, and *then* you drink, so that the liquid has something to soak into, so everything doesn't just leak out of you."

Jesse's new digestive system was like a horrible new pet with endless needs—nagging, nasty, painful. Each day, until she acclimated, she needed to track her every bite in and every bowel movement out. Food had changed from a source of pleasure into little more than a strategy to maintain energy, minimize bathroom trips, and protect against chronic fatigue and dehydration.

We obtained permission to install a fridge in her sorority bedroom. We began what would be a weekly routine of packing the little cube fridge with protein drinks and Gatorade. We filled shelves with prepackaged snacks that combined carbohydrate-binding foods like pretzels and crackers with power protein foods like cheese and hummus. We threw in mini Rice Krispies Treats to be festive. We lined drawers with pre-dosed medicine, skin-care creams and wipes, and trays of medical supplies.

Jesse met with the university's special needs office to obtain accommodations for extended time on assignments in the unpredictable but inevitable ups and downs of her illness. Also extended time on tests, to allow for multiple bathroom visits. We met with the sorority chef to plan for special menus that would help her stay well but not separate her from her new community. Jesse stayed with me at the hotel, both of us falling into bed like stones each night, often holding hands like we had when we'd slept together at the hospital.

This was the scaffolding for Jesse's new life. We tried to look at this new stage as a gift from modern medicine and her resilient body. After all, the J-pouch had provided an escape from the ileostomy bag, and that alone felt miraculous.

Still, none of that negated the emotional and psychological challenge of having to negotiate all of this mess as an eighteen-year-old just starting life as a woman and adult. There was no cover for Jesse from constantly needing to attend to her bowels. And there was no respite from the embarrassment and shame that ran underneath it all like a reverberating current, along with shame's closest companion—isolation.

We knew there were hundreds, probably thousands, of other students struggling in silence with their own bowel diseases, but there was no college community for that. No student organizations for Crohn's disease and ulcerative colitis. No Can't-Stop-Pooping Anonymous. No real source of support. Too gross to discuss. Too embarrassing to admit.

Everyone went it alone.

Our days passed in a flurry of meetings and trips to Target and Bed Bath & Beyond. Jesse struggled to walk any distance, to maintain focus, and to stay awake during the day.

As the week's end drew near, my heart grew heavy.

The morning before I was scheduled to go, Jesse woke up and turned to me in bed.

"Mama."

"Yeah, baby?"

"Please don't go tomorrow."

"Really?"

"Yeah. Stay with me, Mama. Stay."

"Okay, Beauty. I agree; I agree. I want to stay."

She sighed and moved her head to my chest.

I nodded in relief. "I'm so glad you said something."

Neither of us was ready.

Fall session officially began, and it was a struggle. Every class, sorority meeting, late-night theater board meeting—all things that would have been priorities before, things she'd done back-to-back in her freshman year—was a mountain to climb. Each meeting was a test of walking, sitting, and listening. Simply getting through the day was a challenge.

Months before, Dave and I had scheduled an anniversary weekend in Wisconsin. But when the time came, even after having been with Jesse for two weeks, I grappled with the familiar angst of not knowing whether I was abandoning her or doing the right thing.

"How can I leave her when she's still so weak?" I whispered into the phone from the hotel bathroom.

"You have to at some point, hon," Dave said. "It's never going to feel good. And the truth is, you've done everything there is to do. Plus, we've been waiting for this weekend for so long."

"Is Sam still in school?" I asked, my routine joke wrapped in guilt.

"As far as I know," Dave said to make me feel better, but I knew, thank God, that he was kidding. He was right there with Sam, even if I couldn't be.

"She's just so frail and weak."

"That's normal." He was in a doctor mini-silo.

"You really think it is?"

"She's had three major surgeries. Her body is drained."

"You really don't think I'm a horrible mother for leaving while we go off for vacation?"

"No."

We hung up and I came out of the bathroom. Jesse was lying in bed, wrapped in the sheets up to her neck, her copper hair fanned out on the pillow. Her eyes were fixed on me, serious.

"Jess, are you sure you're okay if I leave?"

"Yeah, I'm okay," she said quietly, her eyes drifting to look out the window.

"Really, baby? Because I'll stay. I really can; I'm happy to stay."

"No, you should go. It's going to be hard no matter when you leave. I'm all set up. I just need to get back to my life. Go ahead, Mama, you can go."

I tried to believe she was right.

Later that afternoon, we took a walk around campus. The new crop of freshmen was experiencing the first tender weeks in their new college home. Everywhere we looked, they roamed in loud, loose packs. Most still wore their matching purple Wildcat T-shirts from the previous orientation week. A force field of energy hovered over each pack, signaling a kinetic awareness of the daunting task at hand; their unspoken job was to read the tea leaves and navigate the masses in search of "their people." They picked, chose, and, most of all, longed to be chosen. The situation was clear: each person in purple represented a potential new best friend, romantic partner, future start-up cofounder, or perhaps one day a spouse.

My heart went out to all of the beautiful young souls, their faces pressed with anxiety, hope, and good cheer.

As we crossed Sheridan Road, my eyes locked on the outline of the landmark black iron gate. It had been a little over one year since that awful March Through the Arch, when we'd stood for hours searching for Jesse in the passing student parade and finally spotted her, grimacing in pain.

I tried to believe that time was far behind us. At least now we knew where we stood. I tried to believe that we were on our way to a new chapter, a solid and good chapter.

But, as was the case with every other chapter, there was no way to know.

I reached out for Jesse's hand. It was warm in mine, still so small. I let myself hold it for a moment, gave it a quick squeeze, and then let go.

Thirty-Seven

The Kansas City Star

Dan Fingersh, 26, Prairie Village, KS, passed away Thursday, May 16, 1996, at Parkland Memorial Hospital, Dallas, TX. Funeral services will be 4 p.m. Friday, May 17, at Louis Memorial Chapel; burial in Rose Hill Cemetery. In lieu of flowers, the family suggests contributions to the Hyman Brand Hebrew Academy. Mr. Fingersh attended the University of Kansas and was a volunteer and camp counselor at the Jewish Community Center. Surviving are his parents, Jack and Pella Fingersh, Prairie Village, KS; a brother, Red Fingersh, Kansas City, MO; a sister, Julie Fingersh and brother-in-law, David Rudnick, Boston, MA. Dan was a uniquely strong and gentle person who was loved and cherished by all who knew him.

We have woken up to the day of Danny's funeral. I lie in bed with Dave in my childhood room and think about all the people who are also waking up in Kansas City, thinking to themselves that today they will attend Danny Fingersh's funeral.

I imagine the moment that each of them learned the news. *Did you hear? Danny Fingersh died. What?!? Danny Fingersh? Pella and Jack's son? Oh my God. Julie and Red's brother?* I imagine the shock and intrigue coursing through the community as the news spreads. I imagine the confusion and the questions, the horror. *How did he die? Was it an accident? Was it suicide?*

Most people in our community have no idea what's been going on with Danny. For years, we have brushed off the questions about what he is doing, where he is. *He's in school. He's finding his way.* My parents were resolute about preserving Danny's privacy. *This is no one's business. We don't want people to look at Danny that way. He'll get better and we don't want it to be held against him.* Over time, people stopped asking.

Years from now it will be impossible not to question the real purpose our secrecy served. Who was protecting whom, and why? Of course, we were worried about how people saw Danny, but were we keeping the secret for ourselves, too? In choosing silence, were we also protecting our family from the stigma of mental illness?

Were we hiding from our own shame and grief that a member of our "good" family was so broken and lost?

And what was the cost of our silence to Danny? What was it like for him to know that his life was a secret? Did we unwittingly deny him—and ourselves—the support and love of those around us, keeping us all isolated in the awful and terrifying fourteen-year odyssey that ended with his death?

As is true for most families struggling to support their loved one through mental illness, no one asked these questions at the time. We were too lost in a fog to ask questions. It was impossible to know what was right and what was real. We just kept going. We just plodded on, trying to make it go away.

But what's clear now—at least at this moment, as I lie in my blue-flowered bed, contemplating the day ahead—is that our secret has blown wide open in the most horrible finale imaginable. Today, Danny's story will end on a horrifyingly public stage, for all to see.

We ride in the limousine in silence, holding hands—my parents, Red, Dave, and me. We turn down the street of the funeral home and suddenly see rivers of people we know, walking down the street, blank faced—in couples, in groups, alone—stricken, greeting one another soberly, making their way to the front doors.

Here they all are, I think to myself. *Our community. Here to support us, yes. But also seeking answers.*

The limousine lets us off at a back door. Stan is there to greet us with his Kleenex box, nodding and patting our shoulders.

The rabbi approaches us with the look and gestures of practiced empathy. He murmurs his condolences and then turns to each of us and, one by one, pins to our collars a swatch of black ribbon, torn in half to symbolize our grief. He is saying things to us now, but I can't listen. I just hold on to Dave's hand and fasten my eyes to my mother and father, who are holding hands and wearing black glasses. I try to picture the next two hours being over.

We file out the narrow side door of the sanctuary and take our seats in the front row, without acknowledging the room full of people seated behind us. I can feel everyone's eyes fixed on the backs of our heads. The room is filled and utterly silent. The silence is so loud.

The service is surreal and endless. I stare at the casket, which sits on a marble table a few feet away from us, heaped high with long-stemmed roses, dark red.

Danny is not sitting with our family, as he has a million times. Danny's body is lying in front of us in a pine casket.

Stiggy, are you really in there?

As the rabbi's sermon comes to a close, I know it's my turn to speak. I am giving Danny's eulogy on behalf of my family. It's my job to make this story as right as it can be.

He catches my eye and nods at me. A wave of nausea. I am floating. Everything is slow motion. I squeeze Dave's hand and stand up. I walk to the podium, head down, lay my pages out in front of me. I know my only hope of getting through this is to stay in my own world, keep my eyes glued to the stack of paper. I cannot bring myself to look at the crowd. I cannot face the expressions on their faces. Cannot tolerate them looking at me. I begin.

Those of us who knew and loved Danny are carrying on an endless private dialogue with ourselves, attended with the knowledge that our lives will never be the same.

I continue, telling stories about Danny, about how smart, funny, and kind he was. About how he was a crazy sports fan, that he knew the stats of every player on both the Kansas City Royals and the Chiefs.

I tell everyone how his bedroom was filled with boxes of baseball cards and crates of record albums. That he was so knowledgeable about and sophisticated in his musical tastes that all his friends and classmates counted on him to tell them which bands to listen to next. I speak of his wickedly hilarious wit, his X-ray vision into the thoughts and minds of those around him, his deep love and thoughtfulness. How remarkably perceptive and wise beyond his years he was.

And then I stop and swallow. Get ready for the part that's going to stick in my throat. I close my eyes and draw a big breath. I need to steel myself now, really get a grip on my emotions, because this is when I give the people in the room what they're waiting for. Answers.

We will never know if Danny meant to end his life. He was playing with fire, like many people do in one form or another, and most likely, according to the first responders at the scene, made a fatal miscalculation that he could not have foreseen. We believe the moment was an impulsive one, just as certainly as we know that the risk he was willing to take was predicated on years of mental anguish. "Suicide is a permanent solution to a temporary problem," Danny often said. And yet, how could he not long for an end to his pain?

I go on to share a realization that's only started to become clear for us: the terrible fact that Danny's everyday struggle somehow blinded us to the enormity of his bravery and courage while he was alive. Now that all hope was abandoned, we were just beginning to comprehend the full measure of his inner strength. How we wished we'd appreciated and acknowledged to him what Herculean stamina and tenacity he showed in how he built up his life, came back from setback after setback, always somehow finding the capacity within to start over again. He never stopped fighting to get back to who he once was.

I listen to myself saying the words, but none of this seems real. This piece of paper in front of me, this podium: not real. Me giving a eulogy for Danny, at his funeral: not real.

Here I go, the final stretch.

I pray along with my family that today Danny has found the peace that he deserves. We will grieve for him, and we will each miss him for the rest of our lives—each at different times and in different ways. I ask us all, though, to respect his final hour not with pity or horror but with honor and dignity.

For all of you here who are wondering what to say or do, I have no idea and it is not important. We know that you care. We ask those of you who knew Dan to please never, ever stop telling us stories about him, never stop remembering him to us. He would like to know that he will never stop being remembered, never stop being talked and thought about and loved.

Danny, we love you and adore you and honor the exquisitely brave and dignified life you lived. We miss you today and forever. You will always be a part of our family.

I walk to my seat like a soldier and sit down. Dave's hand finds mine, squeezes it; my mother leans forward, crying and nodding.

Next, the rabbi says kaddish, an ancient prayer for mourners. It is time for the pallbearers to take the casket to the cemetery.

Filmore walks up to take his place at the front of the casket, beautiful and elegant in his gray suit, tears streaming from his enormous, liquid-brown eyes. Danny's friends and cousins gather around the casket, and together they roll the casket on its trolley out the funeral home's back doors and toward the cemetery.

We follow behind them—my parents, Red, Dave, and me—along the dirt path through the green grass and the field of headstones, past familiar names of families long gone, until we arrive at the giant heap of dirt next to the hole in the ground where Danny's body will go.

My parents, Dave, Red, and I stand shoulder to shoulder, black sunglasses shielding us from the eyes of the crowd. We stand facing Danny's pine casket and try to absorb the rabbi's words as they sweep past us on the hot wind.

Then comes the awful metal cranking sound of the pulley that lowers Danny down, down into the ground. One by one, first our family and then the other mourners stand in line to drop a shovelful of dirt into the hole. The sound of the hard earth hitting the wooden casket again, again, again feels like being slugged in a boxing ring, over and over.

This is how it is meant to be. This Jewish ritual is designed to force mourners to face their loss—to see the casket go down, to hear the dirt splatter on the pine box again and again, and to know that their loved one is really dead, so that they can allow themselves to begin the walk through the shadows and valleys of grief and, eventually, back into their own lives.

It is impossible. It is all impossible. We are seeing this, but we are not. We are here, but we are not.

Finally, friends and family say their goodbyes and drift off to the parked cars that snake down the road abutting the cemetery.

We are alone now. My parents, Red, Dave, and I stand in the steaming sun. Red and I are holding hands tightly. Dave's arm is around me and we are breathing, quietly and heavily, together.

No longer needing to hold herself up in front of the public, my mother falls onto the ground in front of Danny's grave, now scattered with the long-stemmed red roses. Lying face down on the ground in her black suit and high heels, she hugs the impossibly green grass and sobs into the soil.

My father goes to her and gets on his knees. He bends his stiff body down, covers her shoulder with his hand.

"Come on, honey," he rasps. "Come on."

Dave and Red and I hold each other, watching, our shoulders heaving, our eyes pouring tears.

It is a strange thing to stand in a moment you've imagined for years.

Seven days after Danny's funeral, I am back at work.

The bridge between my professional and personal life has been obliterated. After years of no one knowing I had a little brother, now he's dead and everyone knows why.

You'd think we would all be good at grief, considering how much of it there is in life. You'd think we'd be able to give and receive comfort as a matter of fact, instinctively. But no. We are alone in it; it is a grim and relentless slog.

I have gone from almost never talking about my brother to throwing myself into a new, close-to-full-time project I've come to think of as Project Grief, the exhausting march of dealing with everyone's uncomfortable feelings about my sad story.

There are lots of pats and pitiful glances, lots of *Oh, I'm so sorry for your loss.* And then there's the particularly unfortunate aspect of the Project, in which we, the grieving, are forced to nod gratefully at tone-deaf advice, listen empathetically about how our loss reminds people of *their* losses, and try not to wince at incessant platitudes like *he's in a better place.*

I quickly become deft at sweeping the awkwardness away. Let's wrap this up quickly. *Yes, yes, thank you. We're all doing fine, really, thanks for asking. But tell me, how is _____?*

In between the painful social interactions, I walk through these early days in a stupor, frozen and numb. Work is a tense distraction, and lunchtime is my daily reprieve. Dave and I never used to meet for lunch during the week, but ever since we returned from Danny's funeral in Kansas City, it has been my lifeline. I watch the morning minutes pass on my watch in slow motion, longing to see Dave's face, to sit with him on a little patch of grass for forty precious minutes before going back to the office and trying to find my work self again.

Family trauma changes your genetic material, I learn—and I do, I change. Without realizing it, the grief becomes a part of me, like water seeping into the soil of my soul.

For fourteen years my family lived in a state of anxiety and panic, where little mattered aside from how Danny was. We lived in a double reality: our individual lives—healthy, normal, flourishing—and Danny's, right there under the surface—haunted, despairing, the future a blank.

Now the blank has been filled with an end more horrible and violent than anyone could have imagined. It will be many years before I will understand that the trauma of living in such a high state of alarm—existing in that relentless, slow-motion catastrophe—for so many years has injected a paralyzing vapor into my body and psychic anatomy and has changed the trajectory of my whole life.

The effect is this: My cells are pumped full of something not normal. I have been enslaved by something I don't understand. I am at once stunted and reeling.

After being a lifelong reader, I can't read. My eyes will not stay on the page. I can't focus. I find it hard to follow conversations. My mind races and splinters, bouncing from one thing to the next. I can't stop. I am powered only by lists.

I go from being someone who is clear, happy, buoyed by normalcy and dreams to someone with blurred vision and a fogged-over brain. I no longer trust in the universe and the safety of the people I love. When it comes to accidents or danger or death, it's all up for grabs, all the time. The feeling of dread is omnipresent. Anything can happen to anyone.

Relief comes jaggedly and in two parts.

One part: I feel capable only of doing the tedious tasks right in front of me; I am driven by a relentless pursuit to check off boxes and bask in the fleeting relief it brings. Relief, relief, always seeking relief. The other part: I burrow deep into the lives of my family and friends, directing my focus outside of myself and into intuiting the expectations and needs of others and racing—fucking racing!—to meet them.

I am like a blind mouse in a science experiment, running through a maze in a panic even though the stimulus is gone. If I ease other people's pain, that will somehow make things right inside. I am so good at it. Except that it doesn't work. I am worthless. My anxiety aches like a phantom limb. This is what is left of me, because my real job is over. I failed that job. And now my little brother is in the cold, bottomless ground.

Thirty-Eight

I waved goodbye to Jesse as she stood on the street in front of her sorority, waving back with a brittle smile on her face—Leila at her side for moral support, God bless her.

Two hours later, as the plane rose over the city of Chicago, I looked down at the patchwork of skyscrapers and green spaces flowing beneath my airplane window.

The night before, Jesse and I had lain together on the bottom bunk in her sorority room, our faces just a few inches apart.

"I'd go to the ends of the earth for you," I whispered.

Jesse's big green eyes languished in my gaze. "I love my mama and I'm going to miss you."

Illness is a great leveler, stripping one's persona and veils. In our case, it had unraveled the separation we'd built to prepare for Jesse leaving the nest a year earlier, temporarily turning her back into my little girl.

As her condition worsened, our emotional boundaries softened and we drifted back to the unfiltered bonds between young mother and child. I continued to search for the line between loving and coddling, and the question was always the same: Was I acting in Jesse's best interest or from a primal need to be needed, a desperate desire to keep her close and diminish my own worries?

I closed my eyes and leaned my head back against the airline seat. Over these last fourteen months, we had watched Jesse muscle through grueling illness, three surgeries, endless IVs and infusions, the loss of a major organ, the indignity of an ileostomy bag, and the anxiety and trauma of her body turned inside out.

Her illness had robbed her of her signature confidence. She had been cracked open—but she had not yet grieved, I could see that. She had not yet raged at the illness that had taken so much from her. I suspected and hoped that she would one day.

For now, she was giving all her energy to building a new reality. She was forging through with strength and extraordinary maturity, buoying herself with a lens of gratitude for all the blessings she still had in her life. I hoped she would eventually regain her moxie and confidence—perhaps a new, even more grounded version of herself, one born from hardship. I would pray and wait for that day.

I thought about my own part in her story of the past year, the unexpected gifts that had studded the hard road we'd walked together. There had been kindness, so much kindness from people along the way— doctors, nurses, the professors who'd given Jesse unending support.

"How's your daughter doing?" hotel staff members had often asked me during my tenure in Chicago. "Hope she's feeling better today." Every one of these gestures provided and fed our faith that she would be lifted up by the kindness of those around her.

I thought often of the quote by the famous rabbi Abraham Joshua Heschel: "When I was young, I admired clever people. Now that I am old, I admire kind people." Never had that felt truer to me than now.

But most of all, I could not deny the primal fulfillment of being able to meet my child's needs in such a constant and elemental way.

One day, I knew I would look back and miss these crystalline moments of pure love and connection—the unexpected graces of illness. I would miss the part of illness that stripped away all the shoulds and coulds, washed away the reflexive urgency to fulfill an endless network of obligations. How it delivered you fully into the present of your life with a purity of purpose and plan. How it made you understand that in the end, all that matters is loving the people you love.

As the plane descended into the cloudy Wisconsin skies, I lay back and closed my eyes. In a strange but undeniable way, I would really miss this time.

Can a vacation be a vacation when your kid is struggling five hundred miles away? Probably not. But since Dave and I had made plans months earlier for this weekend getaway to see the Wisconsin foliage, we were going to give it a try.

I walked off the plane into the airport terminal. It felt surreal to be there, when just a few hours earlier I'd said goodbye to Jesse.

I spotted Dave standing at the foot of the escalator, his face tilted upward and smiling, waiting for me. I trotted down the escalator stairs and into his arms, where I hid my face in his shirt—my favorite green-and-gray flannel—and dissolved into tears.

"Oh my God," I whispered, the weight of the last three weeks hitting me with force.

"I know," he said, and when I pulled back I saw the tears in his eyes.

"I just don't know how she's going to do it," I said. "She can barely walk to class. She can barely make it through the day."

"We'll just have to see," Dave said in his warm, nurturing voice. He was all here.

An hour later, we walked onto the wooden deck of our tiny cabin overlooking the lake. We wiped away the water that had pooled on the seats of the Adirondack chairs and sat.

A tangle of green vines enveloped the deck. Long purple and green grasses arched in the wind, beaded with raindrops. Stalks of purple bells pointed to the ground in little choruses every few feet, each met by a bed of lime-green leaves.

Fall was raining down in colors of brown and orange, yellow and green. Every few seconds, a gust of wind gently picked up and sang the leaves off the branches in waves, sending them down, down, down in scattered columns through the cool air onto the earth's sodden floor.

There was the quick, dark flutter of wings—a little red-and-brown bird hopping from branch to branch. There was the wavy reflection of skies in puddles gathered on the wooden deck.

Dave put his hand on mine. "I feel like we're in a Mary Oliver poem."

I nodded and squeezed his hand. My beautiful husband, my partner through it all.

Suddenly, the wind cut the lake's placid surface into patches of shimmering ripples. Two canoes glided by in the far distance and voices rose above the water, their sound swept in echoes into the darkening woods.

"It's so unbelievably gorgeous," I said.

I thought of Jesse in her sorority house. I imagined her in the bottom bunk, her quilt pulled up high, watching *The Office* on her little iPhone screen.

As if on cue, my phone buzzed.

I picked it up off the deck and trained my eyes on the screen. I stared. *Mama, I don't think I can do this.*

A burst of adrenaline surged through me. She'd never said that before.

What is it, Beauty? I typed back.

The dots waved, then: *I feel trapped and scared and alone. I just don't know if I can do this.* And then: *I need you.*

Those words. My heart dropped.

I forced myself to think, to fight the gravity's pull of desire to immediately rescue. For these last months we had flooded Jesse with care and comfort. We'd carried her through her surgeries, attended to her moment by moment, just as we had *not* done before she landed in the hospital, when she'd shouldered the full burden of her illness on her own.

Our love and pivot of constant attention had helped her—helped all of us—through this summer, but perhaps it had somehow weakened her as well, dissolved too many layers of the independence that she'd so diligently built in herself over the course of all the years before?

In the gauzy Land of Chronic Illness, there was no way to know.

I talked to myself, as I had learned to do—silently, in my head. To be able to regain herself, I decided, she needed to create support systems at school. As painful as it was to force the notion, maybe her best chance of finding her way back to normalcy was for me to hold back my own support, to push her to find her own.

I typed.

Jess, you can do this. I know you can. Call Leila. Reach out to your other friends. They want to help, but they need to know the truth so that they can.

No response. I handed Dave the phone and, after reading our exchange, he nodded.

"That's the right thing to do, I agree."

"Do you?"

"Yes," he said. "She's going to have to be real with her friends. She's going to need to come to terms with it and ask them to be a part of it."

"We all have to learn how to come to terms with it," I said, and I felt the tears, sudden and hot, on my cheeks. "And you and I are going to have to accept that we will never be able to rescue her from this, not ever."

My heart caught in my throat.

After a few minutes, my phone buzzed back. *Okay, Mama. I'll talk to them.*

I tried to bring myself back to the deck in Wisconsin, back to practicing being in my own space without my mind reeling.

"Look, hon," Dave said.

I looked. The sun had cast itself over the woods, little patches of glowing yellow in the grasses checkered with gray blankets of shade. The wind came up again through the forest, sounding its symphony. In the distance, the lake glimmered with its own mysterious, watery life. In the afternoon light, it glowed in glass sheets, an exact mirror of the autumn-kissed trees above, as lovely as any Monet.

We read, we slept, we rested. We called Sam. We tried not to talk about Jesse.

At the end of the day, a text came: *Mama and Dad, I talked to Leila and my other friends today. They understand now. Thank you for helping me.*

The birds called out over the waters before me, and I knew.

She would be okay. We would all be okay.

Thirty-Nine

Jesse had been back at school for three weeks. With each passing day, I heard from her less and less, which I knew was a good thing. Sam was back in school. The summer heat was waning.

Meanwhile, my writing beckoned. It had been one year since the writer's retreat in Montana. I thought back to that morning of my fiftieth birthday party. I'd promised myself that this was the year I'd figure it all out. "It" being: How to enjoy my life and all its blessings without torturing myself. How to become a writer who writes.

I couldn't say that it had happened all the way, but there were definitely some shifts worth celebrating. One thing for sure was that somewhere along the way, I'd subdued the Committee at least enough to keep them from shrieking at my every turn.

But still, I found it a deep struggle to hold focus. To simply *stay with myself* long enough to live inside my own life with the joy it offered. I was still living far above ground, far from my *ma'ayan b'adama*. I also found it nearly impossible to stay with my thoughts long enough to write. The restless beast's muscled tentacles still lived beneath my every day, filling me with a dark, anxious energy.

On a run with Lucy, I bemoaned my seemingly impenetrable struggle to get out of my own way.

"Lucy, I know we are both so sick of talking about this, but seriously. *What is wrong with me?* It makes no sense! I want to write. I know I'm a writer. And I can't fucking seem to do it!"

Lucy stopped short in front of me. "Julie!"

"Yeah?"

"I keep meaning to tell you this and I keep forgetting! My friend Kelly told me about this therapy called EMDR and I really think you should try it!"

"What is it?"

Lucy tried to explain what sounded to me like a voodoo version of hypnosis you'd see on bad TV.

"It's not voodoo!" she insisted. "It's trauma therapy that takes you into past memories and connects them to your present. Kelly said it was developed for veterans with PTSD. She said it really works. I don't really get it, but it's something about inducing you into a REM state but you're still awake."

The Committee roared. *You gotta be shitting us! Bad TV voodoo?!*

I took a deep breath and ordered them to shut the fuck up. If the past year had taught me anything, it was to keep my mind open.

The following week, I sat in a chair facing Greta Bloom, EMDR therapist. She was in her sixties, with kind eyes and a no-nonsense bob. We sat in chairs facing each other, knee to knee. I tried not to laugh nervously.

Dr. Bloom's office was free of feathers and weird statues. I remembered my session with bejeweled Nadine, who had predicted that a week in nature would start me on my journey. She was absolutely and inexplicably right. *Who says we know everything?* I heard my mother say in my ear.

After filling in Dr. Bloom with a quick family history and why I had come to see her, we began.

"Okay, so I want you to describe to me a time when you've felt blocked," Dr. Bloom said. Her ease and confidence gave me hope.

"Okay, well, that's easy."

"Tell me about it like you are watching a scene on a movie screen. You are in the audience. Describe it."

"Okay, well, it's always the same. I go to sit at my writing desk, but first, in preparation, I do all this spiritual stuff that will supposedly get me in the mood. Lighting the candle, looking at my little shrine of tchotchkes, meditating, blah blah."

"Great. Go on."

"I open my laptop and look at what I'm working on. But the moment I look at the blank screen, I'm overcome with a sense of panic. I'm filled with anxiety and will do anything to get away. It's like I'm jumping out of my skin every time I sit down."

"Okay, good." Dr. Bloom handed me a list of words. "Read this over and tell me which words best describe how you feel in this scene."

I looked over the long list and immediately found words seemingly unrelated to writing but weirdly on target: *afraid, overwhelmed, powerless.*

"Okay, now follow my fingers with your eyes without moving your head."

Dr. Bloom held up two fingers and swung them back and forth in an arc through the air. My eyes tracked her fingers for what felt like an eternity.

"Okay, now," she directed, "close your eyes and blink it out. Now tell me what comes up in your mind."

"Nothing comes up." I paused. "Actually, no offense, but actually what comes up are the voices of the Committee in my head screaming that this is kind of dumb and not going to work."

Dr. Bloom laughed. "I know, and I wish I could explain why it works, but I can't. I just know that it does. Now go ahead and repeat the scene."

I took a deep breath and continued. "Okay, I am sitting at my desk and I open my laptop. I'm overcome with a sense of panic and anxiety. I feel powerless and afraid. I just want relief, and so I shut my computer and go do something useful to get away from the feeling."

"Now track my fingers again."

I did. She told me to close your eyes and blink it out, whatever that meant, but I sort of understood.

"Now what comes up?"

I squinted and shrugged. "Danny," I said. "My little brother who we lost." Danny's face was right there behind my eyelids, his huge eyes looking into me.

"What about him?"

Something moved inside me, and words came without thoughts. "I don't know. Just how hard he tried to get better, how much we didn't understand."

"Anything else?"

My mind went blank. "No, not really."

"Okay," Dr. Bloom nodded. "Now again, follow me."

My eyes followed her fingers until she stopped.

"Now close your eyes and tell me, what comes up?"

"I don't know why, but Danny still," and now tears were rolling down my face. I felt like I was floating.

"What about him?" Dr. Bloom asked. "What do you feel? Right now, what do you feel behind your eyes?"

I started to choke on my words. "Just again how sad it is, everything that happened. How could we not help him? We tried so hard once we understood. But nothing ever worked."

"Okay. Open your eyes and follow me again." She began once more, fingers moving back and forth for a small eternity.

She stopped. I closed my eyes.

"What about you?" Dr. Bloom asked gently. "How did you try to help him?"

Something deep inside my body locked. I could not answer.

"What is it?" Dr. Bloom pressed softly.

Finally the words came. "Just that those feelings—powerless, afraid, overwhelmed—that's exactly how I felt for all those years."

I explained how I always thought I'd be a writer, how I was on my way before Danny got sick. "I was so focused and driven, and then it was like . . . who cares about my writing dreams? I was in New York trying to make my start as a journalist, and I just couldn't do it. I couldn't stay the course. It was like, how can I be thinking about writing when this is happening?"

"Can you say more about that?" Dr. Bloom asked.

The words rushed from my mouth like a torrent. "It was just, like, how can I care about my stupid writing career when my brother is fighting not to kill himself, when my mother is barely hanging on? I felt like me being successful would hurt him. He already felt like such a failure. My success would only make him feel worse. He already felt like Red and I were so far ahead of him. My being some big writer—it could make everything even worse for him."

Dr. Bloom put up her hand. "Okay, stop."

My heart was beating hard now.

"So being a successful writer could make him worse," she said very slowly.

I looked at her.

Did I really think that?

"Now," Dr. Bloom said calmly, "follow me again."

After following her fingers, I closed my eyes and the dark, animal force rose in my chest. I saw Danny and me in flashes, like I was watching a movie.

We are little, so little. We are racing our bikes around the block, Danny's brown legs pedaling in a blur. We are cross-legged in the forest, having our secret picnic. We are jumping off the swing set, umbrellas in hand. We are behind our lemonade stand, yelling for cars to stop. Now he is older, and he is walking through the door, face ashen, after being sent home from his Israel trip. Now the phone calls . . . in college, New York, Boston—"Will you stay with me on the phone for a little longer, Jules?" I see myself hanging up the phone after accepting the job offer in Boston to run a nonprofit, leaving my writing career behind. Hanging up the phone with my new boss and feeling both relieved and deeply sad. I see myself putting my head on my desk and crying.

I opened my eyes, wanting to get away. There was Dr. Bloom, nodding at me, waiting in her kind silence.

"Go ahead," she said softly. "Go ahead and close your eyes and just be with your thoughts. It's okay."

I gripped the chair and closed my eyes.

My eyes land on the bandages on Danny's forearms, hugging him in the dark, the smell of cigarettes. The sound of the steel doors closing behind me at Menninger. The sight of him standing in the doorway, watching me walk away. "He's going to die," Red tells me. "He's going to die." My mother lying across Danny's grave, the long-stemmed red roses scattered on the dark soil. My father on his knees with his head bowed. . . .

Jesse's face flashes in. Her little infant hand clasps my finger. Her golden curls bounce in the sun as she runs into my arms. She walks down the grassy aisle, smiling in her Ray-Bans, diploma in hand. She looks up at me from her hospital bed, face pale, eyes wide with fear. "Stay with me, Mama. Stay."

I opened my eyes and looked at Dr. Bloom. My chest felt like it was closing in on itself. Sobs overtook me and I buried my head in my hands in shame. Tears burst from a hot spring inside my heart. The dark force flooded my body as I cried and cried into my hands until I could not cry anymore.

My mind reeled for days and days. There was so much to absorb. Was it really possible that this ancient feeling of dread, this paralysis in my soul, came from those years with Danny? That I somehow recast my future with my past? That those feelings of jealousy toward Jesse had been a cry from deep inside my consciousness to wake up and realize that in her face was the face of the young girl I'd left behind—me?

That weekend, my phone buzzed with a FaceTime call. Jesse's profile picture appeared on my little screen.

Should I share this experience with Jesse? I was processing a realization that changed the way I'd understood the trajectory of my entire adult life. But did she really need to know all that? Does a kid really want or need to know that much of the truth?

Then I thought about the blueprint. *Our* blueprint.

Yes. Let her know my breakthroughs and progress so that she doesn't feel the weight of my struggle. Let her know me more fully. Teach her to know and share herself fully, too.

And so I told Jesse about the session. But first I told her the whole truth about Danny. We'd always told the kids that their late uncle had struggled with his mental health and that he'd died in a fire. She knew that it was thought to be an accident rather than a suicide. Until now, that had seemed like more than enough. Why should I burden her with the whole gory, heartbreaking odyssey? How could it do anything but give her nightmares?

But I was beginning to understand the error of that logic, as well as the damage that family secrets could do. It was that hiding from others—from myself—that had kept me from understanding how Danny's story had impacted my own for all these years. The pact of silence around Danny was a wrench that had tightened the machinery of our family's trauma. Now was the time to disassemble that old machine—and make sure my own children did not become an unwitting part of it.

Jesse seemed to take in the information about Danny thoughtfully and sadly. Then I told her what I was beginning to understand had happened to the rest of us in the process.

"Jess, there's another side to the story of Danny's illness, and that's what it did to the rest of our family. How it changed us, and how it changed me."

"You mean it made you stronger?" she asked.

"That too, but no . . . I mean, I'm just beginning to understand how it changed me as a person in terms of my identity and how that influenced the course of my life."

"Really?"

I felt the space between us become expectant, vulnerable. I was about to tell her something that would change the way she saw me, in the same way that it had changed the way I saw myself.

It was something seismic and fundamental, and I would not be able to take it back. I could not know the impact. I went on.

"Yeah. Remember how I told you last year about this struggle I'd been having—how I saw myself so clearly in you when I was your age? How I was grappling with the regret and mystery of why I never stayed the course with becoming a writer, and that that was kind of all hitting me as you and Sam were getting older and ready to leave home?"

"Yeah." Jesse waited.

I explained how everything was becoming clear and how this EMDR trauma therapy was helping me put it all together. I shared how, as Danny got sicker and sicker, the core focus of my life changed. *Figure this out. Fix this. Find the solution. Make it better now. Save him.* I explained a truth that I was trying to internalize myself. That somewhere along the way, the choice to turn all psychic energy toward saving Danny from his darkness became the driver of my life. That driver made everything else feel superfluous and selfish.

I spoke gently to Jesse, taking care not to be too intense but still telling her the truth. The sicker Danny got, I explained, the harder it became to build my own life. Somewhere deep in my consciousness, I came to equate my ambition with guilt, with a kind of betrayal. The more success I had, the bigger I got in the world, the worse it would be for Danny.

And so I stopped getting big. I suffocated my vision for myself and resolved to devote myself to Danny, just like a good person would. Just like a good sister and daughter would. That's the story I told myself. That's the story I lived by.

So by the time Danny died, my personal ambitions and self-concept were left far behind. Once I disappeared into that caregiver role, I never left. I surrendered the self-value it would take to invest in my own potential. I got very lucky and got married and had wonderful children. And now, with the prospect of an empty nest, my abandonment of myself was coming home to roost.

Jesse's eyes suddenly flashed. "Mom."

"Yeah."

"My being sick—hasn't it brought it all back for you? Because just as you started to try to write again, I got sick. And then do you think it just put you right back in that struggle again?"

I smiled at my girl, so smart, so wise.

"Well, this time I've been trying, really trying, to do it differently. To be there for you without abandoning myself all over again."

"Mom?"

"Yeah."

"I just need you to know that not only do I not want you to give up your dreams for me, I *need* you to pursue them."

I looked at her. I didn't get it. "Wait, what? Why do *you* need me to pursue them?"

And that's when she told me *her* truth.

"I don't need you to fix this like you thought you had to fix Danny. This is my illness, not yours. You can't take it away. You can't find a solution. And actually, if anything, I just need for you to let me be sad and know that it can't be fixed, really."

I looked at her.

"Like, your and Dad's constant need to make things better, find new medications, try new doctors. Really it just makes it harder for me."

My eyes widened. Our search for help was *hurting* her?

She nodded. "In order for me to move on with my life, I really need to accept that things really might not get better, you know? And it's hard to accept that when your parents are unwilling to accept it."

She became quiet when she saw the tears starting to roll down my face. But she pressed on, knowing she was telling me something we both needed to hear.

"I really need you to accept this with me. That *this is my life*. That you can be there for me, but I need to figure this out for myself."

I wiped my eyes, which were now streaming at the heartbreaking truth and wisdom of Jesse's words. It might never get better than this—she was right. And never in a million years had it dawned on me that our preoccupation with finding solutions for her condition was paralyzing her, keeping her from moving forward with her own healing.

I shook my head as it dawned on me that we'd been just the same with Danny—always looking for a better doctor, a better medication, the right program. And it had all failed. And probably just like Jesse, he'd only felt worse with every failure.

I looked into Jesse's eyes. Sadness and regret mixed with relief and immense gratitude. Jesse's words released both of us from the illusion of control that had held me in its grip until this very moment.

"You are my beautiful girl. I love you. Thank you, baby. Thank you."

Jesse's voice came through, strong and clear. "I love *you*. I want to figure out my life on my own. And I want you to follow your dreams. You put them off for so long, Mama. It's your time now, too."

Forty

From the outside, Filmore's red-brick apartment building is small and neat, covered in brown ivy.

How strange it is to stand in his parking lot. How wrong it is that I have never stood here before. How can all the years have passed and never, not once, has any member of our family entered Filmore's world, when he knows every inch, every chapter, every secret of ours?

It isn't until now that I've crossed the invisible boundary between our worlds. And I am only doing so now because I have come to say goodbye.

A tall, handsome woman dressed in a pantsuit answers the door. Her father is dying, and I imagine that she's come right from work, visiting as much as she can. The homestretch.

"Julie?" She smiles, extending her hand.

"Hi, Liz, yes, oh my God, it's so nice to meet you, how are you?" I say, all too fast.

She stands back to let me in. "Oh, we're all doing fine," she says warmly. "Come meet my sisters. They're in the kitchen."

I know almost nothing about Liz, about any of Filmore's children. He rarely spoke about them, and we rarely asked. It reminds me of when Sam was in preschool and we bumped into his teacher at Safeway. "Wait, why aren't you at school?!" he said with great surprise. He'd only seen her at school. He thought that was where she lived.

I walk into the kitchen and stop short of the wooden table, around which Filmore's two other daughters sit. My face flushes as I rush into hel-los, nice-to-meet-yous. What right do I have to be here? What obligation do they have to welcome me into their home during such a sacred time?

Liz introduces me to the two women, who smile at me with their father's face.

221

"We've heard so much about you," one of them says. There is no trace of anything but kindness. The shame is all mine.

"It's so nice of you to come," the other one says.

I shake my head. "I mean, I had to. I wanted to. Filmore is my family. Filmore helped me . . . helped us . . . I mean, through everything." Housecleaning is the last thing on my mind as I say this, but I cringe as soon as the words leave my mouth.

I search their faces and find no offense. And then I think about how one person can live so many lives at once. What version of Filmore, I wonder, do they know?

It wasn't until I was an adult that my mother told me a story about Filmore I'd never heard: He struggled for years as an alcoholic, losing almost everything—including his marriage and contact with his children—in the process. My mother hired him fresh in his recovery, and I understand now what a cliché that made my family, the white saviors. The irony, of course, is that life has evened the scales. There is no question that Filmore saved us, too.

Filmore was the only person outside our family who knew our secrets, our sad insides, and our odyssey. It was Filmore who helped clean up some of the most painful messes of our lives. It was Filmore whom Danny wanted to come get him at college, whom he allowed to see his apartment, rotten with the mess of his rage and depression. It was Filmore who soothed each of us with his singsong voice, Filmore who was always saying to us, like a prayer, "Everything is going to be *all right*."

"How is he doing?" I ask Liz.

"Oh, you know, he's tired. He's getting himself ready, you know."

I nod.

"You go ahead on into the living room, Julie," Liz says. "He knows you're coming."

I walk in and the first thing I see, right on the fireplace mantle next to photographs of Filmore's daughters, are individual elementary school pictures of me, Danny, and Red. I swallow hard.

Filmore lies in a cot to the right of the fireplace. He is tucked tightly into white sheets, wearing his white undershirt, the same one I've seen him in all my life.

His caramel-brown lids stretch over his big eyes. It's strange to see him lying down. My only image of him, ever, is standing, working, holding us all up.

"Filmore," I say quietly as I sit down in the chair next to his bed, and he opens his eyes and turns to me. Instantly his eyes fill with their usual, playful sparkle.

"Well, hello, sweetheart! You came all the way from California to see me?"

The sound of his voice—the playful tone of words unchanged in spite of the fact that he is actively dying—undoes me. I can't play back. I bend my head to rest on his shoulder and my shoulders heave.

"Oh, now, don't you cry, baby," Filmore's hand is on the back of my head. "I'm on my way to see the Lord. That's how it's *supposed to be*, and I'm ready."

I draw back and run my sleeve across my eyes. "Oh, Filmore."

He looks at me intently. "That's right, sweetheart, no reason for you to be sad. *Now*, how are little Jesse and Sam? They all right?"

"Yeah. Can you believe Sam is about to start kindergarten and Jesse's already in fourth grade?" I try to pull on a smile.

"Well, good Lorrrrd!"

We are silent for a moment while he catches his breath.

"Filmore, do you think you'll see Danny?"

"Well, you know I will," he says in his raspy, laughing voice.

"Can you believe it's been eleven years since he's been gone?"

"That's a long time, sweetheart. And I'm gonna watch out for him when I get there, just like I always do."

I nod and look down, trying to keep it together. "You know how much we love you, right?" I need for him to know.

"I know it, baby." He nods and smiles at me and the white whiskers around his unshaven face dance around his mouth. "And I love *you. All* of you."

"I'm so sorry I've never been here before. I'm so sorry I've never met your children. It was so wrong."

"Well, that's just the way things are, you know."

"Yeah, but it's so wrong and I'm so sorry."

I look at Filmore and I can see the exhaustion in his eyes. But I also see the peace in them, like always, the contentment that has comforted me for so many years.

I always thought, when I was young, that Filmore's way sprang from his soul—magically, effortlessly, unattainably. Although it shocked and pained me to learn about his struggle, there's comfort in knowing that he had to make a journey to this place. He went through his own battle in his head, and he came through. Maybe that means that I can, too.

"Filmore, I need to take a picture of you," I say, as if a picture of him in his deathbed will help me later.

"You do that, sweetheart."

As I raise my phone, he turns and gives me his usual playful smile, big brown eyes shining with love.

"Filmore"—I try to smile back—"tell me again: What's the Meaning of Life?"

He chuckles softly. "Baby, you always been searching. You remember what I told you, right? Just to live, baby, to really live!" I can see the effort in his words.

"Yeah," I say, blinking tears down my cheeks. "I know."

It is the last time I will see him, the last time I will hear his voice.

Forty-One

It was my fifty-first birthday—one year since my fateful, soul-searching fiftieth birthday party—and once again I assembled my tribe for a day of self-exploration, overeating, emoting, and processing up a storm about the Meaning of Life.

This time, Lucy rounded everyone up for a morning hike.

"Okay, everyone!" She put her hand in the air. "Let's mobilize!"

We roused ourselves out of our chairs around the firepit.

"So where are we thinking of going?" I asked.

"How about walking Lucas Valley Road up into the hills behind the horse stable?"

"Really?" I asked with a grimace. Lucas Valley Road was a main road, frequented by cars zooming at high speeds. I made a face.

"No?" Lucy said, pushing up her cat-eye glasses. "Why not?"

"I'm just thinking of all those people texting and putting on their makeup. It'd be a big bummer if one of our partygoers got knocked off on our way to the hike, no?"

Lucy was having none of it. "Oh, it'll be fine. It's just a few hundred feet on that road and then we've got a magnificent hike up into the hills."

I surrendered feelings of responsibility and we filed out the door—en masse, water bottles in hand—and into the sunshine that beamed on our golden and emerald hills.

I walked in silence with my friends. My eyes rested on the clear blue sky before us, the birds winging overhead. What a gift to spend my birthday in the company of these precious friends. What a joy.

As we walked next to the paved road, three by three, everyone's personas and defenses evaporated and gave way to their true, open hearts—just like at my fiftieth birthday gathering the year before.

Up ahead, Lucy shrieked, "Oh my God, you guys, look at this!"

We all ran over to where she was bending over looking at something on the ground.

I bent in close. It was a huge dragonfly, the size of my hand, with wings of fine lace that glistened in the sun as they waved slowly up and down.

"Julie!" Lucy grabbed my arm. Her eyes were wide. "Oh my God."

Its body was a brilliant shade of turquoise and lime green, the very same color combination that I love and that figures prominently throughout our house.

I stared down at the exquisite creature and my eyes filled. I thought back to the dragonflies draping our windows the day Danny died. I thought of the dragonfly that dove in front of me as I walked into the hospital before Jesse's surgery, the dragonfly landing at my feet outside my home as I talked about writing. All the many dragonflies that had appeared out of nowhere to bear witness to this last year.

I bowed my head to the ground and the words rushed through my mind. *Thank you, Stiggy. Thank you for showing me the way this year. Thank you for letting me know it's okay to spread my wings. Thank you for showing me we'll always be together.*

I put my finger on the ground, and the dragonfly crawled slowly onto my hand.

"In all our years here, I've never once walked on this road," I said. "How is it that this dragonfly is here, now, on my birthday?"

But I didn't even have to ask. I knew.

"Let's go," I said to my sisters, and the tears running down my cheeks were tears of pure wonder.

I brought the dragonfly to my face, and it looked at me with its giant, seeing eyes.

"Let's go see what this glorious world has in store for us today."

As soon as my words were out, I waited for the Committee to chime in, to have their say. I listened as I walked. There was no sound.

EPILOGUE

A few weeks after my birthday, just one month into her sophomore year, Jesse finally cried mercy.

"I don't think I can do it anymore," she whispered to us on Face-Time, tears streaming down her flushed cheeks. "I'm just so tired. I'm so, so tired."

"Okay, baby—that's it," Dave said, and I could feel us both holding back tears at the slog of her long suffering. "*It's enough*. Come home. You'll take a medical leave, and you'll go back when you're ready."

She was packed up and home in time for that very weekend—back on the couch, back with Scarlett, the relief in her face palpable.

We all knew there was another, less important, but still clear factor that had played a role in Jesse's decision, and that was what had come to pass with Scotch.

After eleven years of dedicated garbage surfing and tricking us into double feeding him, Scotch had begun to refuse food—and kept refusing. We had learned several months earlier that he had stomach cancer. For weeks, he'd suffered quietly, his muscled body turning slowly to skin and bones as he slept the hours away, curled up in a ball on his sunny sofa perch.

One week after Jesse came back, Scotch forced our hand.

He died just liked he'd lived: strong and regal, fully himself, on his own terms until his last breath.

He asked for a walk, and we took him. Scarlett scaled the heights at breakneck speed, and, just as he had for so many years, Scotch trotted lightly and with joy down the dirt path in those golden hills he'd run in thousands of times.

Then, for the first time in his life, he lay down under a bush in the shade mid-run and wouldn't get up. He looked at us hard, shivering, until finally we forced ourselves to listen to what he'd been telling us for days: he was ready.

A few hours later, we took him to the vet, and he lay down and put his head on my lap. Right before he started to drift off, as Dave and I cradled him and whispered love into his soft ears, he lifted his face to mine, poked my cheek with his dry brown nose, and gave me a couple cursory licks—maybe just to be sure we knew the score.

For eleven years Scotch filled our lives with so much joy and so much laughter. Dave said his epitaph should read, "He was a bad boy, and he didn't listen." We laughed because it was true—and because we would love him, like crazy, forever.

The following month, the four of us sat on a plane headed to Kansas City for Thanksgiving, our favorite time of year. The flight was packed with people headed home for the holidays, feeding babies, walking up and down the aisles, and staring, eyes glazed, at the screens in the seatbacks in front of them.

As my family instantly relaxed around me, plugging into shows and movies, I pulled out my computer and maniacally began going through my email inbox.

Dave put his hand on my arm and brought me back. Here we were. We'd made it to another Thanksgiving. I shut my computer and turned to him.

"Well," he said with a smile, "I know it's only because Jess is home on leave, but it's nice that we're together again."

"So nice," I said, and I pulled him in to kiss his cheek. What a long road it had been, this past year. We'd made it together this far. Not perfectly, not without some slipping into silos and excessive perseverating, but we were making it, and we were getting better at it, too.

I looked at Sam sitting next to me, his broad shoulders a full six inches above mine. He was watching one of his shows, laughing softly at the screen. My sweet boy. I thought about these last few years of his young life—all he'd had to live through, all he'd had to metabolize into his psyche. He was on his own journey, I knew that. And he was on solid ground.

I leaned over and smiled at Jesse, who was sitting with Dave across the aisle from Sam and me. She'd been hunched over her tray table for hours, carefully coloring a giant page of flowers. I thought about how much we'd both changed this year.

After a year and a half of fighting to keep her life on pace and on track, Jesse's disease had finally taken her down. She was kneeling before her own life, and with every week that passed, I saw the blessing in it. I could feel her getting stronger. She was calm and centered, with no sense of anxiety about what she was missing back at school, no fear that she was losing ground.

I thought back on the years of her life that had led to this—her relentless drive to achieve, seeded by the generations before her. How her illness forced her to bow before something bigger, something she couldn't muscle through.

Incredibly, she'd seemed to come to peace with losing the carefree life she'd had. Not only was she well on her way toward accepting her life as it was now, but she was learning to see the good in it. Her illness had brought a new clarity, a new way to be in the world that was healing her. Her illness had forced her to slow down. To rest. To color for the pure pleasure of it. And, slowly, I was learning and healing, too.

I looked out the window, marveling at the speed with which we traveled through the darkening clouds. How could we be hurtling through the sky at five hundred miles per hour and yet here we all were, sitting motionless? So much like my life this past year, I thought. All that speed, but here I was, still. I could feel the center of my body, calm and grounded.

Life had spun so fast and so far out of control since Jesse's diagnosis, but, somehow, I'd managed to find my way. This time around I had not lost myself to the illness of my loved one. From my years of struggling with Danny, I had learned—I had earned—an understanding of how to stay in my own life when the world was spinning out.

Danny's death had left me with a feeling of permanent dread, a haunting conviction that something horrible was just around the corner. Indeed, that something horrible came. Our healthy daughter was given a life sentence of a chronic illness. But this time I had not given all of myself away. Again and again, I reminded myself that even if I gave everything, even if I did everything just right, I could not save or protect Jesse from the pain of living through her own journey. I knew now.

I understood now that my desperate need for Jesse to get back on her feet again was born from the residual fear and grief from Danny—the panic that we would lose her to her illness, just as we had lost Danny to his. I understood now that my fear of her staying on the couch was connected to a belief that she might never come back to us.

When I turned fifty, my wish was to free myself from a dread and paralysis I did not understand. I wanted to learn to relish and meet the possibility of my own life and to try to be the writer that had always been inside me.

What I got was a year filled with fear, illness, and a constant reckoning with what mattered. An unimaginably hard year—but the blessing of it was that it allowed me to finally heal and to learn the lessons I needed to learn.

Nadine the psychic had indeed been right. I *had* built an identity around a block of my own making. Its purpose was to keep my self small and out of the way. My cells were finally learning to rest with the understanding that following my own dreams did not put anyone else at risk. There was no need ever again to harbor envy for my daughter or anyone else. Danny was gone, but I was alive. I could belong to my life, if only I would let myself. My life was waiting—and it didn't require my doing, achieving, or being in service to others. Finally, I could free myself of the invisible chain that had kept me from staying by my own side for so many years.

The dark, animal force that had roiled inside me for years was receding now, and what was left was a gathering peace and clarity. With greater and greater ease, now, I could sit down and write. And I could do that because I'd finally realized that I was just a woman in front of a laptop—no one else's life depended on me.

At least for now, the Committee had put down their gavels and gone off to find their next victim. And I could look over at my beautiful daughter, copper hair glowing in the narrow beam of yellow airplane light streaming down from overhead, and be filled with pleasure at the mere sight of her bent over her coloring books, peacefully making beauty for its own, pure sake.

I was finally coming to understand that our birthright is this: We are entitled to our own lives. No matter what happens to those we love, we are entitled. And we don't have to be anything other than who we are.

When the people we love struggle, we can love them, and we can try our best to help them. But we cannot save them.

It is enough to learn how to save ourselves.

A few hours later, our taxi pulled up to my parents' house. My eyes filled at the sight of them, waiting to greet us. *My parents.* My parents, who had lived through the unimaginable, were beaming with happiness and standing together with their arms around each other in the very doorway I'd walked through my entire life.

My mother was her usual Sophia Loren–beautiful, with her deep-red hair and crystal-blue eyes, wearing her yoga pants and her apron, arms outstretched. My father laughed his hoarse laugh and encircled Jesse, then Sam, then Dave and me with his strong, bony arms.

"Kiddies! It's so great you're here!" The love and gratitude in his voice were evident.

I looked up at him, my father. My beloved father, who had weathered the worst and somehow made it through. People would often ask me how they did it, how they were able to go on, but I'd never be able to explain that kind of strength and resilience. My parents had not just survived but also learned to find joy once again—in life, in their children, and in one another, sitting under their big tree every night with their drinks and Cuban cigar. They would celebrate fifty-five years of marriage soon. We were flush with blessings.

"Reddy's family will be here in a few minutes," my father said, his arm still wrapped firmly around me.

Reddy, I thought. My heart swelled with love for my big brother. So many years together. All the years, all the love, all we'd lived through together, witnesses and partners in one another's lives in a way no one else could be. What a gift to spend Thanksgiving together for another year.

Jesse made a break for the stairs.

"I call Danny's room!" she yelled as she bounded up the steps.

"Mom," Sam said, "that's so unfair. Why does Jesse always get Danny's room? I hate Reddy's room. The bed is so uncomfortable."

"Sorry, Sam, privilege of the oldest," Jesse called out. "Plus, I don't have a colon!" This had become Jesse's standard response to get her way.

There it is, I thought, *she's learning to get her swagger back.*

We all chuckled as we rolled our suitcases into the foyer. I watched Sam clamber up the stairs; the red shag Danny and I used to make into balls had been replaced long since by a modern, gray-pile carpet.

My mom and I walked arm in arm to the kitchen. It was gleaming and warm and filled with the ethereal smells of Thanksgiving. I looked through the oven windows at the massive tray of sausage cornbread stuffing and at the bubbling sweet potatoes topped with caramelized apples below.

"God, Mama." I breathed it in. "It's just beyond. It's the essence of home to me."

"Thanks, Lulabelle," she said. "Nice to be home?"

"The best."

We walked over to the large kitchen window and looked at the familiar sight of our yard.

She put her arm around my shoulder. "How's the *ma'ayan b'adama* coming? Are you digging to reach your underground spring? Because it's right there, waiting for you."

I laughed. "It's coming, Mama, it's coming."

"Good," she said emphatically. "You deserve that. Now, isn't my garden gorgeous?"

"It is, Mama, it's *so* gorgeous."

I looked out at the field of flowers, the bursts of burnt reds and yellows fading in the autumn air.

"Look—where your garden is; that's where the swing set used to be, remember? Where Danny and I played Mary Poppins."

"Of course I remember," she said and gave me a squeeze.

We stood there together in silence for a long time.

ACKNOWLEDGMENTS

Anna Quindlen, my girlhood writer crush, had nothing and everything to do with this book. As the *New York Times*'s first regular female columnist, she wrote about life, family, love, and truth—and showed me that I could too. For a fifteen-year-old, red-haired girl from Prairie Village, Kansas, Anna Quindlen gave me a magical torch that lit my way.

One thing I know for sure, like Oprah, is that all roads lead to where you are. And that's why I'll forever be indebted to (a) my big brother, who is my lifelong ally, witness, and cheerleader at every stage, including when he introduced me to (b) Laura Zinn Fromm, who became my OG writing/soul sister from our *BusinessWeek* days, who introduced me to (c) the wonderful Shelley Emling, formerly of *Huffpo*, now rainmaking her way through AARP, which me led to (d) Laura Munson, who wooed me to her magical Montana Haven writing retreat, where tortured writers find freedom, which is where (e) I fell in love with Sally McQuillen, Kristen Moeller, and Brenda Wilkins, my now lifelong writing sisters. ADD and writer's block fell under the sword of these sisters' constancy, wisdom, faith, and love-bullying as I wrote my way through a story I lived in real time. We wrote/edited/laughed/cried/overate/worked. My sisters hiked with me all the way up the mountain. I can't imagine having gotten here without them.

My Haven sisters eventually led me to the next three women to whom I owe inexpressible thanks: Brooke Warner, whose friendship and extraordinary skill and dedication to craft taught me how a book is built (even though, or maybe because, she said things like "Cut that part; you think it's funny, but it's not"); Lauren Eldridge of Lucinda Literary, who believed in *Stay*—and me—from the beginning and whose kindness, savvy, integrity, and character have accompanied me right to the end;

and Jacqueline Flynn, my wonderful editor, who plucked *Stay* out of the pile and brought it into being with enthusiasm, kindness, patience, and generosity of spirit.

I am so grateful to Gretchen Rubin, Kelly Corrigan, Lisa Heffernan, Pam Friedman, Dr. Edith Eger, Chad Olcott, Laura Pochop, Marci Dollinger, Jodi Stolove, and Katie Anderson, whose exceptional kindness and generosity gave me wings that buoyed me all the way through.

Thank you to those in the trenches who transform ideas into projects and files on laptops into books: Karen VanGorp of Encompass Creative, Emi Battaglia PR, Kimberly Wang at Eardog Productions, and Michael Knell, tech superhero, for their extraordinary talent, wizardry, and dedication to this project. Thanks also go to the keen eyes and expert hands of the entire publishing team, especially Patricia Stevenson, Victoria Shi, Susan Hershberg, and Veronica Dove. An extra tight hug goes to Chloe Batch, who designed a book cover that is pure magic.

I owe a steep personal debt to far too many people to name. Whether early fans of my writing, beta readers, word genies, or very helpful friends, each of you has a piece of my heart. Thanks especially to Victoria Love, Chip Fleischer, Rebecca Lien, Jamie Weinstein, Lisa Pavlosky, Hali Lee, Brenda Althouse, Julie Breakstone, Joanne Greene, Molly Bloom, Lori Hillman, Lisa Levy, Heidi Paul, Laurie Dubin, Nancy Muirhead, John Gerson, Ann Becker, and Karen Anderson. Huge thanks, as well, to my Congregation Rodef Sholom community, whose steady embrace gave me the resolve and courage to share this story in hopes of helping other families walking this path.

I give my love and thanks to Molly Shapiro, Julie Krop, and Jessie Baker, who have been treasured partners in life, love, loss, and everything in between, from childhood to parenthood to middle age—and, God willing, as Aunt Etty used to say, "'til they put us in the hole, honey!"

Love and eternal gratitude go to everyone on both sides of my tiny, mighty family, especially to my parents, Pella and Jack, the two strongest, wisest, and most beautiful people I know. Besides giving me life, they have built who I am, what I care about, and how I live. To Susan and Jeffrey Rudnick, who are the most generous, interested, loving in-laws a girl could ever want. And to Jesse and Sam: my love for you is boundless and eternal, and, along with your dad, you are my life's greatest gifts.

And finally, to Dave. What words are there for what you are to me? You are my joy, my love, and my home. You are my daily bread. I could not have done it without you.

POSTSCRIPT

February 2024

Dear Danny,

I hope it was okay to share your letters. I wanted to give your voice the life it deserves.

Keep sending us the dragonflies. They remind us that Mom is right, as usual! The words she had engraved into the fountain in your garden are true: Love is stronger than death.

You will always be part of our family.

Xoxo

ABOUT THE AUTHOR

Julie Fingersh is a writer and freelance journalist. Her personal essays, editorials, and articles cover culture, wellness, parenting adult children, cooking, and how to lead a more sane and meaningful life. Her work has appeared in the *New York Times*, *Oprah Magazine*, the *San Francisco Chronicle*, *Huffington Post*, *Miami Herald*, *Kansas City Star*, *BusinessWeek*, *Grown and Flown*, and more. Her Substack newsletter, *Take My Advice. I'm Not Using It (On Life, Death & Everything in Between)*, is a midlife sequel to an award-winning humorist column she wrote in her twenties for Billboard Publications, Inc., in New York City. Julie also served as founding executive director of Boston Cares, which became a nationally recognized model for community and corporate partnerships and recently celebrated thirty-three years of service to the Greater Boston community. She was a regular guest on NPR and other media outlets and shared the stage as a keynote speaker with Secretary of State General Colin Powell (Ret.) for the inaugural Boston Cares Corporate Volunteer Day, Greater Boston's first-ever day of citywide corporate service. Julie earned a BA in English literature at Swarthmore College and University of Michigan. A Kansas City native, Julie lives in Marin County, California, with her husband. They have two adult children. *Stay* is her first book.

Sam, Julie, David, and Jesse, 2022